THE FORGOTTEN BATTLE

THE
FORGOTTEN
BATTLE

*Overloon and the Maas Salient
1944–45*

A. Korthals Altes
and
N.K.C.A. in't Veld

Translated by G.G. van Dam

CASTLE BOOKS

This edition published in 2001 by Castle Books,
A division of Book Sales Inc.
114 Northfield Avenue
Edison, NJ 08837

Reprinted by arrangement with Sarpedon
An imprint of Combined Publishing
476 W. Elm Street
Conshohocken, PA 19428

First published in 1984 as *Slag in de Schaduw*
By De Bataafsche Leeuw and Uitgeverij de Arbeiderspers,
Amsterdam, The Netherlands

ISBN 0-7858-1420-5

Library of Congress Cataloging-in-Publication Data

Korthals Altes, A.
  [Slag in de shaduw. English]
  The forgotten battle : Overloon and the Mass salient, 1944-45 / A.
Korthals Altes and N.K.C.A. in't Veld ; translated by G.G. van
     Dam.
          p.   cm.
  Includes bibliographical references and index.
  1. World War, 1939–45 – Campaigns – Netherlands. 2.
Netherlands – History – German occupation, 1940-45. I. Veld,
N.K.C.A. in't.
D763.N4K6313   1994
940.54'21924 – dc20   94-33726
                                                       CIP

Will no one tell me what she sings?
Perhaps the plaintive numbers flow
for old, unhappy, far-off things,
and battles, long ago

Wordsworth, "The Solitary Reaper"

CONTENTS

MAPS

INTRODUCTION

What happened between the Peel marshes and the Maas River in Holland might have remained entirely unnoticed in history had not a remarkable initiative been taken in the first few days after the liberation of Overloon. Part of the battlefield, close to the southern edge of the destroyed village, was reserved for an open-air museum where tanks, guns and other war equipment which had been left behind were collected and maintained. Over the years this collection has been expanded with objects from elsewhere. Outside on the grounds fifty large objects, and inside the museum buildings countless other items, are on permanent display. All this has gradually developed into the National War and Resistance Museum (*Nationaal Oorlogs- en Verzetsmuseum*), which is visited by some 170,000 people annually.

What motivates these crowds of visitors to this contemporary Pompeii, this military Madame Tussaud's? How do they look upon the objects left behind in the state they were in — the Sherman tanks, the flail tanks and the Valentine bridge-laying tanks with their protruding tentacles? Walking through the museum-park it is difficult to imagine that this lovely spot was once the scene of bitter fighting, a battle mainly fought by the infantry, which had to face hardships that bring to mind those suffered by their fathers some thirty years earlier during World War I.

No more detailed description of the long and difficult battle between the Peel marshes and the Maas (also called the Meuse) than given in this book has as yet been published. Because of a lack of previously published material, a great variety of sources thus needed to be used, which can be summarized as follows:

First, there were all the military sources, British, American and German. Of these the British were most numerous and varied. The American ones were rather more concise. German sources were and are very difficult to trace and also quite scarce. Only at the highest levels have official documents been saved. The ad hoc nature of many of the German forces involved has meant that records of many of the official "divisions" involved in this battle are nearly impossible to trace, while reports of smaller units were found occasionally but usually only through coincidence.

A distinction should be made between published and unpublished material. In England the authors consulted in the Public Record Office the war diaries of the three divisions most closely involved in the battle. In the United States a number of After Action Reports were made available to us of the 7th Armored Division and also of a few units operating within the Division.

The unpublished German material consisted mainly of the *Kriegstagebücher* (War Diaries) with appendices by the Oberbefehlshaber West (Supreme Commander West) and Heeresgruppe B (Army Group B), together with postwar studies written by German officers at the request of the Americans. The German war diaries are indispensable, but to a degree unreliable; it was obvious that the higher German commanders had a very limited understanding of what was going on on the battlefield, and the officers who recorded the events after the war based their findings to some extent on the unreliable diaries and on the often failing memories of themselves and others. The appendices were most useful, however, because, although orders from Hitler or proposals from Field Marshal von Rundstedt admittedly did not give a clear picture of what was really going on, they gave the authors an idea of what they had in mind and of what they wanted to achieve.

In England sources abound. Not only were the histories of the three divisions mentioned recorded and published, the same was true for virtually each battalion that took part in the campaign. In the history of their regiments one always was able to find one or more chapters on the battalions that fought in the Maas salient. The American division which took part in the campaign merely issued a short brochure and a single, unpublished and incomplete study. In

Germany this battle has scarcely been referred to in publications since the war.

Finally, a word about the Dutch sources. Locally, publications have been issued that describe the war in Northern Limburg. The battle also found a place in several studies by Dutch Army men. In addition, for the campaign as a whole, an unpublished study by the Higher Army Academy has been of great help.

But always the guiding principle of this book, whether it concerns, Dutch, German, American or British aspects in this mosaic, has been the search for eyewitnesses and for what they observed and felt at that time. A valuable source were diaries — some of which have been published — and letters. Many people were willing to recount their recollections verbally or in writing on the events of those days, sometimes with the aid of brief notes jotted down later and of other documents. Whenever possible their words have been incorporated in this book in their authentic form; as nothing has been added, they should speak for thesmelves. For some of the events recorded we had to rely entirely on the material submitted by these people. Sometimes the material thus provided could be used to supplement or to better illustrate an event described, to add a nuance or to fill in a background.

Since the essence of this book lies undoubtedly in the personal accounts of those involved in the campaign, we would like to record our gratitude to the many who have made contributions to the book and who are mentioned in the list of sources and bibliography.

From the very first hour, Harry van Daal, founder and until 1984 secretary of the Committee of the National War and Resistance Museum, gave us every assistance in our initiative. Again and again he provided us with any details he could find, in particular from his own study and work on the history of the battle. Moreover, he was also able to make very useful contacts on our behalf. The contacts in America were coordinated by Harry Matzen, professor of modern history, Ulster County Community College, Stone Ridge, NY. A great deal of cooperation was also given by the historians of the British 3rd Division and the American 7th Armored Division, especially Norman G.J. Jones, Scranton, Pennsylvania, and Norman Scarfe, Woodbridge, Suffolk, who introduced us to various eyewitnesses.

Colonel J.D.W. Renison D.S.O. (retired) was kind enough to entrust his extensive diary to us in manuscript, with staff maps and photographs. The number of Germans willing to assist us in our investigations with personal accounts regrettably remained limited. We are very grateful to Heinz Weber of Büren in Germany, who gave us an astonishing, heart-rending account of his war experiences, and to Brigadier-General Rolf Loytved-Hardegg for the information supplied by him. We are also indebted to Jan van Lieshout, journalist, who placed the diary of the Fallschirmjäger-Regiment Hübner at our disposal, to P.W.L. Weijs, teacher, and to the student of history R.G.W. Kikken, who each made their published studies available to us.

Until today the landscape of the area has remained relatively unchanged in spite of the land having been lotted out among farmers, the canalization of the river Maas (which commenced in 1926), and the construction of two motorways, one the north–south Peel route and the other the road Eindhoven–Venlo. Urbanization and industry here were and still are of a modest nature. The countryside — flat, with the exception of a few sand ridges and the east bank of the river, which is on a generally higher level — accommodated some 100,000 people. To this figure should be added about 90,000 people living in the towns which, in order of their size are: Venlo, Roermond, Venray, Weert and Deurne.

In the Peel area the exploitation of peat moors has quite rapidly been replaced since the turn of the century by cultivation of the land for agriculture, although a network of canals used for the transportation of peat was left intact and was expanded in 1939 with the construction of the Defense Canal for the so-called Peel Defense Line. On the sandy soil between the Peel marshes and the Maas there are small and medium-sized farms that grow various agricultural products, the only variation being plantings of coniferous trees. There is also a lot of cattle farming, plus pigs and poultry, as well as a flourishing horticulture and fruit-growing culture. Numerous brooks and rivulets run into the river Maas, turning the adjacent fields into soggy land. The population, accustomed to lengthy periods of scarcity, is more of a Saxon than of a Brabant-Limburg nature; good Catholics, not exuberant, and inclined to be taciturn.

It has never been our aim to produce in our book an account in which the reader might be able to closely follow each unit from day to day. The book presents a picture which is not the complete reality, nor can it ever be, but it paints what we hope will be vivid aspects of that reality, bringing the essential elements to life again. We have tried to trace back how the battle was experienced by all those involved without interfering with the general outline and cohesion of events.

A prominent position has been given to the "personal" element in this book, as we feel that the supporting and unifying strength of a history such as this should primarily be compassion. Compassion with those who were cast into the melee. This sentiment may now, after fifty years have passed, convey to the reader what war is like, how it is conducted and how it affects the people who have to live through its entire gamut of terror and destruction, filth and boredom, tragedy and inspiration. For that which happened in those one hundred and fifty days around Overloon and in the Maas salient is part of the story of the liberation of Europe, dearly bought by Allied troops from an enemy defending himself stubbornly and with great skill. Many of those troops and many civilians had to sacrifice their lives and property for the sake of freedom. This freedom was their gift and legacy.

CHAPTER ONE

THE FORGOTTEN BATTLE

THE DATE WAS OCTOBER 12, 1944. Over Venray, a small town in southern Holland, the autumn sun climbed slowly toward its zenith, its light obscured only by the clouds of smoke and dust rising upward from the town. The people of Venray, together with many refugees from the surrounding area, sought shelter in the cellars of the houses, listening apprehensively to the sounds of war outside. All morning there had been gunfire, but since eleven o'clock the noise had grown into an infernal din.

Shells were exploding around Mrs. Schmidt's house, which stood in the street that led to St. Anna's Psychiatric Hospital, where her husband worked. Suddenly the ground started to shake violently: bombs, she thought, explosions different from the guns that she had come to recognize all too well since September 30. Since that day, she and her husband had spent most of their time in the cellar. She had happened to be out on the street when these bombs started dropping around her, and dashed to the nearest porch for cover. When the all-clear sounded she rapidly walked back home. Her house was still standing, damaged, but not too badly. She could not enter, however, as the blast of the explosions had jammed her front door. The street was pock-marked with deep craters. Through the smoke she could smell the scent of freshly uprooted earth. Standing there, staring at the destruction and considering what to do next, she noticed a strange object in her front garden. It was half buried under debris and she did not immediately recognize it. She stooped and saw that it was a human torso. She was nearly overcome by nausea.

Four miles north of Venray, guns were splitting the sky. Toward

11:30, as planes were dropping bombs on the town, more than two hundred guns were blasting away. The gunners worked themselves into a sweat, picking up shells, passing them on and pushing them into the breeches of their 25-pounder pieces. Lt. Colonel Sir Nigel Tapp had no time to watch what was going on in front of him. He was too busy directing the complicated fire plan of the twenty-four guns in his artillery battery.

At the edge of the wood Private Roebuck stood among the infantrymen of the East Yorks Battalion, ready to advance, their Lee Enfield rifles with bare bayonets at the ready, Mills hand grenades and clips of rifle ammunition in their pouches. Lined up behind the soldiers, tanks were waiting for the signal to advance to give fire support to the infantry. Shells were crashing in the pine woods on the opposite side of the field. Fighter planes were roving the skies, Typhoons releasing their rockets in steep dives. On both sides of the wood, palls of smoke rose into the air. The noise was deafening. The explosions drowned the sound of cracking trees reduced to splinters by shells. Brownish dust and wisps of smoke drifted like shadows across the sun.

In one of the pine woods two German soldiers were huddled close together in a foxhole with a machine gun, feeling scared and abandoned. For four hours artillery shells had been thundering and screaming over their heads. The two men, their paratroop helmets pushed far back, were Feldwebel (Corporal) Heinz Weber and his orderly, Scheurer, and belonged to Battalion Paul. The twenty-one-year-old Weber had nearly four years of battle experience: in Russia as a wireless operator with the Luftwaffe and later as a paratrooper in Italy. He knew what it was like to be under fire, but so far he had always been lucky and managed to survive. Today, however, he felt depressed and had the uneasy feeling that after all the misery of the past few weeks his luck had run out.

Yard by yard, the advancing barrage uprooted earth, grass and trees around them. Suddenly a man fell across Weber into their fox-hole, his right arm gone. Weber wondered if there were any *Sanitäter* around; it seemed ages ago he had seen one. There was nothing he and Scheurer could do for the wounded soldier. The shellfire increased to a screaming inferno and the two Germans crawled to a safer spot behind a thick tree. There they dug a deep hole, blowing up its roots with their hand grenades. A few minutes later their platoon comander, Bayreuther, crawled up to them to boost their morale. "Sit tight, hold on to your position!" he shouted. Weber saw him crawl back to where he came from, a captured Colt revolver sticking from his too small holster. Weber never saw Bayreuther again.

The destructive barrage blazed its trail forward. The steadily advancing steamroller of noise, smoke and dust gave a feeling of protection to Private Roebuck as he advanced side by side with his buddies.

Feldwebel Weber noticed the din abate as the artillery barrage came to a halt. He realized that the enemy attack was imminent. First he spotted the tanks. How did they get through our minefields, he wondered. Frantically he fired his MG-42 machine gun at the advancing tanks. Behind the tanks he saw the first enemy soldiers. How smart and neat they look compared with our shabby outfit, he thought. The tanks kept coming toward him. Scheurer and Weber thought they still had a chance. They had three Panzerfausts left, effective anti-tank weapons. Weber looked desperately for a better position to fire from. He crawled out of his hole while Scheurer covered him with the machine gun. Weber let himself topple into a half-dug foxhole. But their tracer ammunition had given away their position to the enemy. One of the tanks veered around and headed straight toward Weber. Why didn't they fire their co-axial machine gun? No, they wanted to crush him into the ground, Weber thought.

He held his Panzerfaust ready. The tank or me, he said to himself and counted the seconds. When he felt that the tank was well within range, he fired his weapon. The projectile hit one of the tank's tracks and it swerved off its course. At the same time Weber felt an excruciating pain shoot through his body. He saw that his right leg was dangling and felt numb. Dazed with pain, he heard somebody shout in English: "Komm 'raus, Kamerad! Get out, you bastard!" Hard though he tried, Weber could not move. An English sergeant appeared and pointed his rifle with fixed bayonet at him. What's he going to do with that obsolete popgun of his, Weber thought. . . It will do the job, though. . . Go ahead, pull the trigger, dammit! What are you waiting for? After what seemed to be an eternity, the sergeant lowered his rifle and hit Weber on the head with its butt. Two soldiers pulled him out of the hole and shouted: "Du Offizier?" God, what a nervous lot they are, Weber thought, they must be new to this game.

His opponents were men of the East Yorks and the Suffolk Battalions, tough veterans who had been among the first troops to land in Normandy and who had fought the hard battles for Caen and Falaise. Weber tried to make it clear to them that he could no longer walk or stand up. One of the men tore off his insignia, took his paybook, photos, watch and ring. He was allowed to keep his rosary. As stretcher-bearers started preparing to take him away, the English discovered Weber's earlier position. They were on the point of lobbing a hand grenade into it when Weber shouted, "Scheurer, get out! Put your hands up or they'll kill you!" Scheurer crawled out of the hole. Walking towards the stretcher with arms raised, rifle bullets hit him in the head and neck. He was killed at once. Scheurer was not the last man Weber would see lying dead on the battlefield of Overloon. As he was being taken away between minefields marked with white tape, he saw at the edge of the wood the body of his company commander, whom he had not seen for a week. Weber recognized the Oberfeld-webel only by his uniform as his head had been blown off by a shell. For you and me the war is over, Weber thought.

The war did not come to an end that day for Private Roebuck. His platoon received its first enemy machine gun fire in an area covered with bushes and tussocks. A few men were wounded but they quickly took the German position. Three young Germans, not older than sixteen or seventeen, came out with their hands raised. How young they are, Roebuck thought. Inside the woods, the platoon had to wait for the next phase of the attack. In the meantime the company sergeant-major, much to the envy of Roebuck, ordered the prisoners to dig a deep foxhole for himself. Private Rigby, a newcomer to the platoon, appeared to be exhausted by his first fight. He stood leaning against a tree. Roebuck shouted at him: "Dig, man! Now that we're stuck here, they're going to hit us with all they've got!"

Hardly had they dug in when German Nebelwerfer shells crashed down among them. "Moaning Minnies" the soldiers called them because of the wailing sound they produced as they flew through the air. The "stonk" lasted twenty minutes. Then, out of nowhere, low above the ground, two Typhoons came roaring down at them. Roebuck saw how the fighters released their rockets close to his position. Dammit, he thought, they're going to hit us! But the rockets roared closely over their heads toward the Nebelwerfer. Quickly Roebuck spread out a yellow cloth on the ground to warn the fliers not to fire at their own troops.

Late in the afternoon they passed through a wood which a platoon next to Roebuck's had taken at the cost of a large number of casualties. After he had advanced through what had been an orchard or a garden, he suddenly found himself in the village of Overloon. All the houses were severely damaged and the place reminded him of the desolate scenes in Normandy. German shells began to drop nearby and Roebuck's platoon dashed for cover into a cellar under one of the flattened houses, where they stayed for the rest of the day.

Thus did a handful of people live through that day of war on October 12, 1944, the day that Overloon was taken. One day out of a bloody battle that started in September 1944 and lasted until March 1, 1945. Anyone who was directly or indirectly involved had his own name for what happened during those 150 fateful days; each, according to his own experiences, called this battle such as "The Peel Marshes," "Overloon and Venray" or "Brückenkopf Maas." Most people living beyond the battle area itself know very little about it, as other momentous events were happening elsewhere in Holland at the time. First, the air landings on September 17 near Arnhem, followed by the race against the clock between Valkenswaard and Nijmegen to relieve the British 1st Airborne — a race prematurely halted in the Betuwe area and thus incapable of turning the tide. To some, the battle of Overloon was overshadowed by the spectacular "sinking" of the island of Walcheren by heavy bombers a week later as a prelude to a bloody struggle to clear the Scheldt estuary and open up Antwerp as a supply port. And later, all attention focused on the gigantic German offensive that burst out of the Ardennes to the south.

Yet this battle of Overloon, which has gone down in history without a name, lives on in the minds of all the soldiers on both sides who fought it and among the Dutch men, women and children who found themselves dragged into it against their will and endured the hardships of those miserable, bloody days. This episode of military courage and human suffering does not, after all, require a place name; in hindsight, it would be appropriate to call it "The Forgotten Battle."

CHAPTER TWO

THE BLOODY STAGE

"He that outlives this day, and comes safe home,
will stand a tip-toe when this day is named. . . .
. . . old men forget; yet all shall be forgot,
but he'll remember with advantages
what feats he did that day. . . .
and gentlemen in England now a-bed
shall think themselves accursed they were not here. . . ."

THESE LINES FROM Shakespeare's *Henry V* were read by Major "Banger" King to the soldiers of his company. It was June 6, 1944, around 7:30 in the morning. King's voice reached the men of the East Yorkshire battalion via the Tannoy system of their landing craft. The men were to storm the Normandy beaches as the spearhead of General Montgomery's invasion command. The battalion was part of the British 3rd Infantry Division, which landed on Sword Beach, north of Caen. Montgomery had hoped to seize this vitally important crossroads the very first day. Wishful thinking! In fact, it took him nearly five weeks and even then bitter fighting continued at the front around Caen, where British and Canadian forces continued to engage the main body of German forces. Farther to the west, the Americans, in particular Patton's Third Army, managed to break out at the end of July and by mid-August the remnants of two German Armies were trapped south of Caen. At the same time a combined American-French force landed in the south of France, where enemy resistance collapsed quickly.

7

The battle for Normandy eventually ended in a great Allied victory. At least ten thousand Germans were killed and sixty thousand more became prisoners of war. The Allies, however, did not achieve a strategic triumph. After the landing in the south, the Germans evacuated the whole of southwest and central France; in the north, too, the Allies chased them at high speed, but nowhere could they be trapped on a large scale. On August 20, fifteen days ahead of the original schedule, Patton crossed the Seine River. In the fortnight that followed, nothing seemed to be able to stem the impetuous Allied advance. Over a broad front the tanks and motorized coumns rolled on in the direction Germany. Three British armored divisions pushed onward across the French-Belgian border. Belgium lay open before them. On September 3 Brussels was liberated by the Guards Armoured Division. The next day Antwerp fell to the 11th Armoured. With members of the Belgian resistance as scouts, Lt. Colonel David Silvertop drove through the city in triumph at the head of his Shermans and reached the docks, which were undamaged. On the British right flank, the U.S. First Army crossed the Meuse River at Namur and the Third Army got across the Moselle at Metz.

What next? Montgomery, who, according to the initial agreement, was supposed to hand over command of the land forces to General Eisenhower on September 1, suggested to the latter on September 4 that the time had now come for "one powerful and full-blooded thrust towards Berlin." That thrust, Montgomery felt, had to be carried out by his 21st Army Group. Eisenhower had a different opinion: all Allied units were to advance together on one broad front toward Germany.* But now that the enemy appeared to be beaten, Eisenhower slightly altered his views. He agreed to let Montgomery launch his bold drive to the northeast, but at the same time the advance into the Saar was to continue. For his plans Montgomery had a huge reserve at his disposal: the Allied First Airborne Army, consisting of one British and two American divisions, plus the Independent

---

*Ironically, a similar disagreement had taken place among the German High Command during Operation Barbarossa. At that time, Hitler had championed the "broad front" strategy while most of his generals favored a single thrust on Moscow.

Polish Parachute Brigade. How could he best deploy these elite troops?

Between September 5 and 7 the British 11th Armoured Division had stayed put. In retrospect this was a blunder as the 11th, which had seized Antwerp, had enough fuel left to push on another 30 miles. If they had done so, they would have cut off South Beveland, a peninsula of the Dutch province of Zealand, and that move would have severely hampered, if not prevented, the escape of the German forces that had been squeezed together in West Flanders. General Brian Horrocks, whose XXX Corps this division belonged to, has accepted the blame for the opportunity offered the Germans to escape. This is arguable. The responsibility for blunders of strategic consequence must be looked for in the supreme command. At this stage, when victory seemed so near, however, nobody paid any attention to the Scheldt estuary. All eyes were focused on the Rhine, the last large obstacle that Hitler's forces seemed capable of defending.

Montgomery planned to use his airborne forces to overcome this obstacle. After an initial, smaller plan that was called off because unfavorable weather conditions slowed down the ground troops, he had developed his final plans by September 10. He would not advance northeast via Venlo to Wezel, but to the north, via Eindhoven and Arnhem. His pathway would be paved by dropping airborne troops who were to seize five vital bridges: over the Wilhelmina Canal at Son, over the Zuid-Willems Canal at Veghel, over the Maas at Grave, the Waal bridge at Nijmegen, and finally the bridge over the Rhine River at Arnhem. Eisenhower approved of the plan.

Responsibility for the plan does not lie with one single individual, and the same goes for the gross underestimation of the importance of Antwerp as a supply port. The real reason for the High Command's approval of Montgomery's plan was the general euphoria that existed among all ranks in this second week of September, even though signs of German recovery were becoming apparent. North of Antwerp, along the Albert Canal, later along the Maas-Scheldt Canal and also on the American front, the enemy's resistance was increasing—a fact that many found difficult to acknowledge.

On September 16, Horrocks, whose XXX Corps was to play the

leading role, explained operation "Market Garden" to a spellbound audience of officers in the Roma cinema in Leopoldsburg, Belgium: "XXX Corps will break out of its present bridgehead on September 17 and will advance via the carpet laid out by the airborne troops in order to seize the area between Arnhem and Nunspeet and to continue its drive north towards the Ysselmeer. VIII Corps will be on our right and XII Corps on our left flank. As the bulk of the supplies will be allocated to XXX Corps, VIII and XII Corps will not be able to keep up with us and consequntly we will, possibly for a longer period of time, be on our own."

VIII Corps' task was to cover Horrocks' east flank. The corps was commanded by Lt. General Sir Richard O'Connor. He was fifty-five years old and a veteran of the First World War. The beginning of this war had found him in the Middle East. There he operated successfully in the Libyan desert until his luck ran out. In February 1941 he ran into a far advanced German recce unit, was captured and taken to a P.O.W. camp in Italy where he was held for over two years. Twice he out-smarted his guards; twice he was recaptured. Not until September 1943, in the wake of the Italian capitulation, did he finally succeed in making his getaway, and two months later he reached the Allied lines in a fishing boat. Some speculate whether O'Connor, an able desert general, might have led the Eighth Army at El Alamein had he not been captured. In that case, would there might have "been" no Montgomery.

Unlike most of Montgomery's subordinates, O'Connor got along very well with the Field Marshal. They had gone to Staff College together and both had taught there. O'Connor, reflecting on Mont-gomery, found him to be a great commander-in-chief but prone to being overly prudent; popular with the ranks but not very good at cooperating, since he was not fond of sharing responsibility. Different was O'Connor's opinion of his immediate superior, General Dempsey, commander of the British Second Army: quiet and modest, but as determined as any leader in the army.

At that time O'Connor's VIII Corps consisted mainly of the 11th Armoured Division and the 3rd Infantry Division. His plan was for the infantry to establish a bridgehead across the Maas-Scheldt Canal. When the area between Leende and Weert had been taken, the 11th

Armoured was to advance through this sector toward Helmond. This division was already at the front, but O'Connor still had to bring up the whole of the 3rd Infantry from its rest area in France.

The 3rd Infantry Division's history began during Wellington's Peninsular Campaign against the French and continued through all of England's wars thereafter. In the trenches during the First World War it earned the nickname "Iron Division." Until then its members had been regular soldiers; now only some 30 percent were regulars, a majority of the rest being conscripts. A third, or intermediate, category was formed by the territorials and yeomanry who, prior to the war, had volunteered for weekend service in their own local area. They had a high degree of comradeship and esprit de corps. In 1940 their commanding officer at that time, Montgomery (who had designed the divisional emblem of three black triangles surrounding an inverted red one), executed a successful retreat with the division to Dunkirk. Now they were under the command of Lt. General L.G. Whistler, nicknamed "Bolo," a giant of a man. He was forty-six years old and had already seen action in 1918 and 1919. In the latter year he took part in the British intervention in Russia against the Bolsheviks, whom he called "Bolos," hence his nickname. In the present war he had commanded a brigade at Dunkirk, in Africa and in Italy.

Unlike the "Iron Division," the 11th Armoured was a relatively "young" unit at the end of 1943 — as was its leader, the thirty-seven-year-old General G.P. "Pip" Roberts. The division was formed in 1941 after the British had learned valuable lessons from the German panzers in the first days of Blitzkrieg. Initially it consisted of two armored brigades, but one was replaced by an infantry brigade, again following the German lesson that in a desert war tanks could become extremely vulnerable without the immediate support of infantry. The three infantry battalions of this brigade were specially trained to operate flexibly in close cooperation with tanks, which often led to brigades getting intermingled during swift actions.

The infantry of the two divisions were issued Lee Enfield rifles, with which a well-trained soldier could aim and fire thirty bullets a minute. Apart from this weapon, weighing eight pounds, the solider also carried rifle ammunition, a number of Mills hand grenades, and a shovel. Some men did not carry a rifle but a Sten gun, a lightweight sub-machine gun or a PIAT anti-tank rifle.

The tanks in the division were Shermans. These American weapons, with a crew of five, weighed thirty-three tons and had a 75mm (later also 76mm) gun and a .30-inch Browning machine gun mounted in the chassis. These tanks were considered very maneuverable and easy to maintain. Though often overmatched in battle by the German Panther, during and long after the war the Sherman remained the most widely used tank in the world.

On Sunday, September 17, an air armada of a size never before seen approached The Netherlands. The air fleet numbered 1,036 transport planes packed with paratroopers, 478 planes towing the same number of gliders, other planes for dropping supplies, and an escort of more than a thousand fighters. At approximately 1:30 p.m. the "Market" part of the grandiose plan began. The paratroopers of the American 101st Airborne Division jumped in the area between Son and Veghel, those of the 82nd Airborne at Grave and Groesbeek. Both divisions were about seven thousand strong. The British 1st Airborne Division dropped one para brigade and landed a glider force west of Arnhem, together numbering some five thousand men. Not an hour later the "Garden" half of the plan followed, when Horrocks let the tanks of the Guards Armoured begin the attack from the bridgehead across the Maas-Scheldt Canal, after what he believed to have been a destructive artillery barrage.

Filled with optimism, the Allied ground and airborne forces threw themselves into their task, though few so far realized the weak spots in the hastily contrived plan. In this context special attention should be paid to the piecemeal nature of the operation. Airborne actions must depend for their success on surprise, because the paratroopers are only lightly armed and extremely vulnerable at their moment of coming down. The lack of sufficient air transport, and the objections raised by the air forces against flying two of these missions to The Netherlands on the very first day, led to no more than two-thirds of the Allied airborne corps being in position on September 17. On the second day additional landings followed, which meant that part of the troops who had landed on the 17th, instead of fighting the enemy, were guarding the drop and landing zones. Thus the paras lacked about half of their strength in their attacks on the series of Dutch bridges during that so vitally important first day.

Nevertheless, by evening the British had succeeded in getting about six hundred men to the northern ramp of the bridge over the Rhine at Arnhem. The 82nd Airborne Division captured the bridge over the Maas at Grave and the bridge over the Maas-Waal Canal at Heumen. But they only had two companies in the vicinity of the Waal Bridge at Nijmegen. The 101st Airborne did succeed in taking the bridge over the Zuid-Willems Canal at Veghel, but the one over the Wilhelmina Canal at Son was blown up just as the Americans approached.

Horrocks had expected to make contact with the paras that same evening. Unfortunately, he halted the advance at Valkenswaard in order to allow his troops to spend the night there, as the tanks were in need of maintenance, and to wait for bridgelaying equipment.

On September 18, problems resulting from these delays became evident everywhere. The second wave of airborne troops did not appear over their target until early afternoon instead of in the morning as planned. They were carried in 1,200 planes towing gliders and in 471 transports. All that time the landing zones needed protection, and at Wolfheze and Groesbeek in particular this required a great deal of effort and manpower. On this second, crucial day the Americans were still too weak to successfully assault and take the Waal Bridge at Nijmegen. The American paras did liberate Eindhoven around noon, but the reinforcements from Horrocks' Shermans did not arrive until four hours later. The tanks pressed on to Son. There engineers worked all night to build a Bailey bridge. On the morning of September 19, ground forces at Grave made contact with the American 82nd Airborne. This was a great relief, as the troops at Nijmegen badly needed reinforcements. Because of poor radio communications it remained unclear what the exact situation was further north at Arnhem.

At the break of the third day of "Market Garden" the Allies held their breath. But hope still prevailed. The Third Reich was shrinking daily, not only from advances in the west, but from hammer blows dealt by the Russians in the east, where they had gotten up to the gates of Warsaw. The Allies had now extended their full technical and numerical strength far into, and behind, the German lines. But what exactly was the enemy up to? An enemy that Dempsey's Second Army Intelligence had proclaimed as being "weak and demoralized, likely to collapse if confronted with large-scale airborne landings." Unfortunately, the truth was quite different.

CHAPTER THREE

IN THE WAKE OF "MARKET GARDEN"

THE GERMAN WITHDRAWAL from Normandy, and subsequently from northern France and Belgium, had evolved into a chaotic rout as August turned into September. On September 5, in Holland remembered afterward as "Mad Tuesday," liberation seemed at hand. The Dutch people watched as the German occupation forces and their local stooges began to panic, trying to escape from the approaching Allies on requisitioned bicycles, farm carts or, in most cases, simply on foot, heading east toward Germany. The Dutch were convinced that within a few hours they would once again be free.

But the liberators did not show up, although from a strategic point of view the chances for a further Allied advance at this time were better than ever before. The German 7th and 15th Armies, having partly eluded the trap in Normandy, were being pushed in separate directions. The 15th was headed toward the French and north Belgian coast, where it could only be extricated in the next two weeks by a very risky crossing of the river Scheldt. The 7th, meanwhile, retreated in the direction of Liège and thereafter to Aachen. Between these two disorganized and demoralized Armies a wide gap was formed. It was during those days, as the Dutch were waiting with flags in hand to welcome their liberators, that a remarkable German recovery took place, comparable to the "Miracle on the Marne" in 1914, when Paris had already been considered lost.

This change was brought about by various causes. From the Allied point of view, the sudden caving in of the German position in

France had created an unexpected crisis in supply. Suddenly, all front-line units had extended their lines of communication by hundreds of miles, and though ammunition stocks were kept in fairly good order, gasoline shortages became commonplace. While the Germans were being forced back ever closer to their sources of supply, the Allies had still to ferry petrol and munitions across the English channel (and often before that from America), and then—only when they were on the continent—could these items be forwarded over France to a front that was in a constant state of flux.

Still, supply problems alone cannot be blamed for the stabilization of the front. The Germans, after all, had successfully come the other way four years earlier, and in Russia had launched offensives over much larger distances—and the Allies had certainly had time to prepare for the campaign.

Another factor was the frantic courage and will to fight instilled in many of the Germans as they found themselves pushed back to the borders of their Fatherland. In terms of morale, evacuating foreign-held soil could not compare to defending one's own country. Still, anecdotal reports from this period are mixed. If the Dutch were convinced that the war was about to end, so were many of the German troops, and who among them wished to sacrifice himself as the "last casualty"? It is beyond the scope of this work to make the statistical analysis, but the fact remains that German troops by the hundreds surrendered en masse to the Allies during this period, men who under more positive strategic conditions would have fought on.

The main reason for the German recovery was the same one that had been demonstrated from 1942 onward—repeatedly in Russia, and in Africa and Italy: this German Army possessed a flexibility in its command structure that allowed it, time and again, to pull itself from the very jaws of defeat to reform and pose a new challenge to the enemy.

In those days, from September 4 to 6, a few dynamic German generals succeeded in plugging the gap and building up a new front line, first on the Albert Canal and thereupon, after severe fighting, on the Maas-Scheldt Canal. They performed this feat with remnants of various formations such as second-rate occupation forces, units fleeing from the south, a battalion of the Waffen SS with Dutch volunteers, a police battalion, navy personnel and others. The core of the units flung into battle were hastily recruited regiments of Fallschirmjäger: paratroops quickly assembled into something that resembled divisions and corps. The units thus formed were placed under the command of paratrooper General Kurt Student and were given the rather fanciful name of "1st Fallschirmjäger Armee." This motley force, together with the remnants of the 7th and 15th Armies, formed Army Group B under command of the swashbuckling Field Marshal Walter Model (who himself had a deserved reputation for retrieving near-hopeless situations). Model was subordinate to the Commander-in-Chief of the entire western front, the Prussian aristocrat Field Marshal Gerd von Rundstedt. This was of limited importance, however, because whenever Hitler wanted to dictate strategy and tactics directly to Model, von Rundstedt was casually overlooked.

The paratroops formed the backbone of the German defense on the canals in northern Belgium. Often they were experienced veterans, but there were also young boys of fifteen and sixteen years who had hardly any training at all. Quite a few had never really belonged to the Fallschirmjäger but had served as aircrew or Flak personnel, in offices or on airfields, or even as pilots for whom the Luftwaffe no longer had any planes. All were now being used as infantry and, after a "training" of a few days or weeks, they marched off to the front, trying to make the best of it, which they actually did. In general they fought well and with great tenacity. Whatever they lacked in training and equipment was compensated for by dedication, particularly among the younger soldiers who, more than the older men, had been indoctrinated with Nazi ideology. Many older soldiers felt proud at being members of the Fallschirmjäger, which, along with the Waffen SS, was still being regarded as an elite corps of the Third Reich. Be this as it may, the British succeeded in establishing a bridgehead across the Maas-Scheldt Canal near Neerpelt on September 12. Facing their bridgehead were the Fallschirmjäger units that were to play such an important role in the Peel area in the weeks to come.

It is typical of the decline of the German Army at this time that it is almost impossible to quote the numbers of these units. After severe losses, which were being suffered with increasing frequency, two or three battalions would be regrouped into one new battalion which was then given the number of one of the old battalions. Often the process was repeated after a matter of weeks. The Germans were also following a new policy whereby units were indicated by the name of the commanding officer. For example, Battalion Hofmann of November 1944 was quite different from Batallion Hofmann of October; the only thing they had in common was the commander himself.

By now it had become a general procedure in the German Army to form various units into a Kampfgruppe (Combat Group), a temporary force that was given a specific task. Certain units, varying from a company to a division, were wrongly classified as "Kampfgruppe," adding to the confusion. In this book, whenever the numbering of a unit was not consistent and the unit was also known by its commanding officer's name, the latter indication is used.

One of the Fallschirmjäger units was raised in Halberstadt, Germany, in August, but without receiving proper basic training, for which there was no time. Already by September 5 this newly formed regiment had to leave post-haste for Holland, where it arrived two days later—good time, considering the Allied air attacks and the many transportation problems—and took up positions near Tilburg. Not until then did the soldiers receive their paratroop uniforms and arms, among which were many Panzerfausts. The majority of the soldiers, scraped together from various staffs, signal corps and other Luftwaffe formations, were unable to handle the equipment. Additional training was given for three days, whereupon the regiment was loaded onto trucks and driven to the front on the road from Hechtel to Valkenswaard. This road ran due north from the front in the bridgehead formed by the Allies along the Dutch-Belgian border. It was the natural route of advance for the Allies, and here the main push for the battle to come was to be made.

Two of the battalion commanders of the German parachute regiment had no combat experience; nor, for that matter, had most of the company commanders. The third battalion commander, however, Major Hellmut Kerutt, was an experienced veteran and very energetic. He immediately set up a defensive position on the road.

The German High Command wished to wipe out the entire British bridgehead, but for a strong counterattack more forces would be needed. On September 13 the paratrooper Colonel Erich Walther arrived on the scene to assume command of all the forces in the area, which from that moment on were called "Kampfgruppe Walther." This force consisted of the regiment of which Battalion Kerutt formed the core. On its right flank was the parachute regiment commanded by Lieutenant-Colonel von der Heydte (that was later to play a leading role in the Battle of the Bulge). In addition, two units were provided by the 10th SS Division "Frundsberg": Panzergrenadier Battalion Segler and a Panzerjäger unit commanded by SS Sturmbannführer (Major) Roestel. "Panzergrenadier" meant motorized infantry, but the word in this case amounted only to wishful thinking. The Panzerjäger unit, however, lived up to its name: it had fifteen Sturmgeschütze (self-propelled guns) of 7.5 cm at its disposal. These could also be used as tanks, and, in fact, in a defensive role German experience in Russia indicated that they were sometimes more effective than tanks.

A penal battalion of the Luftwaffe, wearing uniforms for service in the tropics, also formed part of Kampfgruppe Walther. Militarily speaking, even more so than the usual Luftwaffe field unit, the penal battalion was a farce. On the right flank of the battle group was an army division and on the left flank, hastily raised from depot troops, was Fallschirmjäger Division Erdmann, which was fated to play a central role in the near future in the Peel area.

On September 15, Colonel Walther issued the order to counter-attack. It failed, and so did another attempt on the following day. Walther therefore decided to resort to defensive measures, the most important task again being assigned to Major Kerutt, who during all this time had been the "soul" of the fighting on the German side, defending the road to Valkenswaard. The Major set up his HQ just beyond the Dutch border and positioned his companies, well camouflaged, in little woods on either side of the road. A few miles to the rear he placed thirty men with Panzerfausts and a few machine guns as an anti-tank trap, again well concealed.

Old hands such as Walther, Kerutt and Roestel realized that the tough battles of the past few days were merely a prelude. The weather

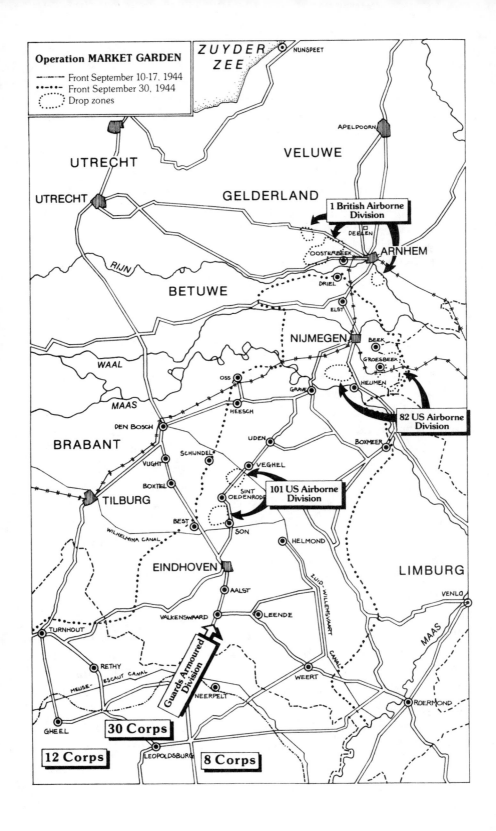

Operation MARKET GARDEN

—·—·— Front September 10-17, 1944
●●●● Front September 30, 1944
:····: Drop zones

ZUYDER ZEE

NUNSPEET

VELUWE

APELDOORN

UTRECHT

UTRECHT

GELDERLAND

1 British Airborne Division

DE ELEN

OOSTERBEEK

ARNHEM

RIJN

BETUWE

DRIEL

ELST

NIJMEGEN

BEEK

GROESBEEK

HEUMEN

82 US Airborne Division

OSS

GRAVE

WAAL

HEESCH

MAAS

DEN BOSCH

UDEN

BOXMEER

BRABANT

SCHIJNDEL

VEGHEL

VUGHT

SINT OEDENRODE

101 US Airborne Division

BOXTEL

TILBURG

BEST

SON

WILHELMINA CANAL

HELMOND

EINDHOVEN

LIMBURG

AALST

ZUID-WILLEMSVAART

VENLO

VALKENSWAARD

LEENDE

CANAL

TURNHOUT

MAAS

Guards Armoured Division

WEERT

RETHY

MEUSE-ESCAUT CANAL

NEERPELT

ROERMOND

GHEEL

30 Corps

12 Corps

LEOPOLDSBURG

8 Corps

had improved and preparations behind the British lines pointed to a large-scale attack. Yet the Germans were wholly in the dark as to what exactly was going to happen.

★   ★   ★

"September 17, 1944 began as any other day. It was a beautiful autumn day, sunny and warm," wrote Second Lieutenant Heinz Volz, adjutant of Major Kerutt. "Toward noon, however, the air above us became filled with an ominous roar, and from behind the enemy lines, at extremely low altitude, a huge armada of gliders and troop carriers flew over. These vast masses of planes were protected by countless fighter bombers, mostly Lightnings, which spotted every movement on the ground and incessantly strafed all the roads in our sector." As there was no German anti-aircraft defense in the area, the Allies had complete control of the air.

At two o'clock a grueling artillery bombardment hit the German positions. Major Kerutt's premonitions had turned out to be correct. An officer of another unit had positioned a number of anti-tank guns along the road instead of in the woods. All the guns, without having fired a single round, were destroyed by Allied artillery and aircraft. Yet Kerutt's companies remained virtually unscathed. Half an hour later the British launched their big tank attack. Kerutt's men succeeded in destroying or severely damaging a number of tanks, although they were not able to stop the powerful thrust completely. What Walther and Kerutt could not possibly know, however, was the race XXX Corps was running to get to Arnhem bridge, and that delaying the British armor for even a few hours brought the paras near Arnhem closer to annihilation.

Toward evening, the British were advancing close to Valkens-waard, but now they themselves began to waste valuable time when Horrocks, much to the surprise of the Germans, halted his corps. This delay was fatal because events near Arnhem were fast developing into an Allied defeat. British XXX Corps could easily have advanced faster. Kampfgruppe Walther had been split and communication with Freiherr von der Heydte's regiment had been cut. It had problably moved to the northwest. Kerutt's battalion found itself mainly east of the road to Valkenswaard, near Borkel and Schaft. With the remnants of the other battalions of the regiment, under his command since September 18, Kerutt now had to avoid being trapped. On the evening of the 18th the British passed Eindhoven (delayed by a German air attack on the town) and made contact with the American 101st Airborne. The Germans could move in one direction only — the northeast — with the constant risk of bumping into British spearheads.

The hodgepodge German front line was crumbling. In the next few days Kerutt advanced along a strange, meandering line to Maarheeze. Together with Kerutt, SS Battalion Segler, the SS Panzer unit of Roestel and whatever was left of Kampfgruppe Walther moved away in the direction of the Zuid Willems Canal. Von der Heydte and his regiment had been lost sight of. Division Erdmann, on Kerutt's left flank, also moved toward the canal. The Fallschirmjäger, on Hitler's orders, fought ferocious reargurd actions in order to protract the "unpelasant situation" in which, in Hitler's view, the enemy found themselves. So far as the sector south and east of Eindhoven was concerned, the Führer was fooling himself — it was in fact the Fallschirmjäger of Erdmann and Walther who in the week following September 17 were forced to retreat until finally the Deurne Canal and the canal running from Wessem to Nederweert turned out to be a formidable obstacle that enabled the Germans to establish a more solid line of defense.

Meanwhile, Horrocks' XXX Corps, led by the Guards Armoured Division, moved towards Nijmegen and Arnhem in their race to relieve the British paras on the north bank of the Rhine. Horrocks' advance guard finally made its first contact with units from the American 82nd Airborne Division south of Grave on September 19. The main force of tanks succeeded in penetrating into Nijmegen via a southeasterly detour that same afternoon.

The British VIII Army Corps had been ordered by O'Connor to advance on the right-hand side of the "corridor." By doing so, Horrocks' flank on that side would be protected. The operations by VIII Corps were not as spectacular and dramatic as Horrocks' advance, yet it is a fact that the battles fought on the flanks by VIII Corps and XII Corps did cost more human lives. Between September 17 and 25, the two corps suffered 3,874 casualties against 1,480 casualties in XXX Corps in the same nine days.

The advance toward the northeast by VIII Corps began the night of September 18. The sky was lit by "Monty's Moonlight" when troops of the British 3rd Infantry Division established their bridgehead across the Kempen Canal. It was the first time they operated under this eerie light from a battery of searchlights which, aimed at the sky, reflected their beams off the low-hanging clouds, thereby illuminating the battle area. In the morning a footbridge was put across and ten hours later a bridge for heavy vehicles was also set in place, despite harassing fire by the enemy.

It was near this Dutch-Belgian border area that the troops were unpleasantly surprised by a new type of mine that the Germans had sown in large numbers in front of their positions: small wooden, sometimes glass boxes without any metallic parts, which rendered the British mine detectors useless. The explosion of this insidious device was strong enough to blow a man's foot off or wound him in the lower body by blown-away clods of earth or stones. These Schü mines, as they were called (*Schützen* means infantryman) form an ever-recurring litany in our story.

In the meantime the 11th Armoured had driven north via the bridgehead near Neerpelt, and from Valkenswaard they veered to the northeast. On September 20 they liberated their first Dutch town, Leende. On the right it would not be until the next morning before the 3rd Infantry Division crossed the Dutch border. That same day the Dutch "Prinses Irene" Brigade drove from the border to Grave, where they dug in to guard the bridge against German surprise attacks. In the late afternoon of September 20, far to the north, Horrocks' tanks, in close cooperation with the American paras, had succeeded in taking the Nijmegen bridges undamaged. But just as the Guards Armoured had at last crossed the river Waal at Nijmegen and was on the point of rushing to Arnhem to rescue the paras there, news came in that the Germans had liquidated the British force at Arnhem bridge. The gallant, battle-weary "Red Devils" had come to the end of their tether, and organized resistance near the bridge had ceased. On the evening of the 20th the Germans were in full control of the bridge and were now using it to rush reinforcements against Horrocks' advancing forces in the Betuwe area, the land between Nijmegen and Arnhem. The Germans had won a crucial battle.

The fighting in the streets of Arnhem and the abortive attempts to relieve Colonel Frost's battalion at the bridge had almost halved the 1st British Airborne Division. The remnants were entrenched in a narrow perimeter around the village of Oosterbeek. There, along with elements of the Polish Parachute Brigade, who had been their only reinforcement, they continued to fight savagely, hoping that ground forces would soon relieve them.

Those ground forces, however, were faced with new problems, not only in their advance through the Betuwe, but also further to the south.

To the 3rd Division, which was stationed at the southernmost end of the sector, it had all started like a piece of cake. The Suffolks in front, followed by the East Yorks, advanced from the border in the direction of Weert through terrain covered with woods, thickets and undulating sand dunes, a terrain which afforded a limited field of view. On the evening of September 21 they reached the railway track Eindhoven-Roermond, having met only sporadic resistance. But in the afternoon of the same day, the 11th Armoured, on the 3rd Division's left, had met an entirely new enemy: this time not infantry with small arms, but heavy German tanks! This had not been anticipated from the supposedly "demoralized" enemy. Where did these panzers come from? To answer this question we must take a closer look at the German strategy of this period.

★   ★   ★

As early as August, when the Allies were racing through France and Belgium, Hitler had entertained certain ideas about the strategy he would like to adopt in the immediate future. The current image of Adolf Hitler as a raving fanatic who, unlike his generals, clung to the idea of holding on to every inch of ground at any price, is only partly correct. Stemming largely from the war in Russia, this reputation was first belied when the Allies landed in Italy, when only Kesselring's arguments persuaded Hitler to sanction the extremely effective defense of that peninsula. It was Hitler who refused on August 31 to allow forces in the north of France to be moved across the Somme, as this would merely have been a waste of troops. It was Hitler who, on September 5, did not want to launch an attack by the Fifteenth Army as proposed to him, but ordered it to be withdrawn to Zealand-Flanders* and the Dutch province of Zeeland. It is true that on his orders the Fifteenth Army had left garrisons behind in Boulogne, Calais and Dunkirk, but it is debatable whether holding on to these ports was unwise. The basic idea of Hitler's strategy was to force the Allies to spread their forces, meanwhile pulling back to strengthen the Westwall, the old defense line along the German border (erroneously referred to as the "Siegfried Line" by the Allies), and also to gain time to raise new divisions in Germany. Once the situation had stabilized, a great counteroffensive was to be launched later.

Hitler was thinking in terms of months, and it may be said that the idea of the future Ardennes offensive was born in the early days of September. Each day that the Allied advance was halted, or even delayed, or each day on which bad weather kept Allied air power grounded, worked to his advantage. In the meantime there was no need for the German Army to be fully defensive. The Allied armies had turned to the north. That would give the German forces in the north of France an opportunity to launch a counterattack against the American flank. The higher commanders on the western front, von Rundstedt and the indomitable Model, were in full agreement with this strategy.

Early in August, Hitler also gave a series of orders to strengthen the Westwall, especially the extension through the south of Holland, along the Maas from Roermond to Nijmegen and continuing all the way to the Ysselmeer. Organisation Todt was in charge of the technical aspects, but the German Nazi Party would take care of the *Menschen-einsatz* — the recruiting of forced labor — both from the Dutch and the German population. In Holland, north of the river Waal, the Reichs-kommissar Arthur Seyss-Inquart would remain responsible as the top

---

*Zealand-Flanders is a strip of land between the Belgian border and the Scheldt River. Facing it, across the Scheldt, are the islands of Walcheren and South Beveland, all part of the Dutch province of Zeeland.

party official in the occupied territory. In the province of Limburg, however, the two heads of the nearby German *Gaue* (party territories) of Essen and Düsseldorf were to act as organizers of the defense so far as they did not conflict with the military. Because of these arrangements, the part of the province of Limburg east of the Maas was to be annexed and "politically and administratively" incorporated into the German Reich.

During the second week of September the party bosses of the *Gaue* took over the local government in the towns of Venlo and Roermond and forced the men of Limburg to dig defense lines and tank ditches.

On September 12 the Americans penetrated the Westwall near Aachen. It was not a major victory, but, apart from the psychological effect — of the greatest importance to Hitler — that the fall of the first German city might have, continued Allied success here would mean a breakthrough to the Rhine. "Every bunker, every block of houses in a German town, every German village must be turned into a strong-point," Hitler ordered on September 16. It was now a matter of "holding the fortress or be destroyed." Every commanding officer was ordered to force his men with drastic measures to hold their ground and — as Hitler put it — "to rouse them to a fanatical frenzy." At the same time, fresh German reinforcements were rushed to Aachen.

As it happened, the Americans did not make make great progress at Aachen as the battle turned into a bloody slugging match. But suddenly, out of the blue on September 17, there were those daring Allied airborne landings in Holland, three divisions now far behind the German lines! Through the narrow trail blazed by the paras, the Allied tanks would now be able to dash into Germany!

The obvious German response was to cut that narrow corridor so that all the Allied forces near Grave, Nijmegen and Arnhem would be trapped.

It so happened that during these days the 107th Panzer Brigade had arrived in the west from Poland. The brigade had initially been earmarked for a counterattack near Epinal in the north of France, but now that the Americans were into the Westwall near Aachen, it was decided to send the 107th to this sector. In two days, from September

16 to 18, the bulk of the brigade was transported by train from Trún in Poland to Venlo in Holland. This was quite an achievement, considering that movement by day was virtually impossible with Allied aircraft continually roving the skies. Due to considerations having purely to do with the rail net, Venlo had been chosen as the terminus for the fifteen trains. "Not bad at all," Hitler said, when he was told the news on the evening of September 17. That day he had been surprised by news of the Allied airborne landings and considered them more of a menace than the American push at Aachen. The newly arrived panzers were in the right place at the right time to thwart the Allied plans.

The 107th Panzer Brigade, commanded by the red-haired Lt. Colonel Berndt-Joachim Freiherr von Maltzahn, had been raised from remnants of the 25th Panzer Division, which had virtually been wiped out during the Russian summer offensive against Army Group Center. In fact, the German Army had not previously used armored brigades. This type of formation was the result of the emergency situation that arose in 1944 regarding personnel and equipment, when it no longer made sense to "pretend" that understrength units were still divisions. The new brigades usually numbered two battalions instead of three, a Panzer Abteilung as tank unit, a battalion of motorized infantry, and a few independent companies. Like many other German units, the 107th Panzer Brigade had been hastily filled out with new recruits after its experience in the east. It had all happened so quickly that the brigade had no artillery at its disposal and the heavy repair units had been left behind on the eastern front.

Still, the 107th Panzer Brigade could not be compared at all with those inferior units scraped together, badly armed and barely trained, that the Allies had expected to meet in Holland. On the contrary, despite its small size, the brigade was a powerful combat force. Officers, NCOs and men were well trained and, having been in action for long periods, in Russian and North Africa, had much more combat experience than their opponents. The brigade was certainly not fanatically Nazi. The atmosphere was rather one of political indifference, combined with a certain professionalism. The men were aware of the situation Germany was in, and they felt it their duty to give all they had in combat. Morale was remarkably high, and arms and equipment, save for the lack of artillery, were very good. The firepower of both the Panzergrenadier Battalion and the tank unit was excellent, and the independent sapper company (also motorized) turned out to be a combat unit to be reckoned with. The term "motorized" stood for more than simply carrying personnel about in trucks. The infantry and sappers used half-tracks that were equipped with heavy machine guns co-opted from the Luftwaffe (though often the right ammunition was not available) or mortars. All units had been abundantly supplied with small arms.

The striking power of the brigade was primarily embodied in its Panzer Abteilung. It consisted of three squadrons of twelve tanks each and a squadron of twelve Sturmgeschütze. The tanks were the much-dreaded Panthers, which, similar to the Sturmgeschütze, carried 7.5 cm guns. The Panther was a tank of advanced design with outstanding features — in many respects better than the Tiger. Much to their dismay, the Germans had become acquainted early on in Russia with the great T-34, which at that time performed better than any tank in the world. The German tank designers learned a great deal from the experience, however, and by mid-1943 answered with the Panther. This tank not only bettered the T-34, but, especially in its second and third versions, was markedly superior to the British and American tanks, including the Shermans that the Allies were using in Holland.

It is understandable that the German High Command regarded the 107th Panzer Brigade as a welcome device with which to attempt to sever the Allied corridor. Its commanding officer, von Maltzahn, however, was totally unaware of any such plans when he arrived by one of the first trains at the deserted railway station of Venlo on the night of September 17. In fact, he had no clue at all what was expected of him, and for hours he tried to make contact with General Student's staff. When he succeeded, he was told that from now on his brigade would be part of the 86th Army Corps commanded by General von Obstfelder, who had his HQ at Hillenraad Castle, just north of Roermond.

As the first few trains of the 107th were being unloaded at Venlo station, delays were caused by interference from Allied airplanes. Von

Maltzahn first received a ludicrous order from Hillenraad Castle to attack Eindhoven, an order against which he protested. Part of the brigade had detrained, but the remainder was still waiting to do so and other units had not even arrived. That very same evening, 86th Corps issued another order to the effect that next day the brigade, with everything that had so far been unloaded, was to attack the village of Son, north of Eindhoven, through which the Allied corridor passed, and to seize the bridge over the Wilhelmina Canal nearby. This order made more sense, although the brigade was not yet at full strength.

Son and its vicinity was in fact already being attacked on the day of the airborne landings by a battalion of the Ordnungspolizei, a police unit from Tilburg, and by a few smaller units which had been quickly transferred by the German command in Holland to the line St. Oedenrode-Best and the Son heathlands. The next day, these forces were joined by three battalions of the 59th Infantry Division. This division belonged to the 15th Army and the three battalions were transferred to the combat area at a speed totally unexpected by the Allies—by train all the way to Boxtel. These measures, so quickly taken, achieved some success, but finally amounted only to a demonstration. The battalions were badly equipped and, like the police battalion, consisted largely of older men. The police battalion had extensive experience in carrying out raids on the civilian population and in assisting the SD (Security Police) in the fight against Dutch resistance, but it was in no way fit to stand against elite Allied units.

As the forces west of Son had already been engaged in heavy fighting for at least 24 hours against the American 101st Airborne Division, it was indeed more important for the 107th Panzer Brigade to attack Son from the east as quickly as possible, rather than wait until the brigade would be up to full strength. The German pincer movement was to cut the narrow corridor near Son before the British tank columns would be able to reach Nijmegen via the bridge over the Wilhelmina Canal and through Son. Presumably, neither General von Obstfelder nor the German commanders in West Brabant had a clue as to whether the bridge at Son was intact or not. The bridge had in fact been blown up by the Germans at the very last moment, but Horrocks had had a Bailey bridge laid over the canal on the night of

September 18, and German observers spotted Allied columns with heavy equipment on their way to Nijmegen: between 100 and 125 tanks, they reported.

Time was running out and von Maltzahn realized that he simply could not wait for the rest of his brigade to turn up. Angered and frustrated, he strongly demanded that 86th Army Corps give him enough petrol for his tanks and other vehicles. To keep the brigade rolling was almost more important than to keep it firing; petrol was at least as vital as ammunition, he argued. He was promised that he would not have to worry on that score. In the actions to follow, however, the brigade would not receive a single drop of fuel from 86th Corps. Lack of it would haunt von Maltzahn throughout the campaign.

CHAPTER FOUR

A MEDIEVAL STYLE OF WARFARE

During that confusing week following the airborne landings, from September 17 to approximately the 26th, there was hardly any front line to speak of. Certainly not in the sector southeast of Eindhoven, where Kampfgruppe Walther and Fallschirmjäger Division Erdman were fighting grim rearguard actions, retreating slowly behind the Zuid Willems Canal and an intricate web of smaller canals that was to be the front line of the German bridgehead in the Peel area. In a way this new front line was, albeit without any cohesion between the retreating units, a withdrawal of the front established earlier by the Germans along the Maas-Scheldt Canal.

North of Eindhoven a "front line" as we know it simply did not exist. The Allies had suddenly occupied positions along a narrow strip of land which in places was only a few miles wide and elsewhere not wider than the road on which their tanks and other vehicles were driving. It was luck that, except at Arnhem, where the 9th and 10th SS Panzer Divisions were nearby, only a few weak German forces were near the drop zones, as the bulk of German troops in the province of Noord-Brabant was tens of miles away from the corridor.

The battles for the corridor, certainly on the German side, began to resemble skirmishes fought in earlier ages, with small feudal armies marching through woods, fields and meadows to fight much farther away, in hostile territory, on small battlefields. In case of victory, the battlefield would be retained; in defeat, the men would make a safe getaway and continue combat somewhere else.

The absence of an actual front line revived another phenomenon of earlier times: the presence of curious villagers who happened to catch a glimpse of these foreign warriors, and moved freely from "enemy territory" to "friendly" areas and vice versa. People from Oploo and St. Anthonis in the northern part of the Peel, at least ten miles away from the corridor, jumped on their bikes to cheer the Allies at Grave. One of the local people who greeted the liberators was Mrs. van den Heuvel, from St. Anthonis, with her children. To her great surprise she encountered her husband, whom she had not seen since 1940 when he fled to England among the soldiers of the Dutch Brigade "Prinses Irene" and who was now guarding the bridge at Grave. A few others, like Len Welbers, realized that if he and his friends stayed in Overloon, they would most likely be forced by the Germans to dig defense systems. They decided to stay with the Allies. Others preferred to sally forth to get hold of a few English cigarettes and then returned home, where the Germans were still in full control. Such scenes were far removed from the twentieth-century concept of "total" warfare, and truly belonged to a medieval era.

The mini-crusade of von Maltzahn's small army got underway on the morning of September 19. This "army," a brigade much under-strength, though later in the day reinforced by a battalion of the Fallschirmjäger, left Venlo to fight a combat much farther away, near Eindhoven. The battle-hardened men even looked like knights in heavy armor, their tanks marked with the black-and-white war cross on their turrets, followed by half-tracks and lorries, and finally the young Fallschirmjäger, dressed in a great variety of all sorts of uniforms, unkempt, but not to be underestimated as foot soldiers, for warriors they were!

All went well and fast as far as Helmond. There the brigade drew up into battle order and steadily advanced toward Son. The weather was a bit foggy, which suited the Germans well since there was no cover against Allied airpower in the thinly wooded area between Nederwetten, Nuenen and Son. The Germans took a few prisoners. A number of them beckoned the Fallschirmjäger to come along. Despite the language barrier the Germans understood that the Americans wanted them to follow them to a farm where there might be something to eat. The plums they found there were consumed with great gusto by Germans and Americans alike. The prisoners, some of whom were extremely frightened, were locked up later inside the farm. The German advance continued.

Strange as it may seem, initially the Allies were unaware that a German force was on the point of attacking their flank, or even in the vicinity. In the late afternoon, when the fog had lifted and the sun was shining brightly, the vanguard of the German tanks under the command of a young officer, Lieutenant von Brockdorff-Ahlefeld, approached the Wilhelmina Canal. On the way he halted his tanks. Standing in his turret, his eyes wandered to the left. There, a few hundred yards away, he saw a column of Shermans standing on the road from Eindhoven to Son. Through his Zeiss binoculars, von Brockdorff saw the British (the Irish Guards) having tea and smoking, blissfully unaware of the prying German eyes. Very briefly the German lieutenant considered shooting up the Sherman column. It was an opportunity almost too good to ignore. With his Panthers and their superior guns, and the advantage of complete surprise on his side, he could have caused trrible havoc on the corridor road. He stifled the impulse at once, however, for all that mattered right now was the canal bridge ahead of him, which, like the one at Arnhem, was the target and focus of this strange and local battle.

Von Brockdorff continued his drive toward the canal, reaching which his Panthers wheeled to the left and up the bank. By now the Allies had become aware that smething was afoot. Shells came down behind von Brockdorff's tanks. Via his tank's wireless he heard that the squadron commander had been wounded and that he was to assume command of the entire squadron. The tanks pushed on. The Panthers had to move with great caution now because they were too big for the narrow canal bank—they might find themselves either in the Wilhelmina or in the soggy grassland on their left. It was touch and go whether they would make it to the bridge or not. And luck was against them.

The Americans of the 101st Airborne Division, who had been surprised initially near Son by the German attack, were now reacting quickly. General Maxwell Taylor, a daring and cunning officer, decided to take part in the action himself. He collected a few men from his divisional staff, one anti-tank gun and a few bazookas. One bazooka was fired at the German vanguard and hit the tank driving in front of von Brockdorff's. The crew of the Panther managed to escape but the damaged tank blocked the canal bank, thus thwarting the German advance to the bridge.

The Germans started to fire their guns on the bridge and the road leading toward it. Von Brockdorff's gunner had to fire closely past the destroyed tank in front of him. As the damaged Panther blocked his field of vision on the left, he was able to fire at the right side of the bridge only. "Get moving, you Panzergrenadiers!" von Brockdorff shouted at his battalion commander.

As it was getting dark, the Germans decided to postpone the attack until the next day, thereby wasting their last and only chance. The fighting for the bridge at Son was the reverse of what was happening at the same time near the bridge at Arnhem. At Son, surprise was one of the principal weapons of the numerically inferior Germans, with time working to the advantage of the Allies. Every hour that passed offered the defenders more opportunities to concentrate their tanks and artillery, and as soon as the weather improved the air forces joined in the fighting. Eindhoven was heavily attacked by the Luftwaffe that night, causing two hundred civilian casualties. Debris blocked the roads in the town for all heavy military traffic, causing some delay to the Allies.

The next day, September 20, the Germans resumed their attack, but it ground to a halt almost immediately due to heavy fire from Allied artillery and tanks. The German paratroops in particular, who had previously occupied positions near Nederwetten, suffered many casualties. One company commander was killed, and the battalion commander, lightly wounded, was taken prisoner by the Americans. His successor was the fanatical Hauptmann (Captain) Hugo Paul, who was to play an important role later in the drama of Overloon. Against the numerical superiority of the Allies, each German tank counted. A number of Panthers could not move because of lack of fuel, the very thing von Brockdorff had wished so much to avoid. The only thing to do was blow them up.

It was obvious to the Germans that they had lost the battle for Son. The brigade slowly retreated via Helmond, fighting ferocious rearguard actions. Hand-to-hand fighting took place with the same bloody gruesomeness as the artillery duels near Son. One of the German paras who had eaten plums with the American prisoners stated, "I would rather not speak about it. In Helmond we blasted the enemy out of houses with Panzerfausts. We also used bayonets and shovels."

On September 21 the Germans abandoned the part of Helmond west of the Zuid Willems Canal and blew up the bridge behind them. That same afternoon the western part of the town was liberated by the British 11th Armoured Division, the eastern sector having to wait four more days. The town of Weert had better luck, for it was taken by the British 3rd Infantry Division on the morning of September 21 without a shot being fired.*

In order to seize the part of Helmond still being held by the Germans, it was decided to bypass them in order to get at them from the rear. To achieve this, the Hereford Battalion of the 11th Armoured established a bridgehead on that same day across the Zuid Willems Canal near Someren, south of Helmond. During the night the Herefords were exposed to savage German counterattacks and in the early morning the bridgehead had shrunk to a mere strip of ground thirty by thirty-five yards. For the Shropshire Battalion that relieved them in order to press on with the attack there was imply not enough standing space! By now the Allied troops were under German shell fire. Major Thornburn and his company, who were the first forces in the bridgehead, sent his Norwegian lieutenant, Bratland, forward with a platoon to push the Germans back.

Bratland and his men, throwing hand grenades, crawled forward through a dry ditch and slowly gained ground. Meanwhile the rest of the battalion were arriving at the Bailey bridge, when Thornburn ran toward them shouting to the battalion commander at the head of the

---

*Occasionally tough fighting took place in this sector. Captain Ken Mayhew of the Suffolk Battalion, for example, was awarded the highest Dutch military decoration, the *Militaire Willemsorde.*

column: "Get them back! I will tell you when there is room to bring them across!" When at long last it was possible to send in the other three companies, a tough battle for the village of Asten lay ahead. Every street in the village was defended by veterans from the eastern front. Supported by tanks, the battalion took 250 prisoners. Co-operation between tanks and infantry was not always that simple. Three of the leading tanks were hit, whereupon the rest of the squadron promptly closed their hatches — very sensible of the tank crews, but awkward for the infantry. When Ned Thornburn wanted to speak to the squadron commander he had to climb on top of his tank with bullets whistling past his ears and bang with his rifle butt on the turret in order to make the commander open the hatch.

On either side of the bridgehead at Asten the Germans were launching counterattacks. Not until the next day could the British deploy their forces when, finally, the Armoured Brigade crossed the Zuid Willems Canal. In the afternoon, the Monmouths Battalion advanced toward Liessel. During the advance they knocked out a Panther and two of the dreaded 88 mm guns. There was much bitter fighting for Liessel, but toward sunset the infantry had driven off the Germans with the aid of tanks and had dug in just beyond the village, lit by a few burning houses.

On September 24 the Monmouths set out on the road to Deurne, accompanied by the tanks that were to enter the town that same afternoon. But again the tanks were defenseless within the built-up town center against all sorts of hidden opponents. The task of mopping up was left to the infantry. Ahead of them were half-tracks under the command of Captain Campbell. His vehicle was leading the column because it had a wireless set on board to maintain contact with the battalion staff.

As Campbell drove into the square in Deurne he saw that his tanks were no longer moving forward. He drove around the square back to the infantry, who, not sure of the situation, came marching up to the square when Campbell shouted, "The place is free!" At the same moment the officer marching at the head of the column fell to the ground — mortally wounded by a sniper. Campbell noticed that the infantrymen were alarmed now that their commanding officer had been killed, and hesitated to go forward. Desperately Campbell yelled, "It's okay! If you won't believe me that the place is safe, I'll show you!" Frightened that the sniper might be aiming at *him* now, he slowly walked toward the dead officer, feeling like a man on his way to the gallows. Picking up the officer's rifle, he handed it to one of the infantrymen. The soldiers regained control of themselves and moved on.

In the late afternoon the British were suddenly fired upon in the outskirts of Deurne. There, standing opposite each other, were the imposing seventeenth-century castle of Deurne and the "smaller castle," a graceful, white building. The latter had been occupied before the war by the family of a legendary doctor in the Peel named Niegersma. In the cellar of the larger castle the twenty-five-year-old owner, Baron Theodor de Smeth, was hiding with three other people, among them his wife-to-be, Maria Snethlage.

Both were active in the Resistance Council, a national organization specializing in raids on rationing coupons distribution offices and in sabotaging German communications. De Smeth was the area commander. After years of dangerous resistance work, the hour of liberation seemed near. A German officer had told him that he was going to defend the "schöne Wasserburg" and through the solid walls the four of them cold hear the noise of battle. What was even more upsetting was that it was getting markedly hotter inside the cellar. When a very worried Maria Snethlage opened the door to the hall, she was met by a wall of flames. Barely managing to escape outside through the fire, she ran into the arms of the surprised British. Unable to do anything to stop the fire, De Smeth watched the castle — which had been the family site for over two centuries — go up in flames with all its irreplaceable art and antiques. The liberation carried with it a taste of ashes.

There were more reasons to make the 25th day of September a memorable one. In the afternoon the Shropshire Battalion, which had had to fight so hard to take Asten, was relieved and the infantry moved on to Deurne. They saw dead Germans lying by the roadside, all wearing riding boots with spurs. Indeed, an incredible thing had happened. It is said that in September 1939 Polish lancers charged German tanks on horseback with lance and sabre — the only cavalry charge against tanks in history, it is assumed. Five years later, here in North Brabant, a similar charge was made, this time German cavalry in a mad charge against a British tank. What had happened?

Toward twelve o'clock that morning Major Mitchell, standing in the turret of his Cromwell artillery observation tank, spotted a few horsemen approaching from the village of Ommel. Mitchell thought they were farmers going off to work. Suddenly, the horses started to gallop and rushed straight toward the section of tanks. German cavalry? he wondered. He ordered his tank to fire. One by one the riders tumbled out of their saddles, none of them surviving the charge. "A useless and rather sad gesture on their part," wrote the artillery historian. This was one of the most remarkable incidents encountered during those days by the British 11th Armoured Division; on the whole, the British had engaged German infantry only—Fallschirm-jäger were largely used as such—who had only delayed the advance. The British were in high spirits. It looked as if the advance to the northeast was ready to resume. But what had happened in the meantime to the roaming force of German Panthers?

★   ★   ★

When the 107th Panzer Brigade pulled back on September 21 via Helmond, von Maltzahn learned from General von Obstfelder, who came to visit the brigade on the battlefield, that from now on the brigade would be attached to Kampfgruppe Walther, which would fall directly under von Obstfelder's 86th Army Corps.

The general explained that same evening that the corridor was to be attacked near Veghel. And again the 59th Infantry Division, to-gether with a few other units, was to attack from the west. Kampf-gruppe Walther, advancing from the east, was ordered to take and hold Veghel, particularly the bridge over the Zuid Willems Canal. All this was to take place the next morning.

Kampfgruppe Walther had only the night and early morning hours to reach their start line near Gemert, via Deurne and Bakel. Objections were waved aside by von Obstfelder—and not wholly without reason. Despite German successes, the situation at Arnhem was still precarious and the Germans could under no circumstances allow themselves to lose valuable time. The plan worked, despite the fact that the combat force consisted of little more than the 107th Panzer Brigade plus a battalion of the 180th Infantry Division. The Sturm-geschütze of SS Major Roestel, SS Infantry Battalion Segler and the paratroop battalion of Major Kerutt were not yet there and there was no longer time to await their arrival. The Germans, as so often in this war, were faced with the prospect of either winning quickly, or not at all.

The story of Son repeated itself in almost every respect: at first a rapid advance from Erp, favored by rainy weather that kept the Allied air force grounded. These same conditions, however, made the ground near Veghel very soggy, especially between the road from Erp to Veghel and the Zuid Willems Canal. The German engineers did not succeed in taking the area from the "excellently shooting Americans," as Colonel Walther's chief of staff noted. Von Maltzahn's tanks came to within five hundred yards of the bridge—there they were halted. As time went by, Allied artillery and tank fire increased and by the afternoon it became clear that the Germans were no longer able to cope with the Allies' superiority in heavy armor and firepower. A night attack by the Germans was beaten off with heavy losses.

The next day, September 23, the weather was better, although, as at Son, this gave the Germans little to be happy about. It meant that the Allied divebombers, *Jabos,* would be active again, but because of the effective anti-aircraft defense of the brigade—in particular the "triplet" machine guns taken over from the Luftwaffe—the damage remained limited. Not so in the ensuing ground battle. Attacks and counterattacks followed each other in wave after wave causing heavy losses to both sides. At least four Panthers were lost and the commanders of both the Panzer Abteilung and the infantry battalion of the brigade were killed. But even now the chance for the Germans to capture Veghel and its bridge would not have been lost entirely, if only the two SS units and Battalion Kerutt had arrived. Around noon small groups of these units arrived at the battle, but where were the others?

The German situation definitely changed for the worse in the afternoon, when Allied gliders suddenly landed on the flanks of the

Germans, between the villages of Volkel and Erp and between the road to Veghel and the Zuid Willems Canal. At the same time, another Allied tank attack was launched from Veghel. The situation of the Kampfgruppe became critical. Finally, however, at this crucial moment the Sturmgeschütze of SS Panzer Abteilung Roestel and Battalion Segler arrived — in time to save the Kampfgruppe from a crushing defeat, but too late to grasp this last chance to cut the corridor.

West of the corridor the Germans were again forced to pull back. The next day, prospects became even gloomier. Not because they were forced to withdraw a few miles again, but because farther to the south the British had entered Deurne and were now threatening the rear of the Kampfgruppe. Hurriedly the Germans had to improvise a line of defense south of Bakel, but they were now being threatened by attacks from three different directions.

Would the Germans have achieved a spectacular, strategic success if they had succeeded in cutting the supply lines to Nijmegen and Arnhem provided the Waffen SS had not arrived so late on that fateful afternoon of September 23? It is hard to tell. The question also arises whether the German attacks near Son and Veghel actually had any effect on the outcome of the battles near Nijmegen and Arnhem. Both at Son and Veghel the Germans had shelled and machine-gunned the corridor for hours, even for days. The striking power of Horrocks' spearhead had been affected badly by often having been forced to wait for ammunition, fuel, equipment and other badly needed supplies. It certainly did affect the battle for Nijmegen, as it prolonged the actions in and around this city, and probably also caused delays in Allied progress over the Waal. But were these German attacks directly or indirectly decisive on the outcome of the battle for Arnhem? Sources are far from unanimous; however it seems apparent that the German attack near Son delayed the capture of the Nijmegen bridge, and thus sealed the fate of the paras near the bridge at Arnhem.

Less than four days later, orders were given to withdraw the remnants of the British 1st Airborne Division, which were surrounded near Oosterbeek and were being attacked relentlessly from three sides in a battle of annihilation. What were the motives for this decision to withdraw?

Not until 1984 did research reveal that Horrocks gave clear-cut instructions during a visit to Driel as early as the morning of September 24. He ordered Thomas (commander of the infantry division which had advanced through the Betuwe with such a painful lack of dash) to make the necessary arrangements for the evacuation with General Urquhart of the airborne. Only the *point of time* of the evacuation was left to their discretion. After Horrocks had given the order, he left for St. Oedenrode for consultation with his superior, General Dempsey. The diary of Dempsey's HQ says that the general left another option open on that Sunday afternoon: either another strong bridgehead across the Rhine or, if this should fail, withdrawal of the British paras. The fact is, however, that at a *lower* command level the decision to evacuate had already been made.

On Monday morning, September 25, Montgomery approved the evacuation of the airborne bridgehead. That this crucial decision had actually been made twenty-fours earlier by Horrocks appears to have been forgotten or ignored later. Our sources do not reveal further insight into Dempsey's option. But it is plausible that the three generals came to their decision because of the disturbing news from the corridor: the continual attacks against their only supply line by Kampfgruppe Walther from the east and by other German units from the west. This fact must have convinced Thomas and Horrocks, even before the latter had seen Dempsey, that they could not carry out a successful thrust across the Rhine in time. And since then, a German attack purused with vigor, this time from the west only, had cut the corridor for 48 hours from September 24 to 26. This may be regarded as justification, in the light of later events, for the sad but necessary decision to give up the British bridgehead across the Rhine.

★   ★   ★

How did the German High Command view the situation? Certainly not with a great deal of optimism. Field Marshal von Rundstedt, the supreme authority on the western front, sent a signal on September 21 to Berlin giving a vivid description of the overwhelming superiority of the Allies, and on the wastage of German men and equipment. On the western front, stated the Field Marshal, there were two decisive battle areas: first, the sector between Lunéville and Metz, and second, the sector between Nijmegen and Aachen. These latter two cities attracted a great deal of attention, both from the public and from the top commanders on both sides. More than any other German commander, von Rundstedt clearly realized how important the area between the two cities was, and his conclusions were utterly pessimistic. Three days later, on September 24, he informed Berlin that he found it necessary, in view of the Allied success near Veghel, "that 15th Army and 1st Parachute Army be gradually withdrawn to the nothern banks of the rivers Maas and Waal and to the extended Westwall south of Arnhem."

It is not clear what the Supreme Commander West had in mind. Did he want to abandon the entire province of Noord-Brabant? Should Student's Parachute Army be withdrawn completely behind the Maas River? It is difficult to reconcile this with another signal of the same day when Kampfgruppe Walther was attacked in the rear from Deurne. This signal was sent by Model, commander of Army Group B, to which Student's army was attached. Model, despite his rank of Field Marshal, was technically von Rundstedt's subordinate and wanted a "large bridgehead on the west bank of the river Maas, about 20 miles north of Venlo," in the eastern part of Noord-Brabant and in the province of Limburg in the area west of the Maas, "from where, after supplies had been brought in, an attack in a northwestern direction can be launched."

A provisional defense with the hope of a breakthrough in Brabant to further isolate the Allied troops near Arnhem and Nijmegen was foremost in the Germans' minds. At that time it was already obvious that the British could not hold on much longer at Arnhem. But for months the Germans, in gross overestimation of Allied power, continued to fear that another large-scale effort to cross the Rhine would be made, if not near Arnhem, then farther west, possibly near Wageningen.

Hitler appreciated Model's optimism. He ordered him to "quickly plug the gap in the front line north of Eindhoven," obviously referring to the Allied corridor squeezed in between the 59th Infantry Division to the east and Kampfgruppe Walther to the east, "by a concentric attack." This was precisely what had already been tried and had failed twice. On the night of September 24, Model advised by telephone that the plan was impossible. First must come the bridgehead and reinforcements; an attack prior to September 29 was quite out of the question. Standing between Hitler, who wanted to stand and fight, and von Rundstedt, who wanted to withdraw all forces behind the Maas, Model had his way. The same night, orders were issued for the formation of the large bridgehead. Colonel Walther received fresh instructions from 86th Corps and it is assumed that they came indirectly from Model himself. Whether he had already received the Führer's orders is unknown. His Kampfgruppe was immediately to disengage the enemy and move to the northeast in order to establish a defensive position along a line running from the Maas bank near Boxmeer through the villages of Oploo and Twist, more or less forming the northern edge of a bridgehead around Overloon and Venray.

Everything had to be done very quickly during that night, but again the Germans proved their skill in improvising by actually carrying out this almost impossible order quickly and without losses. Indeed, *almost* without losses, for at the end something went wrong. But more about this later.

$$\star \quad \star \quad \star$$

The fastest route was via the road from Gemert to Oploo. The Germans preferred not to use this road, however, as the area was too flat and offered them no protection against air attacks. Colonel von Maltzahn set out with his adjutant to reconnoiter a road that was lined by trees and at times crossed through woods. It was a detour, but it offered them a chance to remain inconspicuous to the Allied airplanes. It has never been clear which road this was. According to a German report it was a road leading from the south side of Gemert through Groote Heided, which eventually ended on the road from Deurne to Oploo. Accordingly, it must have been a secondary road, albeit one passable to every type of vehicle, even the heaviest. It is most likely that the Germans took the road from Bakel to Milheeze, then turned left, and continued via the Rips crossroads to Oploo. They may have turned left earlier, in the neighborhood of Mortle. Not only the route followed by Kampfgruppe Walther, but in fact all that happened that night and the next day of September 25, is difficult to reconstruct.

A peculiar incident occurred when the Germans were withdrawing to Oploo and St. Anthonis (or advancing, depending on the way one looks at it) and the British 11th Armoured Division was doing the same. Though the two opponents were following long stretches of the same road simultaneously, both were totally unaware of each other's presence. They were bound to bump into each other and this happened fairly late on September 25. That it had not happened sooner was one of those curious incidents during those seven or eight days that had lapsed since the Allied airborne landings, a week without a fixed front line, with various-sized groups of soldiers of both sides marching across fields, at times engaging or avoiding the enemy and sometimes staying in the same village without noticing each other.

On September 23 and 24 British patrols had already reached St. Anthonis, coming from Grave, and after a few skirmishes with Germans who were still in the village, the British were cheered by the local population. "There were English armored cars at every street corner," wrote someone who had been hiding in the village on Sunday, September 24. "Hurrah, the Tommies are here, we are free," was the general feeling, "but soon we realized that it was merely a patrol. Holy Mass was over and within a few minutes the village square was crowded with people. Excitedly we talked about the arrival of our liberators." Suddenly, shots were fired, scattering the people in every direction. A few German prisoners were taken, "an officer with loose-hanging coat and baggy trosers, his hands raised on his cap . . . next to him a young soldier was running as if being chased by the devil himself. An English soldier gave our spokesman a gas mask and the latter went back home. On the way I met a few Germans on motorbikes and a truck. All were taken prisoner. The people from the villages in the area, knowing that the British were in St. Anthonis, sent any German asking for the way—no matter to which place—to St. Anthonis. Thus the English returned to Grave with loads of prisoners."

The joy at being liberated was indeed premature. The next day Kampfgruppe Walther, after its march from Gemert, arrived in St. Anthonis and Oploo. From what is known of the situation and from what occurred later, it is likely the Germans had taken the road via Rips to Oploo as the last leg of their advance. Most units probably reached Oploo or the area south of the village via this road. Part of the Panzergrenadier Battalion, or perhaps the engineer company, proceeded toward St. Anthonis via a part of the Gemert road. Five German armored half-tracks took up positions at the crossroads on the Peelkant-Gemert road, acting as a rearguard.

Probably Walther and von Maltzahn came to the conclusion that a permanent occupation of St. Anthonis and Oplo made little sense, and that it was better to form a defensive line a few miles to the south, approximately in a line from Mullem to Stevensbeek and from there to Twist, with Kampfgruppe Walter against the Stevensbeek woods and Overloon, partly surrounded by woods, in their rear. Orders to that effect apparently did not reach all units; thus, those who had gone too far ahead found themselves walking into British-held St. Anthonis.

This course of events is supported by what happened to nineteen-year-old Hendrik Jan Ledeboer on the night of September 24. Just before "Mad Tuesday," Ledeboer boarded a virtually empty train to Eindhoven in the hope of an early liberation of the south. For nearly three weeks he had been waiting in vain on the land reclamation project owned by relatives of his near Rips. There he had joined the brothers Jas and Noud van der Ven, important men in the local Resistance. Now a Resistance fighter, Jan Ledeboer participated in spanning ropes across roads and waited in fields during the night for arms that were supposed to be dropped by the Allies. On this particular night he and the van der Vens had installed themselves on the upper floor of the gamekeeper's cottage on the road to Deurne and St. Anthonis, right in the middle of the woods just south of the two crossroads. It looked as if the Germans were in full retreat. The three took notes of anything they heard that might be useful to the approaching Allies. From the direction of Deurne they heard gunfire and saw the sky lit up by flames. Little did they know that the beautiful castle of Baron De Smeth was on fire and would be reduced to a smouldering rubble heap that night.

All at once they heard footsteps on the stairs and two Germans appeared in the doorway: one *Sanitäter* (medic) and an officer. They were barely able to hide their notes. Fortunately, Noud van der Ven

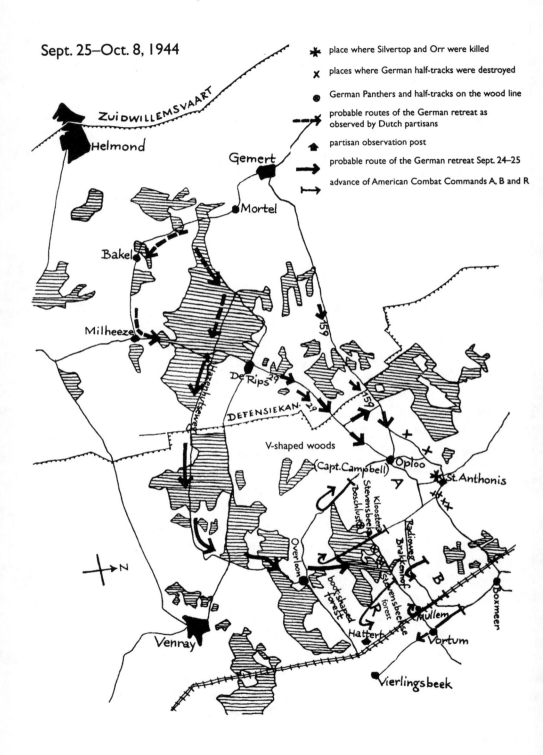

Sept. 25–Oct. 8, 1944

✳ place where Silvertop and Orr were killed

✕ places where German half-tracks were destroyed

⊙ German Panthers and half-tracks on the wood line

➔ probable routes of the German retreat as observed by Dutch partisans

⬆ partisan observation post

➡ probable route of the German retreat Sept. 24–25

⇨ advance of American Combat Commands A, B and R

ZUIDWILLEMSVAART

Helmond

Gemert

Mortel

Bakel

Milheeze

De Rips 29

DEFENSIEKAN·

159

29

159

V-shaped woods

(Capt. Campbell)

Oploo

A

✳ St. Anthonis

Kloosters
Stevensbeek
Boschlust

Radioweg
Brakenhof

Stevensbeekse
forest

B

Boxmeer

Overloon

boot-shaped
forest

R

Mullem

Hatterb

Vortum

Venray

Vierlingsbeek

→N

had earlier said that it would be better not to take their guns upstairs. "Where is the road to Venray?" the officer asked. And then, "What are you doing up here?" "We are refugees, we know nothing of a road." "Come on, show us the way!" bellowed the officer, drawing his revolver. The medic remained friendly and even offered Jan Ledeboer a cigarette, which he eagerly accepted. Again the officer ordered them to come along with him.

In front of the door, a Red Cross truck was waiting and one of the van der Vens was ordered to sit next to the driver; the officer kept his revolver pointed at Ledeboer and told him to walk in front of the truck. Ledeboer knew the road almost by heart. Half a mile farther on there was a road to the right, the Hazenhutse road, which skirted the edge of the wood, then crossed the Defense Canal to continue toward Merselo and then to Venray. He pointed out this road to the Germans. Thereupon the Dutch were allowed to get out and the officer shouted, "You stay put and tell every German soldier to follow this road!"

Hardly had the truck disappeared from sight when the van der Vens and Ledeboer quickly went back to the cottage to resume their observations. They saw small, isolated groups of German infantry taking the road to the right, and at about nine o'clock in the morning a column of at least a dozen Panthers trundled by. Not a single German was seen proceeding to the north; only a few stragglers stayed behind, presumably to surrender themselves as soon as the opportunity arose. After eleven, the road became quiet again. In the village the telephone system was still working. They could dial to St. Anthonis and other places to the north and they asked if any Germans were still around or had passed through. From the answers given, they concluded that the villages were no longer occupied.

Tension was mounting. Would more troops come this way? It was about three o'clock when in the distance a few vehicles came into sight. One, two . . . unknown models, not tanks. Surely they must be British. At the same time they saw Germans make their getaway through the woods. This was the moment of liberation! Ledeboer ran toward the road and saw, first, armored personnel carriers, followed by Sherman tanks that turned out to be from the 23rd Hussars of the 11th Armoured Division. As he was the only one with a fair command of English, he told the British commanding officer the intelligence they had collected: "Farther down the road all Germans have turned to the right, toward Venray. We also have reliable information that the road to St. Anthonis and Boxmeer is clear!" On the basis of what he had seen, it was understandable that Ledeboer concluded that the Germans had gone. Therefore, the British assumed that there were no longer any Germans in St. Anthonis either.

The tanks of the Hussars halted, allowing the Shermans of the Royal Tank Regiment, commanded by Colonel Silvertop, the thirty-two-year-old liberator of Antwerp, to move forward. Silvertop's battalion and the infantry of the Monmouthshire Battalion under Colonel Orr, which had joined him, advanced as spearhead of 29th Brigade via Rips to Oploo, along the very same road which the troops of Kampfgruppe Walter most likely had followed in the morning. During the afternoon the British reached Oploo and then St. Anthonis. A number of Germans still in these villages fled. The English were now waiting for the main force of the 159th Brigade, which was advancing to St. Anthonis via the Gemert road which, or at least part thereof, had probably been used by the German Panzergrenadiers or the engineers company. Inevitably, but to both sides completely unexpectedly, the recce troops of 159th Brigade ran into five German armored cars on the Gemert road. A brief skirmish followed when the five rearguard half-tracks took off at full speed toward the village. Three of them were shot to pieces, but two managed, driving at high speed and firing all their weapons, in reaching the center of St. Anthonis. On getting there they found the village swarming with Englishmen. The only thing left to do was drive on at maximum speed and try to shoot their way out of the village.

In St. Anthonis the commander of the British 29th Brigade, Brigadier-General Harvey, had decided to hold a meeting with the two battalion commanders, Silvertop and Orr, in order to discuss the preparations to be made for the pending contact with the rest of the brigade. They were still unaware of its exact location. In the distance sounds of firing could be heard. The officers must have heard it too, but hardly anyone paid any attention at that time to random firing. Patrols were out all over the place to deal with German stragglers. The

British were moving too far ahead, resulting in minor skirmishes in and around the village. The noise of the clash between the German armored cars and those of the 159th Brigade was, to veterans like Harvey, Silvertop and Orr, merely a background noise deserving no special attention. The three men, together with a major of Harvey's staff, met at the crossroads Lepelstraat and what is now called Col. Silvertoplaan.

Hardly had the four men reached the crossroads when abruptly the two German half-tracks appeared. "At the corner near Simon's," a Dutchman who happened to be there reported, "stood a few high officers who were discussing, their heads bowed over staff maps. Suddenly I heard shots being fired and I saw a German armored car racing down the Lepelstraat. A German soldier, wearing a green camouflage jacket, was firing madly with a machine gun." Later, Brigadier-General Harvey wrote: "On September 25, 1944, we were standing at a T crossing south of the center of St. Anthonis to discuss further tactics. Suddenly two German armored cars came heading straight toward us from the village with machine guns firing. Colonel Silvertop was killed instantly and Colonel Orr was so badly wounded that he died on the way to the hospital. My Brigade-Major J. Thomson was shot through one of his lungs, but has recovered. I myself was only slightly wounded." Just before he died, Orr said, "It was foolish of me to be standing there at the crossroads; I should have known better."

A few minutes later the two German armored cars were destroyed outside the village. They had inflicted a serious loss on the British, however, by having killed two very able and dynamic officers. Two German prisoners dug the grave of David Silvertop in the churchyard close to St. Anthonis church.

The death of Silvertop and Orr made the British a bit nervous. When, some time later, British tanks drove to St. Anthonis via the Gemert road, they narrowly escaped being fired at by their own troops. The next morning Oploo, where the British had briefly been before, and Westerbeek, were permanently occupied. The advance farther eastward to reach the Maas was carried out halfheartedly and at a slow pace. South, to Overloon, the advance made hardly any headway at all. "The reason why was probably known best by the higher army command," wrote the historian of the Monmouthsire

Regiment later, resignedly or perhaps bitterly. The farthest point was reached by Captain Campbell of the Monmouthsire Battalion (Orr's battalion), who took up positions with half of his carrier platoon in a V-shaped wood some three miles west of Overloon, its base facing the village. His was the most forward British position, a small force in front of the line that was being formed. This gave the Germans some respite, in fact only one day, to establish a front line too.

The British hesitation might also have been caused by the knowledge that within a few days an American armored division would take over from them, or because of the loss of the two experienced battalion commanders. Another reason might have been the often cautious, methodical procedure applied by the British as a rule in this sector, which did not go unnoticed by the Germans.

Typically, the Germans would not relax during the respite offered them. Kampfgruppe Walther was simply unaware of what had happened at St. Anthonis, because all the Germans involved had either been killed or captured. In general, the Kampfgruppe was well aware of the British supremacy. As a consequence, and in conformity with their orders, the Germans decided to prepare for a stubborn defense, for which the ground was eminently suited. The front line was now running from the Maas, somewhere between Sambeek and Mullem, along the northern edge of the Stevensbeek woods, then curving to the southwest around Overloon. Tanks and half-tracks, all well concealed, took up positions in the woods near Boschlust. Almost in the middle of the northern edge of the Stevensbeek woods were four Panther tanks, which in the days to come would cause the British a lot of trouble. All around the armored vehicles the infantry had dug in.

The time of mini-wars, waged by small, independent, roaming armies, belonged once more to the past. Modern front-line war, in which every yard of ground mattered, had made its comeback near Overloon.

CHAPTER FIVE

LUCKY SEVENTH "OVER THERE"

"Over there, over there"
Send the word, send the word over there,
That the Yanks are coming,
The drums rum-tumming everywhere."
— George M. Cohan (1917)

THE TRAGEDY AT St. Anthonis was a mere grain of sand in the hourglass that told the Allies times had changed. This grain of sand left its mark. The almost casual manner in which the British maintained a rough front line in this sector was abandoned and replaced by a state of alertness. The enemy had turned out to be tougher and more cunning than expected. Yet the Allied command continued to grossly underestimate the enemy's capacity to recover. This is evidenced by the episode which now commenced, the first battle of Overloon, which was to last a week.

As the British 11th Armoured Division and 3rd Infantry Division were continuing their advance to the northeast along the line roughly following the border between the Dutch provinces of Limburg and Noord-Brabant, decisions had already been made on September 23 to deploy an entirely new force in their sector: the American 7th Armored Division. This division had been part of General George Patton's Third Army, which was fighting around Metz, the obstacle that had finally blunted the impetus of the American tank spearheads. Having landed in Normandy in mid-August, the 7th Armored had been at the head of the victorious columns which had carried Patton right across France as far as the banks of the rivers Meuse (Maas) and Moselle. Cheered on by a jubilant population, they had liberated towns such as Chartres, Melun, Château Thierry, Epernay, Rheims and Verdun. On August 22 they were the second Allied unit to cross the Seine.

The soldiers called the division the "Lucky Seventh"—it seemed as if its men had merely come to Europe to push a few roadblocks aside and receive flowers and embraces. After three weeks, however, an end had come to all this. The division reached the Moselle on the night of 8 September and received its real baptism of fire during the crossing of that river. In forming a bridgehead on the opposite bank, the division suffered its first serious losses. In the meantime, a new destination had been found by the Allied command for the division, the reason for its transferral to the north.

The American division had a slightly more flexible structure than its British counterpart. It did not operate with brigades, but with so-called "combat commands," named "A," "B" and "R" (Reserve). According to the nature of an operation, or of its later development, the division's three tank and three infantry battalions were attached to one of these combat commands, sometimes back and forth from one to another. Usually a tank battalion consisted of 729 men, 17 light tanks and 58 Shermans. An infantry battalion numbered 1,001 men and 72 unarmored half-tracks. The division also had at its disposal a reconnaissance battalion numbering 935 men with 17 light tanks and 32 half-tracks. 1,600 artillerymen in three artillery battalions were attached to the division, as well as a few extra reinforcements such as a motorized anti-tank battalion (tank destroyers) and an anti-aircraft battalion of four batteries.

This was the paper strength, for this division, too, had suffered losses in men and equipment which had not yet been replaced. The actual strength in men of the division for the coming period may be estimated to have been some 14,000. The majority of the soldiers came from the Midwest, Eastern and Southeastern states.

Why was the 7th Armored Division to be transferred to the north? At that time the right-hand side of the "corridor"—the flank of

Montgomery's 21st Army Group facing the Dutch-German border—
was considered to be vulnerable. The ferocious German counterattacks
had clearly demonstrated that. South of the 21st Army Group,
Bradley's American 12th Army Group was operating, comprising
Hodges' First Army, which was directing its main thrust against
Aachen, and Patton's Third Army, which was committed near Metz.
On September 23, Montgomery, his ambitious plan to jump over the
three big Dutch rivers now taking on all the appearances of a far from
successful operation, was still hopeful of being able to cross the Rhine,
if not at Arnhem, then possibly to the south, near Mock through the
German Reichswald, a forest along the Dutch border east of Nijmegen.
The American pressure on Aachen and Cologne would have to be
maintained. The enemy, Montgomery hoped, would in any event be
tied down by Hodges' actions and have to do everything within his
power to delay the clearing of the Scheldt estuary. It was still being
hoped that the "corridor" near Nijmegen would not turn into a dead-
end in the Betuwe, but might be used as a springboard for a new
offensive by the British Second Army, an offensive that would offer
Montgomery the Rhineland and, possibly, a bridgehead over the Rhine
as well.

The Supreme Command fully realized that this made it necessary
to increase the pressure exerted by the 21st Army Group. Eisenhower
gave his approval on September 22. One of the problems to be solved
immediately was plugging the gap that was being formed in the sector
where the Germans were regrouping: between the "corridor" and the
Maas. This gap had to be plugged with fresh troops, and Montgomery
discussed with Bradley how to arrange this. The outcome was that on
September 25 the boundary of Bradley's 12th Army Group was
moved to the north. A few American divisions were to be sent to this
new front, and eventually it turned out that only one division was
available: the American 7th Armored. All by itself it was to deal the
deathblow to the German salient over the Maas. Its attack was to be
supported by a diversionary attack by a brigade of the Free Belgians
to the northeast over the canal from Nederweert to Wessem, and by
an American unit with light tanks which was to attack from Sittard
toward Roermond.

★   ★   ★

On the very evening that the 7th Armored Division set out on its long march to the north, September 25, the remnants of the British 1st Airborne Division were withdrawn from across the Rhine. The debacle at Arnhem had come to an end. It seemed as if both sides were marking time to gather their breath for the next battle, as they also did in the Peel-Maas area. Upon orders from higher command, the British 11th Armoured Division limited its operations to reconnaissance after they had reached the Maas near Boxmeer and Cuyk on September 26. The next night the first British shells fell on Overloon. It was still possible for refugees to reach the British lines from there. Those who did told the British that more and more Germans were passing through their village to take up positions on the road to Oploo and St. Anthonis. Boxmeer itself remained no-man's land.

On September 27 the Germans gave orders for the population of the area to be evacuated immediately — not only Overloon with its 1,300 people but also the inhabitants of a string of villages to the east. Within a few hours the inhabitants, who had to leave everything behind, walked dazed and bewildered toward what was becoming the hinterland of the threatened German front. In small villages like Maashees, Holthees and Smakt more than 3,000 refugees were packed together. In pouring rain, sad crowds of evacuees reached Venray that night, where they found shelter in convents, boarding schools and a psychiatric hospital. Not much later the British ordered the evacuation of Boxmeer. Gradually the British became convinced that the Germans were making determined efforts to establish a front line. Captain Campbell, in his V-shaped woods, destroyed two German half-tracks by bringing down fire on suspicious looking "shrubs" and a "haystack."

On a secondary road that led directly from St. Anthonis to Overloon is a monastery by the edge of the Stevensbeek woods. This monastery was in the three-mile-deep no-man's land in which British patrols moved about. They lost two light tanks there, destroyed by well-camouflaged Panthers hidden on the edge of the woods beyond the monastery. When British artillery began to answer the fire, the monks saw that the shells fell short of the target. They promptly phoned this through to friends of theirs in liberated St. Anthonis. Father van den Tillaart noted in his diary that the telephone system still worked perfectly!

"Early on the morning of September 27," wrote Father van den Tillaart, "Holy Mass was read earlier than usual, for we had heard that the English were going to launch an attack on the wood and we all wanted to be safe in the cellar by the time it started. At about ten o'clock a lively fire from the tanks began, and beyond the Radioweg [a road] English tanks were spotted. The Germans were on their guard and from inside the wood they had an unobstructed view of the flat fields in front of them. They set two British tanks on fire and the other ten retreated behind a smoke screen." That day the monastery received its first direct hit from a British shell.

During the night, neighbors slept in the cellar adjacent to the bakery. In the morning, desks were moved from the classroom to the hall, together with the students' suitcases, for the ceiling in the hall was made of concrete and offered some form of protection against shellfire. "It was a quiet morning and a bit foggy," wrote van den Tillaart. "We heard the roar of German tanks changing positions so to mislead British patrols. We walked through the lanes and, near the farm, we found three pigs killed by shell fragments. A few monks quietly walked down the road to St. Anthonis as they were curious to see what was going on. Quite a crowd had come to take a look at the brewed-up British tanks, but the Germans did not like that. Suddenly their tank guns began to fire and shells started to fall around the burnt-out tanks. Scared to death, the people flung themselves to the ground and lay waiting, wondering whether they would survive. The shells hit none of them, but, cured of their curiosity, they went hurriedly back home along the ditches and hedges." In the afternoon three sorties were made by four Typhoons to strafe the wood south of the monastery. Thereupon the British launched another attack through the fields "behind the monastery, but the Germans were still there and again the British tanks brewed up, billowing big, black clouds of smoke."

That day the 11th Armoured Division managed to destroy one German tank in the woods east of the monastery. Father van den Tillaart went with four other monks to take a look at the tank.

"Perfectly camouflaged, it stood underneath the trees. The gunners had celebrated the destruction of two British tanks with only three shells by bringing out a bottle of champagne. There was a big hole in the side of their tank where the British shell had entered and whereupon the tank had caught fire. The skeleton of the driver was still in the seat."

The Dutch civilians who had stayed behind in the area held by the Germans all had a different impression of the enemy's morale, from very correct to brutal or demoralized. One thing was certain: a large proportion of the front-line troops were very young: sixteen to eighteen years old — the scrapings of the barrel of Hitler's Third Reich. British Intelligence had only vague information as to German strength, but they did have great respect for the professional defense tactics used by the enemy.

On September 29, the Americans arrived in the battle zone to relieve the British units. Some British officers were under the impression that the Yanks took their task too lightly. As the Americans passed along the western edge of the Peel marshes, where units of the 3rd British Infantry Division were stationed near Deurne, Asten and Liesel, a meeting was held between "Bolo" Whistler and the commander of the 7th Armored Division, General Silvester. The diary of the British brigade comments: "This American division does not seem to be more than a covering force of tanks and armored vehicles; have they got enough infantry? Will they be able to commit the enemy so heavily that he will not break through towards us?"

The 7th Armored had received its orders on September 28 from General Crolett, to whose corps it had been attached. It was to pass through the British lines and take up position on the line St. Anthonis–Oploo, where they would take over from the British 11th Armoured. The intelligence officer (G-2) of the American corps had informed Silvester that the "Lucky Seventh" would be facing no more than two or three thousand Germans. In actual fact there were more than 15,000 inside the salient.

The salient could be divided into three sectors: one to the south along the canal from Nederweert to Wessem, the Noorder Canal and a part of the Deurne Canal; a central sector behind the rest of the Deurne Canal and the swamps around the village of Griendtsveen as far as the Deurne-Venray road; and the northern sector with Overloon as the key position. Roughly speaking, the southern sector was held by General Erdmann's 7th Fallschirmjäger Division. The central sector, with the longest front line, was held by the weak 180th Infantry Division.

From a strategic point of view this central sector was the most interesting of the three. The Germans rightly expected the big Allied attack to be launched in the northern sector, where the attackers would not be faced with canals and swamps. In this sector Kampfgruppe Walther had been placed. In the attacks on the "corridor" near Son and Veghel the Kampfgruppe had suffered severe losses: one-fifth of its tanks and self-propelled guns had been destroyed or abandoned, and one-quarter of its infantry had been put out of action. The morale of the troops was still high, nevertheless, and so was their fighting spirit. It is true that the structure of the Kampfgruppe had been altered slightly, but it maintained its character of a makeshift outfit with a number of excellent units and a few inferior ones.

This soon became evident on September 28, when the British launched an attack on the left wing of the Kampfgruppe. The Luftwaffe Bau Battalion, which held that sector, consisted of air force personnel without any infantry training. They came from various branches of the air force, even elderly men who had spent the greater part of the war behind a desk or had been engaged on purely technical jobs. Within minutes the entire battalion had fled in panic, leaving their weapons behind. The battalion commander, an elderly officer from the reserve, was found in Overloon, victim of a nervous breakdown. At that moment Kerutt's battalion arrived and, as he had done on the Dutch-Belgian border a few weeks before, he succeeded in restoring the situation and in retaking most of the lost ground with his Fallschirmjäger.

The front line of Kampfgruppe Walther was as follows: On the extreme right, against the river Maas, near Sambeek, Group Roestel had dug in. SS-Sturmbannführer Roestel was now in command of SS Panzergrenadier Battalion Segler, of his own Panzerjäger-Abteilung, which had been restored to its original number of fifteen self-propelled guns, and six guns put at his disposal by the "mother division," SS Panzer Division "Frundsberg." On the left of this Waffen SS formation was Parachute Battalion Hofmann, and to its left was the parachute battalion of Hauptmann Paul, which had already participated in the attack by Kampfgruppe Walther on the bridge at Son. In the sector on either side of the road from Oploo to Overloon, defensive positions had been occupied by the Panzergrenadier battalion of the 107th Panzer Brigade with, on its left, the brigade's engineer company. Finally, leaning against the weak 180th Infantry Division were more paratroops, Kerutt's battalion.

Not many troops on a broad front, but, generally speaking, good troops. Unlike the panzer brigade, the Fallschirmjäger had only light weapons at their disposal, though these were of outstanding quality: not only the Schmeisser (MP40 machine pistol) but also the Sturmgewehr (MP44 assault rifle) and in particular the MG42 machine gun, nicknamed the "Hitler scythe," with a firing rate of 1,300 rounds a minute. A disadvantage of this air-cooled weapon was that the barrel overheated quickly. In such cases the barrel had to be replaced (with the machine gunner wearing asbestos gloves), which could be done within seconds. Each platoon also carried one Zielfernrohr Gewehr (rifle with a telescopic sight) and rifle grenades. Each company carried mortars and a large number of Panzerfausts. Only Group Roestel and the 107th Panzer Brigade had been equipped with heavy weapons.

The Panther tank was the German trump card. The panzer brigade was basically a suitable instrument for mobile warfare only, and an extremely successful one at that. The question was what role the tanks were to play on the undermanned and rather rigid defense line near Overloon. From Hillenraad Castle near Roermond, where the commander of 86th Army Corps, General von Obstfelder, had his HQ, orders were issued to spread out the tanks along this thinly held infantry line. It seemed the general had forgotten that similar tactics applied by the numerically stronger French Army (with its superiority in tanks) had brought defeat to France in 1940. It was not the first, nor the last, order from the corps commander to cause consternation among his subordinates and eventually to be sabotaged. If von Obstfelder's orders had been carried out, the tanks would have been immobilized and been used merely as anti-tank guns, thereby becoming sitting ducks and wasting the entire offensive power of the brigade.

Brigade Commander von Maltzahn in particular opposed the order. He felt that the tanks should be held as a mobile reserve behind the front line, ready to launch a strong counterattack in case of an Allied breakthrough. Though officers like Sturmbannführer Roestel were in complete agreement with von Maltzahn, von Obstfelder refused to modify his orders. The senior officers of the Kampfgruppe, however, obeyed them at their own discretion. They did position a number of tanks among the infantry — in most cases among the paratroops. "When things threatened to become too hot, the tanks were ordered to withdraw and we had to deal with the enemy all by ourselves," a paratrooper remarked. The other tanks remained in reserve behind the front. Von Maltzahn established his HQ in a laundry in Venray, Walther his in Geysteren Castle on the Maas halfway between Vierlingsbeek and Wanssum. This was the beginning of a disaster that was eventually to reduce this beautiful building to a pile of rubble.

Numerically, the Kampfgruppe was definitely inferior to the "Lucky Seventh," but it was certainly not a force that could be overrun easily in one or two days. What was the reason for this curious under-estimation by the Americans? They had arrived in a sector unknown to them and there had been no reconnaissance at all by any of their own units. Admittedly, their predecessors, the British 11th Armoured Division, had sought and made contact with the enemy, but so sporadically that it had been impossible to gauge his full strength.

General Silvester failed to fully recognize this fact. His feelings were confirmed by his own intelligence officer, who, like so many others of the Division staff, had no experience other than their training in Georgia. One of the musts for the G-2 of a division was to stay in close contact with its recce squadron, the eyes and ears of the division. The intelligence officer of this squadron, the future four-star General Knowlton, had met the G-2 only once — to be precise, at a party in the days when the division was still stationed in England! The rush with which Silvester had had to transfer his division from Metz to the Peel — an operation executed flawlessly — had made it impossible as yet to replace the losses in men and equipment sustained on the rivers Meuse and Moselle. Officers put out of action in battle or relieved from command because of incompetence under fire had been replaced. Of the three combat commands "A," "B" and "Reserve," "B" now had its fourth commanding officer within a month; "Reserve," its eighth!

Despite all this, Silvester felt that wiping out the salient and advancing on Venlo would be a mere walkover, while supporting attacks in the south would take care of the liberation of Roermond. The precise order given to him was: "to clear enemy resistance from the area west of the Maas River in the Peel swamp region."

His plan was to attack the next day, September 30, on a broad front, with tanks and with infantry carried in half-tracks. He dismissed the idea of any reconnaissance; besides, his recce unit had been allocated a very broad area to patrol in the western part of the Peel near Deurne. The attacking forces were divided into two combat commands, each having a strength between that of a brigade and a reinforced battalion. Combat Command A was to attack Overloon under the command of Colonel Rosenbaum. The command was made up of Task Force Brown and Task Force Chappuis. The tanks of the 40th Tank Battalion had been distributed equally between the two task forces; Major Chappuis had three infantry companies and Major Brown only one. They were to attack along the road from Oploo to Overloon and along the road through the Stevensbeek woods to Overloon, respectively.

Combat Command B, under Brigadier-General Hasbrouck, was to attack in the direction of the Maas; its first objectives were the villages of Mullem and Vortum. This command was made up of two task forces, Force I under Major Johansen with three companies of infantry and one tank squadron, and Force II under Major Erlenbusch with only one infantry company and two tank squadrons, probably because he would have to move across fairly open country nearest the Maas, while Johansen would advance west of the railway track to Venlo and was to pass the Stevensbeek woods.

John Margreiter, nineteen years old, a private with the 23rd Armored Infantry Battalion, was attached to Johansen's task force. He made acquaintance with the commanding officer of Combat Command B on September 29. In a speech to the battalion General Hasbrouck said, "I've waited so long for a real combat command and I'm sure that now I really have a good one!" Margreiter looked around him and saw how small the 23rd was after the battle near Metz: it was a far cry from the original 800 men. His own mortar group had no mortars at all anymore; they had been left behind at Moselle. All he would have to fight with would be his M-1 rifle. The next day the order was given: "Attack in the afternoon. And before nightfall we'll be in the outskirts of Venlo."

Margreiter, however, did not entertain such great expectations. If we do not attack prior to 1630 hours, he wondered, it will soon be dark, and does that leave us enough time to reach Venlo today? At 1630 Margreiter was standing near the half-tracks and the jeeps of his company, weapons and ammunition having been checked. The order to mount was given. "Wind 'em up."

The vehicles, parked in the laager, started to unwind from the circle and began to move southward. The last half-track had not started its engines yet when the first 88 mm shell came screaming down over their heads. This was the first time Margreiter and his buddies heard the fearsome scream of this famous German gun. The column suddenly halted and on the order "Dismount!" the men lost no time taking cover in the ditch to their right, where they waited for the advance to continue. During forward movements in combat there are a lot of advances and halts that seemingly take place without the soldiers ever hearing an actual spoken command.

They advanced an undetermined distance past the lead half-track, then crouched in the ditch in single file to see what would happen next. There were several haystacks in the field to their left and across the road; these were some 200 to 300 yards away, and at once it became apparent that they were receiving sniper fire from that vicinity. They learned another lesson here: a bullet closely passing one's head does not whistle as in the Hollywood movies. It pops. And the report is something one can never forget.

Suddenly a captain, still wearing his silver bars, which no knowledgeable combat officer ever did, walked upright on the blacktop road. Looking down on them in the ditch, he exclaimed: "You men cover me. I'm going to walk up to the head of the column." He disappeared from their view shortly and they never learned who he was or what his unit might have been. He was lucky that he was not killed at that point.

Eventually the men continued the advance, receiving no more small arms fire. The half-tracks left behind disappeared from sight. The company came to a crossroads where there were two houses on opposing corners and a wood. Behind them a Sherman tank came trundling down the road to give a burst of fire with its machine gun, hoping to force the enemy into giving away his position, a well-tried technique. The tank rumbled past the crossroads and made a left turn in front of the house. As it was pivoting on its left track a Panzerfaust projectile hit the motor compartment. The Sherman stopped and brewed up immediately. From his ditch Margreiter saw how the crew hastily abandoned the tank through its turret and its forward hatches and made for the ditch. One of them was shot through the leg, but they survived.

A moment later the Americans began to receive a severe mortar concentration on their position in the ditch and again experienced the grinding fear of bombardment. After a time it stopped, and they again rose upright to see what was going on. Then it began again, and after a while the order came: "Fall back! Fall back!" This time the shells were not as close to them as they had been before, so they rose and began to walk back in the direction from which they had come, staying in the ditch beside the road. In the back of Margreiter's mind the phrase "the troops retired in good order" appeared from something he had once read. They had scarcely begun this retrograde movement when an old dogface behind him tapped him on the shoulder and said: "Kid, up here when they yell 'Fall back!' we don't walk, we run! Now, shag ass!" With a great sense of relief they all began to pound their way along the ditch away from the mortar barrage. As soon as they reached a point of safety they began to walk again. When it was getting dark, Margreiter did not find himself in the outskirts of Venlo but in a culvert beneath the road, not far from the farm of "Brakkenhof," just north of the Stevensbeek woods.

All along the line the Americans had similar experiences. Hasbrouck's attack on Mullem and Vortum ground to a halt almost at once against a strong German screen of anti-tank guns, minefields and dug-in infantry with anti-tank weapons. The tanks had advanced in single file on the roads as they used to do during their march across

France, brushing aside occasional roadblocks. The nature of the ground in Brabant, however, made deployment off the roads virtually impossible. The fields were too soggy and crisscrossed with ditches and canals.

Suddenly a figure appeared next to Margreiter. It was the platoon sergeant, Elvin Saxberg, the "Swede." As the men wriggled into their harness and picked up their weapons, it became obvious that one of them did not want to accompany them back up the road. The soldier became quite agitated and literally shouted at Saxberg that he had had enough and that his nervous system would not and could not take it anymore. Saxberg told him that he was a coward and that if everybody felt that way the United States would never have made it out of North Africa. Eventually the soldier was left in the culvert and the others proceeded back up the ditch in single file.

At one point during the night, they passed a burning house and crawled past it just in case any Germans might be observing from the edge of the wood. At this point Margreiter remembered a poem from his college days: "I have a rendezvous with Death at midnight in some flaming town." He tried to remember who the poet was. Rupert Brooke, he thought. Much later it would come back to him that it was Alan Seeger.

Finally they dug in near the same crossroads where they had been that afternoon. "Did you see that dead man there in the middle of the road?" whispered Margreiter's buddy. "Look, Bob, you don't think they go around putting sheets over bodies in the front line, do you?" In the flickering light of the fire the body turned out to be that of a big, white sow.

In the doorway of the burning house the figure of a man was outlined against the fireglow, and another, and another. Margreiter was getting excited. "Goddam, Bob," he whispered, "those are Krauts! I'm going to shoot the next one that passes in front of that fire." He put his gun to his shoulder and peered through the sight at the doorway. After a few minutes it occurred to him that maybe they were his own men after all. He put the safety catch back on and dozed off in his hole. Later he learned that the burning house had been occupied that night by the HQ section of his own company. During the night mortar fire rained down again on their foxholes. Two men were killed. It took one of them more than an hour to die, but nobody was prepared to leave his shelter and take the man to a medical aid post.

A cloudy day dawned: Sunday, October 1. Slowly they moved forward again. At the crossroads Margreiter saw the burnt-out Sherman tank once more. The hollow charge of the Panzerfaust had burnt a hole in the side with a diameter of approximately nine centimeters. He touched the hull with his hand; it had cooled off.

Beyond the crossroads a pine wood began, through which the company slowly advanced in the usual battle formation: two platoons next to each other, Margreiter's in the rear, as support. Somebody pointed out what to him looked like a bundle of rags. It was the first dead German he had seen so far. A few moments later, shots were heard: the scouts had made contact with the enemy. All Margreiter could do was wait, and while lying there on his side he started to dig a slit trench, a very exhausting job if you have to keep your head down for fear of being shot.

Thus, Combat Command B became stuck again in the field and in the undergrowth near the farm of "Brakkenhof," halfway between Mullem and Stevensbeek. Their last resort was the artillery, and fortunately the British guns also came to their support. On October 2 seven artillery battalions fired 1,500 shells into the German positions within two minutes. This brief, ferocious barrage helped the Americans take their first Dutch village, Vortum.

That night at 1930 hours the village had been taken by Erlenbusch's Task Force II of CCB against little resistance. But south of Vortum Erlenbusch's tanks ran into strong German defensive positions. Farther west Rosenbaum's CCA had also met fierce opposition during two similar attacks on Overloon. On October 1 a few Sherman tanks penetrated as far as the small hamlet of Heikant. But here, too, the infantry's advance was very slow, no more than a few hundred yards. It bogged down under fire from mortars, artillery, Nebelwerfer and small arms.

Like any other front-line soldier, Margreiter was unaware of all this. He only knew what was going on in his own area. He had spent October 1 and 2 in the woods, occasionally under fire. The flank of his platoon was facing fire from a Schmeisser sub-machine gun. "How could we make the German give away his position?" he was asking himself. A soldier lying in front of Margreiter shook a few twigs on a nearby bush and Margreiter peered over the edge of his trench to observe where the fire was coming from, but the German did not react. During the night Margreiter slept in his trench on a layer of hay with room enough for two men. It did not rain and sometimes they passed apples to one another. On the second day a man was shot through his leg right in front of Margreiter. "Medic, medic!" cried the wounded soldier, notorious in the platoon as the man who, back home, had both a pregnant wife and a pregnant girlfriend. The sight of his first wounded buddy upset Margreiter, but he would soon get used to such scenes. A German rode into their positions on a bike. Three or four nervous shots failed to hit him and quickly he raised his arms. He is just as frightened as we are, thought Margreiter.

What were the emotions of the Germans? Were they really as frightened as Margreiter and his buddies? Facing the Americans were the Fallschirmjäger battalions to which Heinz Weber had been attached. Twenty-one years old, but, with all his front-line experience, now feeling a great deal older than the seventeen- and eighteen-year-olds who were being dispatched over the Maas as if on a conveyor belt for cannon fodder. A week earlier Weber had been promoted to sergeant in front of the troops. The battalion commander, Captain Paul, had addressed him. Paul was a tall man with an aquiline nose and light blue eyes; Weber had never seen even the shadow of a smile on his face. "Feldwebel Weber," Paul had said, "promotion calls for even greater fulfillment of duty. It means that you should be an example to your men!" "Yes, Sir!" said Weber, and thought: An example of what? Of how to die?

With eight men of his platoon he went on a night patrol. His orders were to find out whether their opponents were British or American, where their positions were and to fire a green signal flare when it was safe for the rest of the company to join them. The signal was also a warning to the nearby infantry dug in with the Nebelwerfers that they must no longer fire into the area where the patrol was moving about. They reached their objective and fired their signal flare, but nevertheless the infantry brought down fire on Weber's position. It was not uncommon for soldiers of either side to be killed or wounded by fire from their own troops.

Often the shellfire was less bad than one's hunger. The panzer brigade, with its own supply company, was much better off than the average infantryman near Overloon. Now and then a few Fallschirmjäger were given bread or fish by the tank crews, but it did not help all that much. Weber had to report regularly to Overloon, and on one of his visits he found potatoes and even butter in the deserted parsonage. Immediately he lit a fire in the open hearth in the kitchen. A pity there was no bacon in the house! The frying pan was hardly warmed up when shells began bursting on the church and on the parsonage, and Weber quickly jumped down into the cellar. Again no warm meal!

As he walked past the church after the shelling had stopped, Weber thought: Should I go inside to pray? No time for our Lord. He must protect us, but we have no time for Him. How bitter, hard and unsensitive have we become, me and my men. All around there is nothing but death and misery — and tanks! Even against two infantrymen they will use their guns. And if you're hit by an armor-piercing shell there's not much left of you. A few days before, Weber had found the body of his orderly, Vogt. He had covered it with a piece of canvas of their tent and buried it.

Now Weber was lying at the northeast approach to Overloon. His assault troop numbered seven men. Again an American tank approached, making use of a depression in the ground to protect its vulnerable chassis. From there it fired high-explosive shells at Weber's troop and after a while there was nothing left but a tangled heap of mutilated bodies. Weber found that only one man was still alive, a fellow sergeant, who had sustained a severe back wound. When Weber cut the man's jacket with his knife he saw how his breathing pushed the lungs against the splintered ribs. Very carefully Weber pushed the crimson-foaming lungs back into the lung cavity. When the wounded man regained consciousness, he moaned. Now and then he uttered a few words about his wife and his four children, mentioning their

1. *Flight and pillage: German soldiers driving stolen cattle along the Venlo road in Roermond, September 3, 1944.*

2. Schanzarbeit *(digging defense systems): female Russian labor on their way to dig trenches. Wilhelmina Square in Roermond, September 1944.*

3. Royal Dutch Brigade "Princess Irene": reconnaissance unit north of Boxmeer, September 22, 1944. In the Daimler scout car in front on the right sits the youngest soldier of the Brigade, the barely 19-year-old Corporal Jonkheer M.L. de Brauw, future Dutch Minister of Science (1971–72).

4. *A peasant family in Brabant, between the villages of Heeze and Leende, cheering the advancing British 11th Armored Division.*

5. British infantry and Sherman tanks crossing a Bailey bridge over Lock 11 of the Zuid Willems Canal near Asten.

6. Infantry of the 11th Amored Division in Asten, September 24, 1944.

7. *A 105mm howitzer of the American 7th Armored Division in action near Overloon, October 5, 1944.*

8. *Brigadier General Hasbrouck, Commander of Combat Command B (and soon to be commander of the 7th Armored) studies a map in the vicinity of Stevensbeek/Radioweg.*

9. *The American advance from the south, towards Roermond, became stalled. A Sherman tank of the Cavalry Group engaging the enemy in front of Nieuwstadt on September 29, 1944. The front was to remain rigid for another four months.*

10. *One of Wemple's Sherman tanks, currently on view at the Museum in Overloon, was destroyed near De Hattert on October 5, 1944. The crew was killed. One direct hit from a 88mm gun dislocated the turret; below in front the tank was hit by two 75mm shells.*

1. Suffolks and Churchill
tanks of the Coldstream
Guards advancing toward
Overloon, October 12,
1944.

2. During the afternoon
of October 12, 1944, the
South Lancashire Battalion
attacking west of Overloon,
supported by a Bren carrier.

13. A Nebelwerfer, abandoned at the battlefield, is currently on view at the Museum grounds in Overloon.

14. A captured NCO of the Fallschirmjäger, Overloon.

15. A German 88mm gun operating in a wood in Brabant.

16. The Loobeek in 1955: an unpretentious stream in a flat countryside, heavy flooding made it a formidable obstacle for the British in 1944.

17. Venlo found itself subject to constant air raids. This was taken after the first raid, October 13, 1944.

18. Loobeek: on the main road from Overloon to Venray a bridgelaying tank toppled with its own bridge into the "beek's" bed.

19. Vic Watkins, Army cameraman, covering three young Germans with his revolver on the Overloon road in Venray, October 17, 1944.

20. East Yorks moving forward cautiously into Venray.

21. East Yorks, D Company, waiting in Venray for the next dash forward.

22. Sister Marie-Godelieve, assistant manageress of St. Anna Psychiatric Hospital, Venray, at the end of October 1944.

*23. Major "Banger" King during the evacuation of St. Servatius Psychiatric Hospital,
Venray, at the end of October 1944.*

24. The 23rd Armored Infantry Battalion (7th Armored Division) in a trench near Griendtsveen, October 17, 1944.

25. Counterthrust in the swamp: a German Sturmgeschütz in re-captured Meyel,
October 27, 1944.

26. British 5.5 inch howitzers near Asten, firing at the German bridgehead of Meyel,
November 1944.

names to Weber. After some time he begged Weber to put an end to his life. "Shoot me!" Weber could not do it. "Please, do it, Heinz," the sergeant pleaded. Weber sat down beside the man and cursed for feeling so powerless.

Each time he tried to raise the sergeant to a more comfortable position, pushing his shirt against the fist-sized wound, the tank sprayed their position with machine-gun fire. Their only protection was a snapped-off tree trunk. Finally, Weber tied his leather belt to his own feet and to those of the wounded man. Crawling away from the spot, yard by yard, he lifted the man on his shoulder and carried him into Overloon where he walked up to one of the Panther tanks. Exhausted, he sat down with his load propped against the tank. But the sergeant had died on the way.

There was no letting up for Weber. The Americans were luckier. On October 3, Hasbrouck's Combat Command B was relieved by Colonel Ryan's Combat Command R. Meanwhile, Combat Command A remained engaged in the attack on Overloon. CCA, supported by Johansen's Task Force II, had in fact reached the village from the west and northwest but had been halted on October 2 at the southern edge of the Stevensbeek woods. The village itself was being shelled by artillery and bombed and strafed by Thunderbolt fighter bombers.

The monks in the monastery of Stevensbeek began to lose faith in the American attack. Two French captains attached as liaison officers to the 7th Armored in France told them that the division did not have enough infantry to mop up the woods and that its tanks had run into minefields laid in the roads during the night by infiltrating Germans. Now, even though army chaplain O'Neill told them with great conviction: "We've got everything, we can do everything, we've got too much!" the monks' faith in the Americans could not be restored.

And rightly so — for the Germans even launched counterattacks near Overloon. The first attack, on the evening of October 2, caught the Americans off balance and surprised them by its ferocity. They had dug in and were able to repulse the attack, however, thanks to their artillery. On October 3 the Germans launched two more counter-attacks from the woods and the western approach to Overloon. Both times they were driven back with artillery and air support, but the front line remained just where it was, and more tanks were lost.

On the same day, the Shermans and the infantry of CCR went into action. Task Force I under Colonel Wemple and Task Force II under Major Fuller were to attack Overloon from the north. But in this sector the well dug-in Germans and their concealed anti-tank guns, Nebelwerfer and mortars inflicted heavy losses to Wemple's two tank squadrons. Moreover, the attackers ran into minefields. That night they had not advanced a single yard beyond their original positions. Task Force II was halted by German fire within 500 yards of Overloon in what was to be referred to later as the "boot-shaped wood" because of its shape on the staff map. It all looked like a reversion to the First World War. The After Action Report stated: "Entrenched positions changed hands in bitter hand-to-hand fighting; bayonet and hand grenade were the weapons of those days."

On October 4, Wemple's Task Force tried its luck in a night attack by infantry with sappers, in an effort to blaze a trail through the minefields so that tanks might follow through. The first part of the assignment met with success, but when the tanks probed their way forward in the darkness, German resistance was found to be as strong as before. Neither the tanks, nor the infantry, which suffered heavy losses, gained any ground. The same day, more German counterattacks were launched — seven in all.

Heinz Weber took part in one of them. At five o'clock in the morning they had to move forward, their captain commanding them to shout "Hurrah." This shouting served them probably as a substitute for heavy weapons, Weber cynically observed. At battalion strength they dashed for the edge of the wood, where, instead of infantry, they found tanks waiting for them. The tanks hunted the Germans down and early in the afternoon the majority of them had been killed: "Among them, the captain who had made us shout 'hurrah' had received a one-way ticket to hell."

As a matter of fact, it was not only the tanks that halted the German counterattacks. The three artillery battalions, each with eighteen 105 mm howitzers mounted on tank chassis, inflicted heavy losses on the Germans. On October 4 alone, one of the battalions fired 2,762 rounds. A field artillery battalion with eighteen 4.5-inch guns, attached to the Division for the whole autumn, also took part in the action.

On October 5, Wemple made a desperate effort to outflank Overloon from the east. Here the ground was more open, with meadows and hedgerows on each side. One of his tank squadrons was to lead the attack with eighteen Shermans, the other squadron was to follow. Again opportunities for deployment were limited and the attack had to be launched in columns. Yet it looked as if the plan might succeed. The enemy's forward positions were overrun and the tanks advanced nearly a mile. But, hidden from the Americans, the Luftwaffe Festungs-Battalion X had taken up positions in the garden of a small castle called "De Hattert," just north of the road from Overloon to Vierlingsbeek. It had one of the most feared anti-tank weapons at its disposal, the notorious 88 mm gun. Within a few seconds, thirteen to eighteen tanks were blazing in the fields. If only General Hasbrouck had sent out patrols before!

Wemple immediately asked for air support in order to get beyond the enemy's positions near "De Hattert." Fighter bombers made an attack with rockets, reducing the castle to a smoldering pile of rubble. But the air attack did not affect the outcome of the battle. The tank crews who survived the murderous fire were literally forced to crawl back to their own lines. Others waited for darkness in order to make a getaway, and some of them were taken prisoner.

Despite all these setbacks, the BBC and the press, ironically enough, reported that night: "Overloon taken." There could be no sadder refutation of this premature news item than the burnt-out hulls of the American tanks near "De Hattert." Heinz Weber knew better. He saw the Shermans brew up in front of him. One exploded just after the crew had bailed out. Weber covered another tank with his Schmeisser. At first the crew were not keen to abandon the tank—they expected that Weber would shoot them—but soon they were forced to crawl out of it in order to save their skins. Weber shouted: "Come on, hurry up! Throw your weapons and hand grenades behind you— off you go!" The Americans apparently understood him and did as they were told. Weber let them keep their watches and other personal belongings.

In the meantime, farther west, the 23rd Armoured Infantry Battalion, after two days and nights of rest and maintenance, had dug in at the same edge of the wood it had left on October 3. During the night the Americans heard their own artillery firing at the wood, and going forward the next morning, they met no opposition. All the treetops had been razed by shell fragments and on the ground they found scores of bodies, Germans, lying in the attitudes in which they died when the shells hit them. The first body they saw held them spellbound: a typical young Aryan, with wavy blond hair, well built, lay on his belly with his arms outstretched and his head turned to the left. A shell fragment had gone through the front of his helmet, sheared away his face and the front part of his skull and then struck his rifle, bending the barrel to an angle of forty-five degrees. Part of his brain had spilled out on the pine needles on the ground.

The "Swede," Margreiter's platoon sergeant, walked toward the group which stood staring at the ghastly corpse. Saxberg kicked the dead German on one buttock and said: "That's the way we like to see you, you sonuvabitch!" Why does he do a thing like that—to shock us? wondered Margreiter. No matter what Saxberg did, to Margreiter he always remained the tough sergeant you'd better obey, no matter what his orders were.

Beyond the dead Germans the Americans found over a hundred abandoned bicycles. The Germans had come to the wood on bikes that night and had tried to infiltrate the American positions on foot via the woods. Yet this scene of destruction did not give the Americans any cause for joy. What had happened to the Germans might also happen to them. As a precaution, they would cover their own foxholes during the nights to come, with wood cut from surrounding trees.

On the evening of October 7, the platoon had just finished digging new foxholes when Sergeant Saxberg gave the laconic order: "Pick up your gear, we're moving!" For the sixth time within twenty-four hours they had had to dig a hole, this time in a recently planted wood, so dense that a lieutenant went ahead of them to cut a lane with a machete. In order to dig a slit trench the soldiers first had to pull out the small trees by their roots.

But on the morning of October 8, a surprising order was received.

The entire 7th Armored Division was being pulled out. The order came in during the evening of October 6 from HQ First U.S. Army through XIX Corps, and was executed on the following two days. The British 3rd Infantry Division and the 11th Armoured Division were coming back to take over. The American positions now faced Overloon in a gentle curve, in general only one or two miles farther from the line they had inherited a week before when they were so full of confidence. And at what price? Between October 1 and 6, the 7th Armored Division lost 452 casualties (killed, wounded and missing), 29 medium tanks, a light tank and 43 other vehicles.

Near Overloon, the German defense had proved beyond all doubt that it could not be overrun by an armored division alone. The Germans turned their equipment to the best advantage. The 107th Panzer Brigade had never committed more than single tanks, dug-in in static positions. By day they produced harassing fire, in particular against Shermans, which had a reputation of being fast on the road but also fast in brewing up, and then used to withdraw during the night between Overloon and Venray, where the brigade maintained its tactical reserve.

The Americans had grossly underestimated their task. They had relied on the scanty information from the British units which had only probed the front line sporadically here and there. But had the Americans themselves made full use of their eyes and ears? Their artillery observers had six light air observation planes which, because of the overcast weather, had been unable to carry out reconnaissance flights effectively. Yet the Division had left its reconnaissance squadron at the village of Rips in the Peel, where it did hardly any useful work during this first week in October.

Farther south, nothing of the original plan had been realized. Neither the Belgians near Wessem, nor the Americans near Sittard, had succeeded in gaining an inch of ground in the direction of Roermond. As early as October 2 and 4, respectively, these units were obliged to call off their actions.

It is sad to reflect that dynamic action by the 11th British Armoured Division, provided it had been coordinated with the 3rd Infantry Division, which at the time was still nearby, might have cleared the whole area between September 25 and 27, before the Germans were able to transfer their troops to the area of Overloon. The Americans told a reporter of the London *Daily Sketch* that "each grassblade in front of Overloon was a bayonet."

"The 3rd British Infantry Division," their historian wrote, "watched unappreciatively as the Americans pulled out and drove away to the south." No wonder. They were moving toward a very quiet front sector in that part of the Peel between Deurne and Weert, to lick their wounds. It was the British foot soldier on whose shoulder the unenviable task was placed of continuing the battle. This was the dawn of a new phase, not just for Overloon, but for the whole northern sector of the front as well.

CHAPTER SIX

CONSTELLATION: OVERLOON

M ONTGOMERY WAS DISAPPOINTED. His "full-blooded thrust" to the Ysselmeer (formerly the Zuider Zee) had bogged down in the Betuwe area. The biggest airborne operation ever in history had failed to fulfill its promise: outflanking the Westwall from the north, thus cracking the Rhineland open for his Army Group. Besides, to the south, Bradley's Army Group appeared to have been halted as well: Hodges near Aachen, Patton near Metz. In hindsight, the question may be asked whether the Allies should not have pursued a different strategy by simply smashing through the weak German front *between* these two cities, with Patton in the lead. Indeed, Patton himself suggested on August 23 that he should continue the advance toward the north instead of going farther east; but the Supreme Command considered that this was in conflict with "the plan": pushing forward on a broad front to the German border. Patton rightly said that one must not make a plan and try to adjust the circumstances to it. One must try to adjust the plan to the circumstances. He also added that he believed the difference between success and failure in supreme command depended on the ability of army commanders to do just that.

When, on September 26, the battle for Arnhem was over, Montgomery still failed to recognize that times had changed dramatically. He did appreciate, though, that he was being faced with three major problems. In the first place, the opening up of the Scheldt. Hardly anything had been done so far to achieve this: only the eastern part of Zeeland–Flanders had been liberated, without bloodshed. In the second place, securing the corridor to Nijmegen, because of its shape ironically referred to in Washington as a "dangling appendix," had become his responsibility. And, finally, the German salient west of the Maas stuck like a thorn in his flesh.

Yet all this did not cause Montgomery to adjust his plans. On the contrary, he still believed that not only would he be able to solve this threefold problem within a few weeks, but also that he would be able to launch a great offensive to seize the Rhineland. His directive on September 27 was that the British Second Army in the sector Nijmegen-Gennep was to attack with all available means and try to cross the Rhine, preferably near Wezel. In the meantime, Hodges was to support him by launching an attack toward Düsseldorf and Cologne, and the 7th Armored Division was to mop up the German salient west of the Maas.

We know what the outcome of the American effort was. Was Montgomery really so unrealistic? The most plausible explanation lies in the self-imposed isolation of the Field Marshal. Relinquishing command to Eisenhower on September 1, he had felt himself demoted and, more than before, he set himself apart from both his superiors and his peers. A perhaps-telling detail: on Montgomery's desk stood a cage with Herbie, his canary. Its shrill, constant chirping made any sensible discussion with the Field Marshal impossible. Solitary as a monk, an abbot surrounded by a few young lay brothers who never dared contradict him, he began to make new plans for the October campaign.

In these plans an extremely heavy task was assigned to the Canadian First Army. They were to take the western part of Zeeland-Flanders, which the Germans had turned into a fortress, and also were to force open the road from Antwerp to the isthmus that connects the island of South Beveland to the mainland.

Opening up the Scheldt, an operation which started at the end of September and was not completed until the first week of November, would exact a heavy toll each day, much greater than had been anticipated. Not only the military but the civilian population as well was sorely tried because the western part of Zeeland was devastated in the process and the saucer-shaped island of Walcheren was inundated after RAF bombers breached its sea dikes.

So much for Montgomery's first problem. While the American 7th Armored Division unsuccessfully tried to solve his third problem—the German salient west of the Maas—Montgomery's attention was riveted on his second of how to secure and exploit the corridor to Nijmegen. Around October 10 his offensive against the Rhineland, called "Gatwick," was to be launched from this sector. Horrocks' XXX Corps was to launch the attack from the northwest, and O'Connor's VIII Corps was to make a frontal attack on the Reichswald. To implement this plan a number of British divisions were to be involved on October 1, one of them being the British 3rd Infantry, which at that time was stationed at Mook, not far from Nijmegen.

Within a few days the British commanders began to have their doubts about the feasibility of "Gatwick." Dempsey and O'Connor were very worried. Whistler told O'Connor that an operation of this magnitude would require more manpower. Finally Montgomery, too, realized this. On October 7 he informed Eisenhower that he would have to postpone "Gatwick" because he would need more infantry and also that the Maas salient would have to be wiped out first. To do this he agreed with Bradley the next day that the boundary between their Army Groups should be restored to its previous position to the south. British troops would then take over from the American 7th Armored Division, which would come under command of O'Connor's corps to support the coming action. These changes on the Allied side had not gone unnoticed by the Germans. What were their conclusions?

Despite their defensive success at Arnhem, the Germans were profoundly impressed by the daring Allied airborne landings. Anything the Germans observed since then was seen in the light of these operations. They completely failed to realize how heavily the Allies had drawn on their reserves in manpower and equipment. Arnhem had been a shock—both to the Allies and the Germans. To the Germans in that they were convinced that any moment another airborne landing might occur, since they believed that in England three or four more such divisions were waiting. The shifting of the boundaries of the British and American army groups led the head of the intelligence service of Heeresgruppe B in early October to the conclusion that "the enemy would stick to his original plan to launch a decisive blow against the Ruhr area from the sector north of the rivers Waal and Nederrijn [Lower Rhine]; that furthermore another large-scale airborne landing could be expected as part of such an operation." The intelligence officer of Student's Fallschirmjäger Army already had a premonition of where it was to take place: with further airborne landings the Allies would now try to break through to the Ysselmeer at a point west of Arnhem. As for the how, what and where, the German Staff Officers were in utter disagreement, but they all felt that an Allied attack toward the north or northeast was most likely. The intelligence officers of other staffs also anticipated a dangerous American move on Aachen in conjunction with Montgomery's large-scale attack.

German intelligence of the Allied side varied from fair to very good, though their conclusions were often distorted by the operation at Arnhem. The striking power of the Allies was overestimated or, better put, the caution of the Allies after Arnhem was underestimated. The shifting of the boundaries of the army groups was, of course, intended to be temporary and with a limited goal. In reality, the Allied high command did not dream of another "Arnhem," though they did yet contemplate launching an offensive from Aachen.

As already noted, Montgomery was still being faced with two problems: those of the rivers Maas and Scheldt. Tactfully he informed Eisenhower that the Scheldt was to have priority. Less tactful was his letter of October 10 in which he complained of the leadership being too remote from the front. "The pursuit phase after Normandy is over. We are back again to the 'dog-fight' battle as in Normandy. This asks for a commander on the spot." This was a provocative letter from a man who was trying in vain to resume the command which he had had to relinquish to Eisenhower on September 1. We will see later how great the consequences of Eisenhower's reply will be. It should be realized that up till now Eisenhower had restricted himself merely to pointing out to Montgomery the importance of an early opening up of Antwerp, and, for the time being he let him have a free hand, first to attack toward the Maas, and thereafter to move into western Noord-Brabant.

The attack toward the Maas was planned by General O'Connor for his VIII Corps under the code name "Constellation." To carry out the operation he had approximately 90,000 men under his command:

two infantry divisions, two armored divisions, a tank brigade and the Belgian Brigade. By implementing "Constellation," O'Connor hoped to trap the enemy. Air observation had revealed that the German main defense line was in the north. There the 3rd British Infantry Division was to launch the initial attack (Castor). After Overloon and Venray had been taken, the 11th Armoured Division was to pass through the 3rd Division and to attack southward. In both phases the "Lucky Seventh" was to attack to the east so to make contact with the British west of Venray (Pollux). If these actions should result in luring the main force of the enemy to the north, the 15th Scottish Infantry Division, held in reserve, was to launch a surprise attack in the south towards Roermond (Sirius) and in the final stage the two armored divisions were to link up with the Scots near Venlo (Vega).

On paper it was a very imposing array of stars indeed, but would it ever be possible to keep the presence of this Scottish Division hidden from the Germans?

★   ★   ★

On the Overloon front a temporary lull in the fighting had set in on October 7. The weather remained wet. The Germans, mainly because of an inadequate supply system, suffered more from this trenchlike warfare than the British. On October 8 a soldier of Fallschirmjäger Battalion Paul wrote to his girlfriend: "The Tommy is only 200 yards away from us and treats us every morning to a loud reveille with half an hour of artillery fire. You get used to it eventually. It is simply a matter of luck whether you're hit or not. Last night my canteen was shot off the parapet of my trench. You really must fight for your life here. Hopefully we'll be back in reserve soon. I have not washed for a week. No, this is not exactly my idea of a good life: sleeping in a hole, eating whatever grub they can get through to us, usually with dirt in it. Yesterday a shell dropped nearby. Promptly our hole caved in and we had to dig another one again." The letter was never dispatched and fell into British hands a week later.

Heinz Weber was lying with his orderly, Fritz Scheurer, in a foxhole. They felt lonely, fifty to seventy yards away from their comrades. In a wistful mood, Weber's thoughts went back to the time he spent at the air base of Soesterberg in Holland, when he had been billeted in the town of Bussum: what a marvelous life compared with here in Overloon! There were times when he felt tempted to get away from it all: "Weber, beat it back to Bussum!" But yet he did not desert. He also failed to understand how Winter, an old corporal, could have slipped away to the American lines. Winter must have told the enemy everything he knew, for it did not take very long before a loudspeaker from the other side summoned all the Fallschirmjäger in his sector to surrender. A few of them were mentioned by name and rank.

Even in those days of severe setbacks the Germans had relatively few deserters. The greatest barrier to desertion was fear: every soldier knew that at even the slightest suspicion of desertion, standing orders were that soldiers showing such tendencies were to be shot on the spot by their own men. Even if a soldier was lucky and got away, there was always the risk of the Gestapo taking it out on his nearest relatives. There were also, of course, the usual horror stories — unfortunately in some instances only too true — of how the Allies dealt summarily with German prisoners. Hadn't they clubbed a number of wounded Fallschirmjäger to death with rifle butts at Cassino? With all this in mind Heinz Weber did not feel inclined to fall into the enemy's hands alive.

Apart from fear, there was also the widespread propaganda. Following the Soviet example of the "political commissar," Hitler ordered at the end of 1943 the appointment of so-called "National-sozialistische Führungsoffiziere" (officers for the promotion of Nazi ideology). Their main task was at division level, but they also indoctrinated smaller units with Nazism. Naturally they reported on the morale of the troops to the Nazi regime. Toward the end of September 1944, all Germans to be sent to the front were read the order of the day, which had been drafted by the NS-Führungsoffiziere attached to von Rundstedt's HQ. Here is a specimen of their pompous talk: "The Bolshevik menace with which the Western plutocracies make common cause threatens to destroy Germany. There is only one answer, comrades! There is no either/or, if we want Germany and the Germans to survive: we must fight to the bitter end, with all means and with all our strength, with utmost dedication and if necessary making the supreme sacrifice! Rather dead than a slave! Thus, as brave soldiers of our Führer, we shall march on toward the final battle and victory."

Weber had to stand at attention as he listened to this farcical speech made by the NS-Führungsoffiziere, who worked themselves into an ecstasy. But as soon as the first enemy plane appeared, the two officers scurried for cover. "Goddam s.o.b.'s," Weber swore.

In the meantime, the population of northern Limburg was faced with the true nature of Nazism. October 8 became a "black day." The Germans carried out a ruthless manhunt in the villages of Helden, Sevenum, Heythuysen and Helenaveen. In Sevenum, German soldiers surrounded the church as Mass was being read. Latecomers were assured that it was merely a routine check of identity cards. A German armed with a sub-machine gun entered the church and bellowed: "Come on, all men outside, or else we'll shoot!" Shouting, "Are there any men in here?" Germans searched every house in the village.

Outside, all men between sixteen and sixty years of age were lined up in rows of four and counted. They were told that they would be put to work digging defense systems. It would only take four days. These promises soon turned out to be idle. The men, rudely dragged away from their homes, were to be separated from their families for more than seven months. As if they had a premonition that the Germans were not telling the truth, weeping women and children stood around the men. The Germans pushed them away, saying: "We don't want any women or children."

That afternoon the pitiful catch of the manhunts reached Venlo — hundreds of men, the older ones loaded in trucks, the rest following on foot. There they were crowded together in cattle trucks — like many thousands of others in the winter to come — to be taken away to Germany in a slowly moving train. After a day in transit camps these Limburgers were moved to an unknown destination. Finally they arrived in Braunschweig, where they were put to work as slave labor. They were given various jobs; many were sent to the Hermann-Goering-Werke where in pouring rain and bitterly cold wind they unloaded wheelbarrows with red hot slag or carried steel girders and sheet iron.

The clothes they happened to be wearing when they were rounded up, often their Sunday best, were soon torn to tatters; within a few days they had become a shabby, dirty group, always hungry, digging in the fields for potatoes or turnips left after the harvest, plagued by lice and suffering from dysentery. A dozen of the four hundred men from Sevenum died from physical and mental exhaustion. Once only, in mid-November, did the deportees get in touch with their relatives in the villages beyond the Maas.

In the meantime, the British had completed their plans. On October 10, General Whistler issued his detailed orders to the 3rd Infantry Division for an attack the next morning. The attack was to be the first phase (Castor) of O'Connor's operation "Constellation." It was orthodox in concept, reminiscent of the Great War. First would come an "opening barrage" on the enemy positions, followed by a frontal attack behind a "creeping barrage" by two battalions of the 8th Infantry Brigade, one on each side of Overloon, a third battalion following in their wake. Guns of other divisions and of the army group, totaling 216 25-pounders and 68 heavier pieces, were added for the barrage to those of the Division's three field regiments of 24 guns each. In addition to artillery, extra mortar and machine-gun units had been placed under the command of the division.

More modern equipment had been included in the plan as well. Air support — including an air raid on Venray — was not lacking. In addition, two battalions of Churchill tanks had been placed at the disposal of the 3rd by the Grenadier and Coldstream Guards. These battalions belonged to the 6th Guards Tank Brigade, an independent unit; it was not permanently attached, but was allocated to whatever unit needed it. Thus, approximately one hundred tanks came to the support of the infantry. The two tank units had worked together before in the battle of Caen in Normandy. Finally, "flails" and bridge-laying equipment from another independent unit were to appear at the front. The "flails" were Shermans fitted with a rotating drum to which heavy chains had been attached, and they were used to beat a path through minefields.

The Churchill, at 40 tons, was heavier than the Sherman. With its speed of 25 kilometers per hour it was slower, but it had armor plate approximately four inches thick and usually had a 75 mm gun and a 7.92 coaxial machine gun in its turret. The crew consisted of a commander, a gunner, a signaler-loader, a driver and a co-driver who could also fire a machine gun mounted in the front of the tank. Like most tank crews, the Guards literally lived with their tanks. When necessary, they used to dig a slit trench at night and carefully park their Churchill over it, thus protecting themselves against shellfire and rain. Their only fear was that in their sleep the ground might start to sag and the tank bury them alive.

The tanks were more than just machines: hence the staff of the 2nd Squadron of the Coldstream tank battalion had named their four vehicles Tiger, Jaguar, Rock and Jackal. Sergeant Johnnie Lambert was in command of Jackal. His battalion was to join in the attack on Overloon the following morning. Within 48 hours he was to lose both his legs when Jackal (on display in the museum grounds at Overloon) hit a mine. Sergeant Tom Jeffrey, the twenty-four-year-old commander of a tank in the 1st Platoon of the 1st Squadron Coldstream, felt fairly secure from HE (high explosive) shells behind his heavy armor plates. But he was scared to death of armor-piercing (AP) shells. In action he cringed when he heard the sharp bang made by AP shells narrowly missing his tank. He used to offer a little prayer and rely on the four crew members with whom he had shared all the ups and downs ever since the landing in Normandy. It was not only the Germans the British tanks had to deal with. In Overloon they met another formidable enemy: the terrain. The last few weeks of September had been abysmally wet and the first week of October had brought long spells of dull weather; but from October 9 onward there were pouring rainstorms and toward nightfall of the 10th it was decided to postpone the attack for 24 hours, until October 12.

Nigel Nicholson described how the Grenadier Guards of the 6th Tank Brigade felt about that depressing autumn: "It was not the Germans, nor even the interminable mortaring, that made these battles seem like one long, bad dream. It was something far more terrible — mud. When the Grenadiers reached Oploo, rains came lashing down and within a few hours the surrounding area had been transformed into a sea of mud. From then on, anything the Grenadiers did, anything they could do, was dictated by this terrible concoction of Nature. Everywhere there was to be mud, bogging the tanks so deep that sometimes even the recovery vehicles could not pull them out, putrefying anything that came in contact with it, seeping into the tents at night, making everybody cold and dirty and miserable from dawn to dark. Holland in that bleak winter was a far cry from the land of flourishing tulips and smiling burghers that many had imagined it to be. It was as desolate as an enormous Irish peat-bog in the depths of winter."

On October 11 the skies began to clear; the attack could be launched the next day. Heinz Weber, old hand that he was, sensed the lull before the storm. "Fritz," he said to his orderly, "something is afoot. We'll be getting such a licking here that we will no longer know our arse from our elbow." And how flimsy was their HKL (*Hauptkampflinie*—main defense line)! He also worried whether the other two men would still be within hearing in their foxholes.

★   ★   ★

October 12 broke as a radiant autumn day. Between Wanroy and St. Anthonis there was feverish activity. Private Roebuck had been awakened early in his billet, a barn in the vicinity of Wanroy; his battalion, the East Yorks, had been billeted in and around the village. Not until a few hours before the action began did the company commander issue his orders. Then they climbed into trucks to be driven to the Stevensbeek woods. This had been arranged by the battalion's staff, who felt that it was better to get up early and be driven to the front rather than to spend another cold night in mud-soaked positions. The second-in-command, Major J.D.W. Renison, had carefully studied the ground to be attacked by the East Yorks, unfortunately only on a map. He would have given anything for good aerial photographs, for the woods in particular differed markedly from their positions on the map because of new plantings and earlier woods having been cleared.

On Renison's map the first objective of the battalion had a peculiar shape. The Americans had called it "the boot"; the British officers thought that it resembled a Scottish terrier because the "animal" was sitting on its hind legs, trying to snatch a "biscuit" dangling in front of its gaping mouth and with a "puppy" wood behind its tail. First, the

East Yorks would have to make their way through this dog-shaped wood if they wished to seize control that night of the woods south of Overloon, nicknamed the "kennel." In their assembly area the men were given a warm drink. They needed it badly, for everything was still soaking wet. On the right of the East Yorks the Suffolks were to lead the first attack; it would take them that night to the southwest of Overloon. On their way to the Stevensbeek woods the infantry saw large numbers of guns on each side of the road, ready to fire, a very encouraging sight.

At 1100 hours the guns started to roar. Four artillery regiments with medium guns and a battery with heavy guns, altogether 68 pieces, made the earth tremble. Twenty minutes later the air force went into action. Venray was the target of 36 Marauder bombers of the 9th American Air Fleet. The population had already grown accustomed to being shelled, but this unexpected air raid became their worst ordeal. From east to west the bombs drew their destructive furrows through the town: Venray's Schoolstraat, Henseniusplein, Paterstraat, Grote Straat and Hofstraat were all in ruins, covering many dead.

The town was, unfortunately, chock full of refugees: within two weeks the population had increased from 17,000 to 25,000. Yet, and this may be called a miracle, the number of casualties were only 32. Of the Marauders, seven did not unload their bombs, many were dropped in the open fields, and because ever since the shelling started people had been hiding in the cellars, the number of victims fortunately remained small. In the psychiatric hospital of St. Anna, just north of Venray, 1,500 female patients from the various wards had been packed together in the cellars of the hospital. Each direct hit raised clouds of coal dust that covered patients and nurses with a grimy layer of dust. A previous air attack on September 30 had already killed 16 people there. Presumably the British believed that the buildings were occupied by Germans.

What St. Anna had to endure in those days has been recorded by a woman of outstanding character, the forty-six-year-old Sister Marie-Godelieve (Maria Billiau). She belonged to the Belgian congregation of the Sisters of Mercy, which ran the hospital. Her story is a moving account of those tragic days. Just before "Mad Tuesday," the patients and staff of St. Anna had celebrated in grand style the silver jubilee of the Medical Superintendent Dr. Schim van der Loeff as if there was no war going on. Even the merry-go-round with its street organ had been taken out of storage and had been set up on the large lawn. A few weeks later Sister Marie-Godelieve heard organ music outside in the playground and left the ward to see what was going on. The merry-go-round was crowded with German soldiers who were having lots of fun. The Germans always respected the buildings of the hospital, but they did use the road between Overloon and Venray, which traversed the hospital site, thereby offering to some extent an excuse for Allied shelling and bombing.

From October 1 onward the patients had been moved downstairs to the cellars. Those giving the most "trouble" had been kept on the ground floor where they could be cared for only when the guns stopped firing. During those pauses the sisters and nurses, assisted by a few men, shifted coal and coke out of the bins in the cellars, thus making additional space downstairs for more patients. Somehow the staff managed to keep the kitchen going to feed this community of 1,700 people. Oddly enough, it seemed as if being continually in danger increased their appetites.

On October 5 there was a direct hit in one of the wards where the worst patients were being treated. The victims had to be removed under fire. Doctor van der Loeff said that the first sight of the ward where the shell had exploded gave him a terrible shock — it was a real bloodbath. In spite of all this, efforts were made to provide at least some form of entertainment for the nurses who were under such a heavy strain. On an old gramophone in the bicycle cellar, which had been converted into a temporary nurses' home, a record of Mozart's *Eine kleine Nachtmusik* was played. Then, on October 12, a terrific artillery and air bombardment raged over St. Anna.

Said the sister: "We believed that everything would be destroyed; the cellars shook, the walls seemed to move, explosion followed after explosion. It had never been so bad. Those who were not in their own ward had no earthly chance at all of getting back there, so we all worried about the others. I was visiting the cellar of St. Vincent's and could not possibly go back to the nurses' home. A man came in looking for his wife; he had walked for hours during the shelling to find her. As he entered the cellar, dull thuds were heard outside; his wife ran toward him and embraced him: 'Paul, help me.' He held her, spoke to her as to a child, comforted her. She grew quiet. His being there was enough to calm her down and make her forget all the uproar around her. How safe and protected we should feel, we who have a Father in Heaven, an almighty Father who loves us. Our minds should be at peace in the Love of our Heavenly Bridegroom, Jesus who is our strength. This thought gives me peace and strength to remain calm, to give an encouraging nod here and there and to go on praying, without stopping. . . . Finally the din of the explosions abated. . . .''

Five miles to the north it certainly did not get quieter at the front. At 1130 hours the 216 25-pounder guns joined in a devastating explosion of fire and half an hour later they switched to the start line of a creeping barrage. At 1215 hours the East Yorks left the edge of the Stevensbeek woods in order to cross the open field in front of them and get across the Vierlingsbeek road to the north and the east of Overloon. The Suffolks advanced across the open ground of Hazenbroek and Peelkampsveld. The barrage that preceded them lifted at a rate of 100 yards every five minutes. This turned out to be too slow and delayed the advance of the infantry. Sometimes the Suffolks encountered the ingenious, so far unfamiliar Schü mines. Resistance was met occasionally, but by two o'clock B Company had captured nine men from Battalion Paul and the attack seemed to be making good progress.

Then information was received that A Company was in trouble. This unit got stuck near a burnt-out windmill and the company commander and six other men were killed by snipers. A sergeant took over command. The battalion commander, Colonel Craddock, who had gone to the mill himself, decided to let C Company pass through the positions of the weakened A Company in order to attack in the direction of A Company's objective, a small brickworks a few hundred yards off the Overloon-Venray road. At 1530 hours this new phase of the attack commenced. C Company succeeded in establishing itself on this road south of the village. Thereupon A Company was also able to continue the advance, and finally D Company followed and occupied the wood northwest of the brickworks. In the afternoon there was sporadic resistance only and all the companies began to dig in for the night. Later in the afternoon the South-Lancashires advanced southwest of the Suffolks. They met very little opposition and by dusk reached the woods that had been their objective.

It was quite a different story, however, for the East Yorks Battalion during their advance through the dog-shaped wood. The Churchill tanks of the Coldstream Guards and the Crocodile flame-throwing tanks hit mines on tracks which had been considered passable. Their support, on which the whole plan of the attack had been based, soon became too weak, which enabled those Germans who had survived the shelling to hold their fire until the infantry came within range. Thus the British ranks were decimated.

In taking the biscuit-shaped wood, D Company lost all of its officers and its sergeant-major. A corporal took over command. Battalion HQ lost touch with this company, which was eventually found to be inside the "front leg" of the dog, no longer capable of reaching its objective—the east side of Overloon. B Company had come to its assistance and succeeded after heavy fighting in occupying the houses on the Vierlingsbeek road, which had all been destroyed. Only the cellars had remained virtually undamaged and the bottles with fruit and vegetable preserves were still standing in neat rows on the shelves.

C Company had also received a lot of German fire inside the dog-shaped wood, but A Company followed closely on its heels, turned left toward the tail of the dog-shaped wood and advanced towards the "puppy" wood north of the Vierlingsbeek road. This enabled C Company to cross the road and take up positions around a house on the opposite side at the edge of the large woods surrounding Overloon on the south.

The Germans kept plastering the area with mortar and Nebel-werfer fire. The battalion commander, Colonel Dickson, was thrown onto the ground by an explosion. He appeared to be unharmed, but later it turned out that he had been affected badly. The fighting inside the village was less fierce than had been expected. Dickson had asked for the artillery to direct a heavy barrage on the Vierlingsbeek road.

This did not leave the Germans hiding in the ruins enough time to recover and fight the East Yorks, who followed close behind the barrage. Eventually the tanks of the Coldstream Guards were able to give active support in mopping up what was left of the village. But their support, as already noted during the attack of the East Yorks on the dog-shaped wood, had not been as effective as had been expected.

In the case of the East Yorks, the nature of the ground was mainly to blame for that, and elsewhere the minefields and the very effective German defensive fire. When the attack began, two squadrons of the Coldstreams were committed, both advancing from the Stevensbeek woods, No. 3 Platoon passing along the road to Overloon in a southerly direction to cover the right flank of the East Yorks. No. 1 Platoon advanced in a southwesterly direction to accompany the Suffolks through somewhat more open ground. No. 2 Platoon was to follow this squadron later to give cover on its right flank, farther west. The battalion's HQ platoon was to coordinate the attack with tanks and infantry. But, because the East Yorks, according to the historian of the brigade, turned left and the Suffolks turned right, the HQ platoon suddenly found that it was heading for the northern edge of Overloon all by itself, that it had moved too far ahead and had become dangerously exposed.

Not being used to such an advanced position, the platoon commander halted the tanks to consider the situation, and the infantry, seeing this, halted too. This resulted in a deadlock. The HQ platoon wanted to find a way out by continuing the advance, hoping that the infantry would catch up with it. But two tanks were halted by a type of mine which was new to the Coldstreams: *Riegelminen,* rectangular in shape, powerful enough to rip open the bottom plate of a Churchill tank. The HQ platoon commander's tank hit such a mine, but managed to continue waddling forward. This left him in touch with the infantry, but he became separated from the rest of his platoon and found himself fighting all on his own near Overloon. To make matters worse, two more tanks of Squadron No. 1 were hit inside a small wood by AP shells fired from a well-concealed Panther. The commander of one of the tanks was Tom Jeffrey. His impression was that he had been in action much longer than half an hour when a fire broke out suddenly near the containers underneath the turret in which the ammunition was kept. "Everyone for himself!" yelled Jeffrey through the intercom, and his crew knew exactly what that meant: get out of the tank as quickly as possible because it might brew up at any moment.

The driver and the co-driver each had his own hatch through which to escape, but if the turret had been swung into a certain position these hatches became blocked and the only way out in that case was a small emergency exit in the side of the tank. The signaler-loader had his own escape hatch. Jeffrey could see him through wisps of smoke inside the tank and thought: The man must be suffering from shock! Together with his gunner, Jeffrey tried to make his way out through the other hatch in the turret. This proved to be very difficult since the gunner had been badly wounded by the hit in no-man's land and the Germans opened fire on the crew at once. All were killed except Jeffrey, who crawled for cover. All he could do was wait and see if the infantry would find him once they advanced again. After some time, the infantry moved forward and Jeffrey was brought back to the rear, the sole survivor.

Not until the Suffolks had committed their C Company into the battle at 1530 hours did the cooperation with the tanks improve and they were able to advance together at the same pace. Infantry and Coldstreams arrived simultaneously on their objective, the brickworks southwest of Overloon, on a sandtrack parallel to the road Overloon-Merselo. On the access roads north and west of Overloon, flail tanks were called in to clear a path through the minefields. By the end of the afternoon the roads were free and tanks and infantry started mopping up the greater part of Overloon.

Farther to the west, the tanks of the 2nd Squadron, together with the South Lancashire Battalion, started their attack. Their objective was the woods south of Peelkant and Kamphoef. Mines delayed the advance of the tanks, and without their support the infantry was unable to drive the Germans from shelter there. By dusk the tanks withdrew in the flickering light of burning houses and a blazing Churchill.

When night fell, the greater part of Overloon was in British hands. Major Renison wandered through the ruins and tried to find his way in the flickering light. Overloon was in British hands; yes, for "liberated" was hardly a fitting word since there was not a living soul left among the ruins to be "liberated."

Much to their surprise, British soldiers found a small group of frightened civilians in the cellar of a farmhouse outside the town. They had defied the German orders to evacuate the place and lived through the bombardments and the terrible barrage. The oldest of the group, Crooymans, had a small dairy farm and also grew roses and small trees. In order to fool the Germans he had blackened his face to make himself look much older; his wife, her face wrapped in a scarf, was lying "ill" in bed. Thus they deceived the Germans, who came to check if all the people of the village had left. Crooymans' daughter Drika was allowed to stay behind, together with her husband and their two children. Her brother Sjaak and his friend Piet Poels stayed behind in a neighbor's house. A German soldier caught them as they were looking after the cattle—the cows were lowing with pain because the shelling made it impossible for them to be milked regularly. Although the Germans told them that they would be shot as partisans, the boys managed to get away and hid in a haystack for three days, living on apples. Later they plucked up enough courage and crawled into an underground shelter dug by Sjaak's father. Hardly were they inside when a German tank drove over it. The walls caved in and Sjaak got stuck among beams and boards. It took hours to dig him out, and for six days he had difficulty walking or standing up.

Again the boys ran off: first to the cellar of the Crooymans family, which was found to be too small, and then to the cellar of another house. There, like shipwrecked sailors, they tried to live through the hurricane of war. Whenever the noise outside abated, vegetables were collected from the fields and the cows were milked. They also had a stock of salted pork and preserves. Drika managed to bring a cow from the meadows to the stable so that milk for her baby was close at hand.

The German front-line soldiers were not unfriendly; sometimes they brought bread and foodstuffs which they had probably taken from the deserted shops in the village, and even medicines when Crooymans suffered from stomach cramps. Some of them frankly admitted that the war was lost. When the shelling started again for the umpteenth time, prayers were said aloud; Drika clutched her rosary

Oct. 12–19, 1944

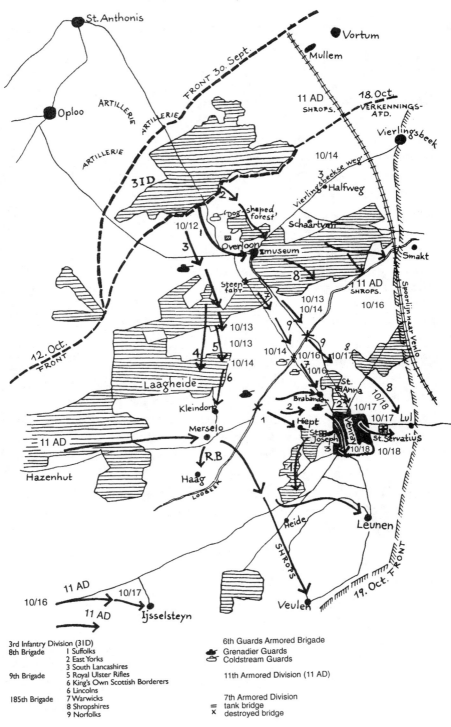

3rd Infantry Division (3ID)
8th Brigade	1 Suffolks
	2 East Yorks
	3 South Lancashires
9th Brigade	5 Royal Ulster Rifles
	6 King's Own Scottish Borderers
	6 Lincolns
185th Brigade	7 Warwicks
	8 Shropshires
	9 Norfolks

6th Guards Armored Brigade
Grenadier Guards
Coldstream Guards

11th Armored Division (11 AD)

7th Armored Division
= tank bridge
x destroyed bridge

in one hand and with the other she held a whistle to be used as an emergency signal in case those in the cellar should be buried underneath debris.

The artillery bombardment on this last day raged over their heads like an unending terror, like thunderbolts in rapid, deafening succession. The adults protected the children with their bodies. Then, suddenly the shelling stopped. It was five o'clock in the afternoon. Cautiously Drika went upstairs, entered the farm yard and waved a white napkin. British soldiers were approaching, rifles at the ready. They took her back into the cellar and, holding the burning candle, they examined each face. The first thing they asked for was something to drink; sweat was pouring down their faces. Thereafter the people were told to leave the cellar because it was too dangerous for them to stay there with the Germans only a few hundred yards away. They started to walk down the road from Overloon to Oploo, the two children in their arms, subjected to continual firing. That they had lost all they had did not matter to them; they were still alive. The image of their fiercely burning village remained engraved on their minds, however. Also they were deeply impressed by the long columns of tanks that came rolling toward them from Oploo.

These were Churchills of No. 1 Squadron and of the HQ platoon of the Coldstreams. Although the capture of Overloon is frequently described as a "tank battle," there was also something reminiscent of the trench warfare of September 1916. At that earlier time, the very first tanks ever used in battle trundled forward on the Somme front, dispersed among the infantry, but hampered by the pot-holed, shell-cratered ground, unable to carry out any independent task except that of spreading terror among the enemy. Thus, the battle for Overloon is more an echo from the past rather than an example of modern, mechanized war of movement, which had been characteristic of the fighting during the preceding months.

The story of the "tank battle" is not the only part of the legend of Overloon. Equally persistent is the story that some thirty SS men fought to the last man in the churchyard of the St. Theobaldus Church and that literally each of them had to be shot. Not a single British source, nor the War Diaries of the British Public Record Office, nor any eyewitnesses have ever confirmed this bloody story. On the contrary, although Waffen SS were prominent elsewhere on the Maas front, intelligence reports mention no more than a possible presence of SS in the woods southwest of Overloon. Heinz Weber, who had spent nearly a fortnight around Overloon, had seen only SS Pioneers who, without consulting the Fallschirmjäger, had sowed minefields in front of their positions and then left again.

October 12 was characterized by skirmishes between groups of infantry against infantry, by isolated tanks which fired at infantry, by self-propelled guns and anti-tank guns firing at tanks, and by infantry who fired their bazookas and machine guns at anything and anybody. The day of the liberation of destroyed Overloon was a link in the chain of battles so vividly remembered by those who took part, but which is only briefly mentioned in the official history of World War II.

CHAPTER SEVEN

CONSTELLATION: LOOBEEK

O N OCTOBER 13, THE SECOND phase of the operation by the 3rd British Infantry Division commenced. Originally the plan was for 9 Brigade to pass through the positions occupied by 8 Brigade the previous day and advance on Venray. 185 Brigade, which was to have remained in reserve if all had gone well, was also thrown into the battle. Committing the entire reserve shows how difficult the 3rd Division's assignment was. Reveille was earlier for the tankmen of the Grenadier Guards: 0245 in the night. "Friday the thirteenth," they grumbled as they warmed up the tank engines in the cold autumn darkness. Two squadrons of their battalion had received orders to support 9 Brigade in mopping up the woods southwest of Overloon. This task had been assigned to two infantry battalions: the Royal Ulster Rifles were to clear the woods west of the Overloon-Venray road, the King's Own Scottish Borderers farther west of this area.

For the tank squadron of the Coldstream Guards this would be the second day of the battle. They were to support 185 Brigade, whose objective was the woods east of the Overloon-Venray road. The first push was to be made by the Warwicks and the King's Shropshire Light Infantry. They were followed by the Norfolks, who were to launch the final attack on Venray.

Again there was a great discrepancy between plans on paper and reality. Eventually the first phase of O'Connor's plan "Constellation" was to take six full days instead of two. The first few days were used to reach the Loobeek, a canal which traversed the battlefield from the southwest to the southeast and crossed the Overloon–Venray road halfway. On October 15, preparations were made for the crossing of the Loobeek, and in the next 24 hours this obstacle was overcome, after strenuous efforts and at the cost of many casualties.

Finally, the three infantry battalions of each of the three brigades were committed in succession, allowing each battalion a brief rest period to recover from their ordeal. Also, in accordance with the plan of VIII Army Corps, two other divisions came to support the operation: old acquaintances, the British 11th Armoured Division and the American 7th Armored. The Warwicks and the KSLI each let two of their infantry battalions bear the brunt of the attack. The opposition was so ferocious and they suffered so many setbacks that the two remaining battalions which were to follow could no longer go into action that day.

In the west the Ulsters attacked first, then the Borderers on their right. Both had to advance through woods which in some places were thick enough to be impenetrable. Both battalions encountered snipers and Schü mines. Having passed through the woods, they ran into heavy machine-gun fire in the open field. Sometimes the tanks of the Grenadier Guards had to operate on their own, the infantry being pinned down by enemy fire and unable to advance. Three tanks that supported the Ulsters were lost; another was hit by an 88 mm gun. Major Ivor Crosthwaite saw the tracer ammunition of the gun, some five to six hundred yards in front of him, heading for his tank — like the waterjet from a hire hose, he thought: "The first time that I realized that fear can cause a stabbing pain in your side!" He fired off a smoke shell to hide his tank from the enemy and tried to find a less vulnerable position from which he could ask for artillery support.

This pattern repeated itself: unexpected opposition, obstacles — and then artillery support. Crosthwaite saw the infantry being pinned down in a treacherous minefield, again the ubiquitous Schü mines. The results were terrible. Within a few seconds, seventeen victims were lying in the open field. From each a foot had been blown off. Only tanks were able to rescue them as Schü mines didn't have the explosive power to damage them. The tanks drove close to where the wounded were, the crews climbed down and, following the tanks' tracks, walked toward the victims. Eventually all the men were saved, put onto a tank and driven to the rear. To Crosthwaite it seemed as if they were too stunned to be in great pain.

That night the bivouac of the two battalions of infantry reminded them of the worst days in Normandy. In this eerie wood, devastated by Typhoons and shells, they felt deserted as the tanks withdrew for the night to load up with fuel and ammunition. Crosthwaite was told: "You're letting us down!" The bivouac turned out to be inaccessible to the field kitchens. Even jeeps could not get beyond the rear companies of the Ulsters. Blankets and greatcoats for the soldiers in their foxholes had to be delivered to them on foot through the woods. Finally, the Germans infiltrated the bivouac area during the night and the soldiers did not get much rest.

The two battalions which had attacked east of the Overloon-Venray road were relatively better off. By noon the Warwicks and the Shropshires entered the woods, preceded by a creeping artillery barrage. Here, too, events repeated themselves. As soon as the battalions had crossed the southern edge of the woods they encountered furious machine-gun fire and fire from SPs in the open fields. The tanks of the Coldstream Guards could do very little against this and two of them were hit. During the whole day a special unit of the 3rd Division gave extremely welcome support to the infantry; these were the mortar and machine-gun units of the Middlesex Battalion. This battalion had been split up among the three brigades and had been trained to give close fire support. On a day like this it was demonstrated how useful and necessary their training had been. The Middlesexers fired 1,400 mortar bombs and 140,000 rounds of machine-gun ammunition; on the day before, it had been twice as much.

In the meantime, Venray was continually being attacked by planes and artillery. Among the buildings hit was St. Anna's Hospital. At three o'clock in the afternoon, Sister Marie-Godelieve was startled in the cellar by heavy explosions. She dashed upstairs and smelled smoke. "My God, save us. Not fire, no, not fire!" A few moments later she was told the bad news: the patients' ward had caught fire after an attack by Typhoons. They thought they were shooting at Germans. Inside the burning building were 200 women, all of them mental cases.

Sister Marie-Godelieve immediately called the nurses to take the women to safety: "Don't panic!" she said, so they set to work. "Some 30 to 40 young people went about their duty in the face of death; we heard shells hurtling over our home, the hissing noise of the flames grew louder, an acrid smell entered the building, but in our midst, among all the hustle and bustle, quiet and order prevailed. Mother Mary was with her children. Two young nurses picked up their suitcases, their only personal belongings left. I felt very sorry having to tell them to put them down again: the patients had to be looked after first. The worst patients were taken away first. Some had already fled from the other wards . . . Notre Dame and St. Ghislain.

"I assured them that this would be the last time for them to move. Some of them had asked me whether it would be dangerous to go outside and, as I heard shells roaring over our heads, I told them that they were safe, that Mother Mary would look after them; their minds at rest, they let themselves be taken away from one danger spot to another. But what else could we do? The acrid smell became stronger; would there never be an end to the influx of patients? Standing at the bottom of the staircase I felt like a captain on a sinking ship.

"Most patients nodded to me, asking if I would like to come with them. Thank God they remained calm; now and then someone complained that she had lost her shoes or coat. We gave them whatever we found lying around and they moved on. Forty patients who needed help and 120 walking cases filed past me and found their way out via the steep cellar staircase. I followed them with my eyes, at the same time listening intently to the piercing noise of the shells. Oh, God, let them all get away safely! Don't let anyone get hurt. I prayed over and over again, asking for mercy. The patients were gone now, the cellars were empty.

"Outside, women volunteers were milling about. All kinds of household utensils had been removed from the refectory and the kitchen; a pile of mattresses and blankets was lying on the grass; it looked like a jumble sale. I walked down to the front of the building. Flames were crackling and hissing, the whole second floor was ablaze, large pieces of the roof were crashing onto the terrace. It was terrible. There was not the slightest chance of putting out the fire: the new fire

engine bought in anticipation of such a disaster stood deserted on the
road. The work of many years went up in flames. I watched and
thought that God was nearer to me now than in the days of prosperity.
The fire raged with growing fury, sparks flying round and threatening
to set the woods on fire. Twice, three times we had to throw ourselves
on the ground as shells whizzed past.

"It would have been a crime to risk any more lives here any longer.
I ordered everyone to leave the grounds. Anxious to help, many
demurred, but another round of shells added emphasis to my words
and away they went, with bowed heads. They so much wanted to risk
everything to save what they could. The nurses from Santa Maria
reluctantly left the scene of disaster. We went to St. Ghislain. We were
powerless to save our home, our beautiful home, but we were so
grateful that nobody had gotten hurt. In the cellar we thanked God for
His having saved us all and we started to sing the Magnificat; we had
so often thanked Him for the good things we had been allowed to
enjoy in our home for the past few years. How often had we thanked
Him after a pleasant family party for the pleasant atmosphere in our
home, our cozy home, and for all that was so secure, trustworthy and
good in our family life. Now we also wanted to thank Him in our days
of trial: He gave, He took, blessed be His name."

Much further behind the front, Venlo also made its acquaintance
with total war on this Friday. Curiously enough, Venlo had so far
hardly been bombed, even though the Allies must have known that its
roads and bridges were vital supply lines for the enemy. Air reconnaissance showed that the Germans were unloading armored vehicles
at its station. The day before, a German manhunt had driven the male
population into hiding, but bombs now forced the entire population
of Venlo to go underground. A direct hit on the Rembrandt Theatre
buried alive a number of young men who were hiding in the cellar. The
whole area was a smoking heap of ruins, from which cries for help
were heard from those who were trapped. Red Cross, air-raid wardens
and fire brigade were unable to muster enough men. Ceilings had to
be jacked up, jagged pieces of stone, glass and rubble had to be cleared
with bare and bleeding hands, some of the rescue workers had no nails
left on their fingers. People covered with dust staggered away from

the area near the Keulse Poort, over which gray clouds of ashes were
towering. This air attack on the town center killed fifty-nine citizens.
It was a sad prospect that more air attacks were inevitably to follow—
for the real target, the bridges, had not suffered any real damage.

In these days of bitter fighting, first for Overloon, later for the area
between the village and the Loobeek, the exhausted and decimated
German troops being pushed back toward Venray decided to do
something about the situation, probably on orders from their corps
commander von Obstfelder at Hillenraad Castle, whose orders did not
always excel in clarity or brilliance.

First there was a change of command at Geysteren Castle. The
paratroop Colonel Walther was replaced by an army officer, Colonel
Rudolf Goltzsch, who brought with him the staff and a few supply
units of the former 344th Infantry Division. What was known as
Kampfgruppe Walther was now renamed Kampfgruppe Goltzsch, or
the 344th Division, although the word "division" was misleading. The
units of the Waffen SS which operated as Group Roestel on the right
flank were replaced by a Fallschirmjäger-Lehr Regiment under the
command of Lt. Colonel Hermann. Apparently the corps staff at
Hillenraad Castle felt that in an emergency the Fallschirmjäger could
be relied upon to plug the holes in the front and hold it—not an entirely
unrealistic view, for Lt. Col. Rolf Loytved-Hardegg, the Commander
of Parachutist Regiment 21 (to which, in fact, Battalion Hofmann had
been attached) was dispatched from the southern front of the salient,
where Division Erdmann was engaged, to Venray with a few units.
It was intended that he take over command of Battalion Hofmann and
Battalion Paul (or what was left of it), merging the whole into a new
force. In the rosy view of Hillenraad Castle it was believed that this
would also make it possible to relieve the Panzergrenadiers of the 107th
Panzer Brigade. Loytved-Hardegg was to replace von Maltzahn as
"Kampfcommandant" of Venray.

Loytved-Hardegg had a successful career in the Luftwaffe behind
him. In the spring of 1944 he volunteered for parachute training and
thereupon took part in the fighting in Normandy. Typical of the

situation in the German Army in those days, he received orders from General Student at the end of August 1944 to form a paratroop regiment to be ready for action in two or three weeks—which he actually managed to accomplish. The regiment was thrown into battle at the beginning of September in northern Belgium as part of Division Erdmann, and as such joined in the withdrawal behind the canal front line in the southern Peel.

During their retreat the Fallschirmjäger could hear the cheers of the liberated population from the villages they passed. Loytved-Hardegg, with part of his regiment, marched to the crumbling northern front line of the salient, where his first battalion, that of Hofmann, was trying to halt the British advance. This unit did not worry him so much, but his main concern was Battalion Paul, which was desperately trying to hold on in the woods south of Overloon. On the road from Venray to Overloon, Loytved-Hardegg encountered soldiers from the battalion fleeing to Venray, exhausted, no longer capable of putting up a fight, and without any hope. Against the Allied tanks and planes, they said, there was nothing they could do. The superiority of the enemy was simply too overwhelming.

It had been Battalion Paul which had born the brunt of the defense of Overloon, as confirmed by its number of casualties. Of the 147 prisoners taken by the British on October 12, 109 came from Battalion Paul. In the period between October 2 and 14, 81 men were killed, 80 wounded and 241 were missing, most of them taken prisoner. With a total loss of 402 men, the battalion had virtually ceased to exist.

Had some of them been a bit too eager to surrender? The day before the attack on Overloon, the British had learned from a few German deserters that quite a few men in the battalion were willing to desert, but dared not do so because of fear of reprisals against their relatives in Germany. But these same Germans said that if the British should attack the village, the Fallschirmjäger would fight hard to the very end. And that was exactly what happened.

In this sector of the front—certainly in the case of the Panzer-grenadiers and the Fallschirmjäger—desertion was an exception. Most German soldiers still believed that the tide would turn and that Germany could still win the war. The officer corps was more skeptical.

When Loytved-Hardegg visited General Student, he heard him speak to Goering and was amazed by the general optimism of the conversation. Student, having put down the receiver, said: "We don't fight because we expect the new V-weapons to bring us victory, but simply to obtain the best possible terms for an armistice." Other officers held similar views; it was a justification for continuing the massacre, the tremendous sacrifice in blood, by hanging on to the defense lines here in Overloon. Loytved-Hardegg had not a clue as to the number of casualties, but the sight of the soldiers stumbling back along the road made him realize how grave the situation was. Shortly afterward he met the battalion commander. The exhausting battle had left its marks on Paul's face, and even this tough, fanatical man, deep in his heart, shared the feelings of his subordinates.

The decision to retreat could no longer be postponed. Under the mounting pressure of the British attacks on October 13, Colonel Goltzsch had no choice but to withdraw all his forces behind the Loobeek, to turn the ground in front of it into one huge minefield and to flood the banks. There was no time to waste, and the pressure became so great that mines were sown at random, without marking them on maps.

During the night Loytved-Hardegg went to his new HQ in Oostrum. On his way, he heard in the darkness the screams of the patients of St. Servatius, a psychiatric hospital for male patients. In the morning, very important visitors suddenly called on him in the barn, half sunk into the ground, where he had established his HQ: Colonel Goltzsch and General von Obstfelder. Loytved-Hardegg began to explain the very difficult situation at the front, but the general showed very little interest and suddenly interrupted him, saying: "Yesterday's orders have been canceled. Our previous positions in Overloon must be retaken at once." Loytved-Hardegg was bewildered. He answered that the order was irresponsible: random minefields had been laid, the ground along the Loobeek had been flooded, it would mean a senseless waste of the Fallschirmjäger battalions which had already been mauled so badly.

As Loytved-Hardegg addressed the General, Colonel Goltzch rose to his feet and looked at him meaningfully. "This is an order from the Führer! Do you understand?" shouted General von Obstfelder and hastily left the barn to return to the comfort of Hillenraad Castle. Loytved-Hardegg became even more confused when Goltzsch then said to him: "Of course you must send out recce parties. Why don't you try to get a few patrols to Overloon, then we'll see what to do." This was an interpretation of the orders from the corps commander that verged on sabotage.

Loytved-Hardegg felt himself involved in something he did not like, but he refrained from opposing Goltzsch's interpretation. He was adamantly opposed to sacrificing his men in a mad and useless assault. He did in fact send out two patrols which did not get beyond the flooded terrain which was infested with mines. An SP gun which was to cover the patrols hit a mine and both tracks were damaged. This was the only result of the Führer's orders to retake the positions near Overloon.

★ ★ ★

October 14 brought variable weather, rainy with occasional bright intervals. The ground just in front of the Loobeek was still being stubbornly defended by the Germans. This made it necessary for two battalions which so far had been held in reserve to be thrown into the battle. The Lincolns joined 9 Brigade in the west and the Norfolks joined 185 Brigade in the east. It proved impossible for the Lincolns to get through the hail of German shellfire in the morning.

At half past three in the afternoon the division's artillery went into action. Closely following the barrage, the Lincolns advanced in good order as they had done in the morning. Again the German fire rained down on them. "Those who fell — and they were many," wrote their historian, "stayed behind waiting for stretcher bearers to collect them. The others pushed on. There was not the slightest cover." Lt. Colonel Firbank went ahead of his soldiers, firing a sten gun from the hip.

The attack by the Lincolns brought back to Major Larkin, who was at the head of his company, images of movies he had seen of the Great War: soldiers going "over the top" from their trenches and storming forward into no-man's land. Two days passed before the battalion found the time to bury its 28 dead. East of the road to Venray, the Norfolks managed to reach the Loobeek in three assaults that took them a whole day.

Tanks of the Grenadier Guards succeeded in occupying the Laag Heide woods within the hour. It is most likely that here, in the south-east corner of the Laag Heide, the most bizarre weapons of the whole battle were used: two handbows. During a brief stay in Overloon, Major Crosthwaite had been in a café where in better times a local bowmen's club must have held its meetings. He took two bows from the wall and a couple of arrows and ten minutes later was supporting with his tank an infantry attack on a wood beside a road. Standing upright in the turret, Crosthwaite shot his arrows toward the enemy's positions. "The handbow has a long tradition in the British Army," he remarked. The next day Crosthwaite searched in the wood. He did find a few dead Germans, but none with an arrow in the chest. "He would have died without having believed it."

The Coldstream Guards were not so lucky. South of the woods of Overloon they were halted by three Panthers. Four of their tanks were lost; their shells had hit the first Panther and had no effect at all — they bounced off the front plate of the tank like tennis balls. The Division's concern was not only the Loobeek in front, but also their flanks. The 11th Armoured and the American 7th Armored protected the 3rd Division's right flank. But the left flank, after the first jump to the south, was exposed in the direction of Vierlingsbeek. For this reason the South Lancashires had to join the battle for the second time, now as spearhead. They were to advance through the woods (where the War Museum stands today), south of the Vierlingsbeek road, terrain with poor visibility, intersected by mud tracks. During their advance they came across a corpse more horrible than any they had ever seen; whether it was friend or foe was impossible to tell from the uniform rags. A troop of tanks had rolled over it.

Ferocious resistance and minefields slowed down their advance. The South Lancashire reports show a reticence which is typical for many people from the north of England. What they had to go through may be gathered from the fact that three officers were awarded the Military Cross and two other ranks with the Military Medal, rare decorations for bravery. Eventually the South Lancashires got as far as the railway track to Venlo. They bagged 102 prisoners. The action was supported by a squadron of the Grenadier Guards. Near the hamlet of Schaartven three tanks were hit, one of which, abandoned by its crew, rolled burning with its engine in reverse gear back into the wood, over a distance of 800 yards.

That day, Major Renison jotted down: "Overloon marked a return to the utter devastation of the Normandy battlefields. Dead cattle strewed the landscape. The trees were stripped bare of their bark and foliage; above all the coming and going of transport and the rain had reduced green fields and pleasant gardens alike to black, slimy mud. Hardly a human soul was to be seen, except the British Army. Here and there a broken doll or the pathetic debris of the infants' school. Once more it was war stripped of any softer tones — naked and beastly."

Not only Overloon but Venray too was gradually being turned into rubble, including its pride, the Church of Saint-Petrus-Banden. The church was a sort of basilica, with remarkably high side aisles, resembling a hall church. Built in the latter half of the 15th century, its straight tower was a few decades older. The tower was called the "Pearl of the Peel." The Germans had set up an observation post there which reported the British positions and movements to the German artillery and Nebelwerfers. A heading in the *Daily Mail* of October 16 rightly said: "Church tower halts Dempsey." When the newspaper reported this, the fate of the tower was sealed.

During the whole afternoon of October 14 the church was the target of squadrons stationed at Eindhoven. Thirty-six Typhoons fired 284 60-pound rockets over Venray. The British artillery also aimed their guns at the tower. Within a few minutes the church was reduced to a pile of rubble; the tower, however, though heavily damaged, was still standing. All around the church the heart of Venray was burning: the Hofstraat and also the Jerusalem boarding school for girls, where 800 refugees had hoped to find a safe hiding place. German film reporters were busy filming the exodus out of this inferno for the German *Wocheneschau* (news). "Toward the evening the sky was lit up by a tremendous fire," wrote Sister Marie-Godelieve in St. Anna. "Sparks were flying all around and caused a threat to the whole neighborhood. The cattle were lowing sadly. The burnt smell penetrated everywhere and we could no longer hide it from those in the cellars. We were getting terrified. It was as if the entire town was on fire, and sparks were being blown toward our main building. Guns sounded dull in the distance, shells whizzed past our home. Would this be the end of everything? We hardly dared go to sleep. Fortunately the wind changed and the risk of fire was averted." Not only in St. Anna, but all over the land of northern Limburg the glow of Venray on fire could be seen.

On Sunday, October 15, the front seemed to grow quieter, although shells continued to fall behind the German lines, and in the grounds of St. Anna more wards were hit. Sometimes a patient managed to run away, which, considering the circumstances, could not always be prevented. One of them stole a scarf from a nurse and sneaked off unnoticed from the group of patients; she was brought back and said that "she had wanted to speak to the English general to ask him to hurry up with their liberation." Others managed to go farther — even through the lines — and soldiers, much to their surprise, saw people wandering about as if there was no war on, people vague as to where they came from but definitely knew that they were "going home."

Yet the number that managed to run away remained small according to Dr. Schmidt, assistant director of St. Anna. He lived in a house on the street that led to the entrance gate to the hospital. There he remained with his wife in the cellar, but as soon as the noise outside abated he would hurry to the wards to help where he could. The very mentally disturbed patients reacted with a sort of aloofness to the uproar around them: they continued to live in their own secluded world. The milder cases, however, started to panic, to use abusive language or to scream. Many of them had to be put in straitjackets to prevent them from attacking each other. The greatest worry of both Dr. Schmidt and the nurses was the increasing squalor of the place as there was no longer any water available. It had virtually become impossible to wash patients who had dirtied themselves.

The food situation had also deteriorated. The kitchens were still working but food was becoming scarce. Apples were in plentiful supply and so were sedatives. As time went by, Dr. Schmidt noticed that the continuous strain and fear, together with the care for the patients who required so much attention, was gradually becoming unbearable for the nurses. With the buildings continually being shelled, they seemed to become petrified, in medical terms in a state of catatonia. As the shelling went on, they were overcome by a feeling of being doomed to total inactivity in the cellars, where there was nothing they could do, isolated in confined spaces, the walls closing in on them. But Schmidt also observed that as soon as the nurses were able to resume their duties these symptoms would vanish within hours. Being able to do something, to be active again, was a very good therapy. On the shoulders of Dr. Schim van der Loeff, the medical superintendent, rested a heavy responsibility for these 2,000 helpless people. What more would they have to go through when St. Anna would become the center of the battle scene? His own resilience had its limitations, too.

Back to the problems of the British: One way or another they had to get across the Loobeek. Support had been promised to General Whistler for his already sorely tried infantry by corps commander O'Connor, even though the first phase — the capture of Venray — had not yet been completed.

At the same time the Loobeek was to be crossed, units from the British and American armored divisions would go into action. In the area between Rips and Deurne they were to draw the Germans away from Venray, to the northwest sector of the front. If this should work, the second phase of "Constellation" could immediately be followed up by the third, the attack by the Scottish Division in the south.

In the afternoon of October 15 it began to pour again. The 3rd Division had completed its plans for the crossing of the Loobeek. During the night the infantry was to reach the other side by means of kapok bridges, 185 Brigade with its battalions of Norfolks and Warwicks on and west of the main road from Overloon to Venray; farther west the Suffolks would be followed by the East Yorks, both from 8 Brigade. Tanks were to support them from the north bank. On the main road and west of it, engineers were to prepare a crossing for tanks with Bailey bridges. Where the Suffolks were, tanks carrying fascines—bundles of brushwood—would form a solid bridge by dumping these into the stream.

When looking at the Loobeek today, one can scarcely imagine how this narrow stream could have been such a formidable obstacle. The continuous rains in those October days, and the raising of the water level by the Germans, however, had widened the Loobeek to approximately six yards. Besides, it had steeply sloping banks. And even on its bed, it was known, mines had been laid.

"We received our orders after dark," wrote an officer of the Norfolks, "and in the usual downpour the unhappy company commanders made their plans, while we with hooded torches struggled to read the map." The infantry, shivering on their soaking wet groundsheets, barely got an opportunity to sleep. Major Renison was very concerned: to him the whole plan seemed to depend on so many interrelated factors. "I was extremely unhappy about the (original) plan. It seemed to me a most extraordinarily casual way of coping with a maneuver, the failure of which might spoil the whole attack!"

In the early hours of October 16 the forward troops of 185 Brigade carried their kapok bridges to the waterlogged banks. At first everything seemed to be all right. Between four and five o'clock in the morning the Norfolks and Warwicks silently crossed the "beek." But the tanks got stuck in the muddy fields before even reaching the stream.

The first tank bridge was laid beside the main road crossing, which had been demolished by the Germans. Here the tank which had put the bridge across was the first to topple into the water, taking the bridge with it. No more Churchill tanks would cross the Loobeek at this spot and the Norfolks, deprived of tank support, advanced only a thousand yards before they were pinned down in German crossfire, suffering many casualties. Farther to the west the Warwicks had had a tough time in their small bridgehead. At nine o'clock in the morning the engineers, who drove up to the Loobeek along a mud track, defying German shellfire, succeeded in putting a bridge across. During the day the Warwicks, with support from tanks of the Coldstream Guards which had also crossed the bridge, were able to infiltrate the northwest part of Venray via Brabander. In the evening the first patrol entered the woods of St. Anna and signaled to the divisional artillery that "two thousand bad women" were there, causing a lot of wild speculation among the gunners until it became clear that "mad women" had become garbled.

Farther west, beyond Kleindorp, the Suffolks ran into trouble. After the first company had crossed at seven o'clock, they were met by heavy fire; they also found that they were advancing straight through a minefield. Two of the fascine-carrying tanks bogged down on the soggy north bank of the "beek"; the third tank's fascine alone was not big enough to ford the stream.

There was no alternative but to ask for additional bridge-laying equipment, and that would take time. Despite the fact that the Suffolks would have to do without the support of the Churchills and their own carriers and anti-tank guns, Colonel Craddock decided to establish a bridgehead on the opposite bank. He ordered two other companies forward with their kapok bridges and at ten o'clock they made a successful crossing. But in the wet weather the wireless of the battalion was barely functioning.

An hour later, still without any news from his men on the other side of the Loobeek, Craddock himself went forward to see what was happening. While crossing a field where scores of soldiers had gone before him, he had a foot blown off by a Schü mine. Lying there, Craddock had no idea that he was in the midst of a minefield. He thought he had been hit by a shell. Lying on his back, he used his hands to try to crawl back. The stretcher bearers also seemed unaware of the danger. They walked toward the wounded commander, and as they laid him on the stretcher one of them also stepped on a mine. The blast of the explosion hit the man full in the face and blinded him permanently. The colonel toppled back from the stretcher into the mud.

The Suffolks remained exposed to intense mortar and shell fire and still there was not a single tank in sight. The East Yorks were the last battalion to be committed in the struggle, this time with a new company commander. That night, Major Renison was asked by his brigadier if he felt that Colonel Dickson was still capable of leading the battalion. Renison was reluctant to answer the question. He was then given the embarrassing task of explaining to Dickson that he was to be replaced — by Renison himself — who felt quite badly about it. "It was a horrid moment for me after all our banter about 'dead man's shoes.'"

When, in the early afternoon, the East Yorks marched toward the Loobeek, the four companies forming a long column, Major Renison found there a "sad congestion of men and equipment." He had no alternative but to let his troops take cover in the verges on both sides of the road and sweat it out while German shells were dropping all around them. Finally, by three o'clock, something approached that to Renison looked like an "infernal machine, a tank with a 32-foot ladder bridge mounted on it in a vertical position. It looked for all the world like the Tower Bridge driving past, and I waited, in vain, for every gun in the Boche artillery to open up on it; it looked too tempting for words!"

The huge machine managed to make its way toward the "beek," 50 yards north of the spot where the fascine tanks had failed. Here the bridge dropped properly in its place and the Grenadier Guards could begin the crossing in order to extricate the harassed infantry from their awkward position.

Again fate intervened. Three Churchill tanks which had just crossed the stream got stuck in the mud, thereby blocking the advance route and making the crossing unusable. Yet the commanding officer of the Suffolks decided to move his battalion forward, no matter how. Because of the congestion it was already dusk when the East Yorks crossed the Loobeek. A number of them got lost in the darkness among the troops of 185 Brigade; the main force, dispersed and under continuous enemy fire, succeeded in establishing itself in the hamlet of Brabander. On their right the Suffolks had fought their way into Hiept. On digging in for the night, they had been brought a warm meal and a very welcome ration of rum. They had lost their battalion commander, three company commanders and forty-five other ranks.

The crossing of the Loobeek had been written in blood, but all along the front the infantry had now reached the outskirts of Venray. Of the Guards Tank Brigade, two squadrons of tanks of the Coldstreams had crossed the "beek" and the next day a squadron of the Grenadiers was to follow over the only bridge available for tanks.

After a period of suffering lasting more than two weeks, the hour of liberation for Venray had come. To General Whistler, commander of the 3rd Division, Venray's liberation was a source of great worry. Usually of a very cheerful disposition, it had now become obvious how deeply he had been affected by the heavy losses of his troops: he hardly slept or ate. Would there again be so many casualties in the days to come?

CHAPTER EIGHT

CONSTELLATION: "ABORTED STAR"

O N THE MORNING OF October 17, later than planned, and delayed by minefields and artillery fire, the troops all along the front began to prepare for a concentric attack on Venray. They were unaware of the fact that this attack would comprise the premature end of Operation "Constellation" — not the decisive push that was to wipe out the entire German salient west of the Maas. "Constellation" was about to be aborted.

The front near Venray, viewed clockwise, presented the following picture. West of the town the Suffolks were advancing through the woods between Hiept and Venray in a southerly direction, supported by tanks which had crossed the Loobeek on October 17 via the only available tank bridge. Later, more bridges would be laid by the engineers. On October 17 and 18 the East Yorks had the far from enviable task of fighting their way from Brabander into the northern part of Venray. Their advance started at 9:30 and within three hours they had reached their first objective. On the Overloon road they were harassed by machine-gun fire. Fortunately the commander of a flail tank offered to drive ahead and demoralize the Germans with his gun and rotating flails. A few Churchill tanks followed in his tracks.

Pvt. Roebuck's platoon carefully moved forward past the houses, taking cover in doorways wherever bends in the street might hide unpleasant surprises. After the third bend, a German 88 mm shell exploded right behind Roebuck and he saw that his company commander was badly wounded by splinters in the stomach and arm. At the next street corner the platoon was raked by machine-gun fire. The man in front of Roebuck was hit in his belly and, virtually sliced in two, fell on the ground. The German who had shot him came out of his shelter with his arms raised. The man had bandy legs and arms too long compared with the rest of his body. "What a bloody monkey," Roebuck thought bitterly. "I should shoot the bastard. First killing a man with a senseless blast from his machine gun and then trying to save his own lousy skin!"

The German was taken to the rear and the East Yorks continued to mop up the area until, at dusk, they were given orders to find a place to spend the night. Major Renison wished to avoid his troops' becoming involved in confused street fighting during the night. He had every reason to be satisfied: his soldiers had penetrated the center of Venray and, during the night, they beat off a counterattack by the engineer company of Loytved-Hardegg's Fallschirmjäger Regiment 21, the commander of which was killed.

Roebuck had spent the night with eight others in the deserted café of van den Oudenhoven on the Overloon road in Venray. A dead German was lying in front of the door. They had mounted their Bren gun on top of the cafe's bar. They were very tired, but the corporal in charge of Roebuck's section had enough common sense to put a few men on guard. At daybreak, guard duty was limited to one man.

Roebuck posted himself behind the bar and to while the time away he took the Bren gun apart and started cleaning its components. Having finished, he did the same with a German Sturmgewehr (assault rifle) that he had found in the café. Much to his annoyance, he could not put it back together. The fact that this weapon was lying around should have been a warning to him. An hour or so later, after he had been relieved from sentry duty, a number of soldiers came walking down the street toward the café. They turned out to be the South Lancashires, with orders to mop up the southern part of Venray. They were visibly spent and one of them, carrying a small case, had obviously gotten tired of it. He flung it into the doorway of the café and, on opening it, the sentry found a collection of watches, rings and other items taken from prisoners. "A nice stroke of luck for my mate," thought Roebuck, "but it's another load to carry."

Suddenly they heard a noise from under a row of chairs stacked against the bar. The sentry shouted, "Who's there?" and to their surprise a German crawled from beneath the chairs, stick hand grenades (nicknamed "potato mashers") tucked under his belt. "It's *his* gun I've been taking apart," Roebuck thought. "He might have killed me as I was cleaning our Bren gun." After the first shock there was a feeling of comradeship toward the prisoner. He was given a cigarette, which seemed to restore his self-confidence, and on being questioned by the sergeant-major he became cheeky; he was then knocked down and given a good hiding.

On this last day of the operation — October 18 — mopping up the southern part of Venray turned out to be much easier than expected. The South Lancashires (whom Roebuck had seen file past in the early hours with their loot) advanced with support from Churchill tanks of the Grenadier Guards which at six o'clock in the morning came rumbling down the streets of the town. Beyond the Marktplein (Market Square) the leading tanks were halted by a group of monks. They told the tankmen that mines were hidden in the streets. "The Church was right," so recorded a grateful historian in the war diary of the Grenadiers. By mid-day, infantry and tanks, harassed by German artillery fire, had completed their assignment. At six o'clock in the evening the BBC announced: "*American* tanks have entered Venray!"

Thus the greater part of Venray had been liberated by troops of the 8th Brigade. The northern and eastern sectors of the town had become the objectives of the 185th. The Lincolns, having lost 200 men in the past few days, of whom fifty were killed, were spared further action. The struggle of the last two days had been left to the other two battalions, the Warwicks and the 2nd Shropshires.

On the night of October 16/17 the Warwicks had occupied positions at the edge of the woods of St. Anna. Early in the morning they entered the hospital grounds. Excited nurses came dashing down the stairs into the cellar, where Sister Marie-Godelieve watched over her patients: "The Tommies have been in our cellar!" they shrieked. Despite this happy news she did not really feel any joy. She still worried a lot. The first thing to do was deliver a letter to the commanding officer asking him to help them in their desperate situation. While shells, German ones this time, continued to rain down in the grounds of St. Anna, a messenger went on his way. When Sister Marie-Godelieve was told that the British had placed a gun in position inside the bakery close to her cellar, she decided to go upstairs. She now saw her liberators for the first time in the flesh.

"I failed to realize that we ought to welcome them as our liberators," she said. "I only knew that we must get rid of them before the Germans became aware of their presence and involve us in more fighting. Suddenly it crossed my mind how we, in our dreams, had imagined what our first welcome to our liberators would be like. Illusions and reality! We decided to send another letter, for we were terrified of being shelled by the Germans. Another ordeal like the one on Monday would be too much for us to bear. In our letter we wrote how the Germans had always respected our buildings and we asked the British commander to do likewise, in order to save our patients. The letter was again delivered under shellfire."

The Warwicks advanced along the street where Dr. Schmidt lived. In the morning a German tank had driven past the house, retreating to the south. The tank commander had shouted from his turret: "We are the last Germans. After us you will see the Tommies coming. The war is over for you. But stay in your cellar, it's still too dangerous!"

Like the East Yorks, the Warwicks remained in positions right among the houses of Venray during the night of October 17/18. Toward evening a patrol penetrated as far as St. Servatius Psychiatric Hospital. Not a single German was found there, only a large number of insane male patients. The Ursuline Sisters had found shelter there when on October 14 their boarding school "Jerusalem" went up in flames. For days the Sisters of this elite school for girls had had to live among men. Whenever they had to make use of the toilets, a torrent of abuse and obscenities was shouted at them by the male patients. When on October 18 the Warwicks — somewhat incautiously — went to occupy the hospital and its grounds with their main force, they were met by machine-gun fire, which could not be silenced until two platoons of tanks of the Coldstream Guards appeared on the scene. Here the Germans again followed their familiar strategy of pulling out of a position during the night and returning at daybreak.

On the Warwicks' left flank the 2nd Shropshire Battalion had finished the arduous task of clearing the woods and fields northeast of Venray, which were infested with mines. Supported by Churchills of the Coldstream Guards, seriously hampered by anti-tank mines, the Shropshires advanced as far as the road leading from Venray to Oostrum. Their losses were limited to just under a hundred men. They were the forces that liberated the hamlet of Lull on October 18.

Guus van Dam, barely nineteen years old when he was drafted for the *Arbeitsdienst,* a paramilitary labor service, had escaped in February from the camp in Overloon and gone into hiding at the nearby farm of the Stappers family. After the evacuation of Overloon he and Piet Stappers had eventually found a place to stay at an old farm in the hamlet of Lull. Now and then he spoke with Germans on their way to or from the Overloon front line. Many of them were younger than he was. Some intimated that they were fed up with the war, others were drunk. One even asked for civilian clothes in order to desert (they were given to him), and a sergeant asked where he could find a whore—in Overloon of all places! It struck van Dam that the Germans still managed to supply their forward troops with a warm meal, the leftovers sometimes being given to him and the other refugees at the farm: macaroni with ham (a welcome change after days of soup made of horseflesh) and porridge with salt.

On October 17 the approaching artillery fire forced Guus and the others to hide in the damp, low-ceilinged cellar. From the German firing orders which he heard through the cellar's small window, he understood that a machine gun had been mounted near the farm. He sighed with relief when finally he heard the command: *"Feur einstellen! Munition mitnehmen!"* (Cease fire! Take the ammunition with you!)

Gradually it grew very quiet outside and was quite dark. Then, all at once, the trapdoor to the cellar staircase was thrown open and a German, his helmet camouflaged with tree leaves, peered down into the dimly lit room. Van Dam expected him to throw a hand grenade, but to his surprise the German shouted something like "Just a few more minutes and Tommy will be here! Stay in your cellar, he won't harm you!" He slammed the door shut and his footsteps died away. A few minutes later, wisps of smoke came though the cracks of the door. One of the people sitting near the cellar door opened it, looked inside the kitchen and yelled that the farm was on fire. The refugees panicked and scrambled up the stairs, fleeing the farm through the kitchen.

Outside, German soldiers were watching the fire. Was it one of them who had set fire to the farm? A few of the Germans helped in escorting the women to a barn at the far end of the farmyard. The stable was also burning and a few cows were straining at their chains and lowing pitifully. Van Dam, unable to watch this any longer, walked up to a German soldier, tugged at his sleeve and asked him if he would shoot the animals. The soldier was very obliging and killed them expertly. Closely packed together, the refugees spent the rest of the night in the barn. Their cries and prayers were drowned in the hellish noise of exploding shells. Fortunately they survived the ordeal. At daybreak the Germans had gone. Van Dam left the barn and cautiously walked down the Smakterveld road from which direction he expected the first British troops to come.

★   ★   ★

So far the exploits of the 3rd Division in the week's fighting for Venray have been followed closely. What had happened to the support from the other divisions, as promised by General O'Connor to Whistler? That support was given during the last three days of the battle. The 11th Armoured launched an attack northeast of Venray on October 16 by the 4th Shropshire Battalion and to the northwest by the Rifle Brigade Battalion.

The Shropshires assembled in the woods southwest of Overloon. They advanced through difficult terrain dotted with sand dunes, heading east toward the railway line Nijmegen–Venlo. There Fall-schirmjäger were dug in, and they kept up a crossfire with their machine guns that pinned the Shropshires down. A short, robust sergeant left his cover. He was George Eardley, twenty-seven years old, who had joined the battalion as a volunteer. Known as a tough fighter, he was not afraid of taking great risks. Armed with a sten gun and a couple of hand grenades he dashed forward through a hail of bullets toward the German position about 80 yards away. Firing his sten and throwing one hand grenade, he killed the machine-gun crew. When another Spandau started firing at him, he charged forward over the open field and silenced that machine gun, too. A few minutes later yet another machine gun halted the advance of the Shropshires. Eardley motioned to his men to keep their heads down while he crawled forward. They watched spellbound as Eardley with a single hand grenade knocked his third Spandau out of action.

For his courage and daring Sergeant Eardley was awarded the highest decoration for bravery of the British Army, the Victoria Cross. Rarely awarded—during the whole war no more than 182 were given out—most of them were posthumous. After the battle for Arnhem this was the fifth and last VC awarded for actions on Dutch territory.*

The Shropshires reached their objective, but were then pulled out to the main divisional area, where their support was required in the initial stage of "Pollux," already started in the northwest. Here patrols of the Rifle Brigade had found a crossing over the Defense Canal, which the Germans had not destroyed.

General Roberts ordered three battalions of infantry, supported by tanks, to cross the Defense Canal and advance to the southeast. They encountered the usual obstacles and the ubiquitous Nebelwerfers. Hendrik Jan Ledeboer, who had joined the Rifle Brigade as an interpreter, found himself under fire from these rocket launchers. How vulnerable and lonely he felt in the "stonk," as the British called such a concentrated fire. It struck him that the men, cringing in the slimy mud, were clinging to one another like drowning men, for moral support. When the firing ceased Ledeboer saw a half-track driver who had been wounded in his buttocks being carried away on a stretcher. Lying on his belly, the man was shouting, "Gimme my loot!"—for the troops carried on a very lively trade in watches, rings, money and other items taken from prisoners.

Ysselstein, Merselo, Leunen and Veulen were liberated. Only in the latter hamlet did the troops of the 11th Armoured Division encounter resistance of any significance. Here three Sherman tanks,

---

*Earlier in the war, the VC had been awarded to pilots for bravery shown over Dutch territory.

which accompanied the infantry, were surprised by a German tank. Major Thornburn watched helplessly as the first one brewed up. The second tried to dodge the shells and turned like a lumbering, frightened animal, until eventually it too was hit.

When the Germans counterattacked, Veulen could barely be held. The next day, October 19, while trying to advance, the British encountered fierce opposition. Yet, in the past three days, the 11th Armoured had bagged 450 prisoners and General Roberts was therefore very optimistic.

It did not take long for the American 7th Armored Division to become involved in the fighting in the desolate Peel after their rest period. The 23rd Infantry Battalion had established a bridgehead near Griendtsveen. The men spent five days there in a situation which John Margreiter, for one, found unable to describe adequately. Rains lashed the peat bog. During the night he stood in a foxhole filled with a few inches of water. There was little or no warm food in their advanced positions. They lived on K-rations (canned food, rich in calories but not very filling) which they carried with them and were eaten without being warmed up. The infantrymen griped about the field kitchens, which did not show up until October 20. When British sappers began to blow up German mines in the area, one of the men of the field kitchens shouted: "We're under fire!" and off went the vehicle with its eagerly awaited warm chow. The Americans were relieved that night. Nearly 90 percent of the men had to be treated for trench feet. A few had to be carried away from the swampy fields.

Yet the overall impression was that the 3rd Division had succeeded in breaking the backbone of the German resistance and that a continuation of the attacks by the two armored divisions on the flank might be successful. The thing that mattered now was to deal a decisive knockout blow to the German salient between the Peel and the Maas. In this action the 15th Scottish Division was to play a cardinal role. The Scots, already assembled in the south, were to start the third phase of General O'Connor's Constellation: "Sirius."

On the evening of October 16, O'Connor considered the time ripe to begin preparations for "Sirius." Reports had come in that German units had left the southern sector of the salient and had been spotted near Venray—the very thing O'Connor had hoped for. His staff was already busy drafting the first orders for the Scots when the telephone rang: "Operation 'Constellation' must be discontinued!" It turned out that while infantry and tanks were exposed to all the hardships of the fighting, the Supreme Command had been making far-reaching decisions. The front line was to remain where it was: from the river Maas near Maashees in a curve to the southwest through Venray and Veulen to Griendtsveen, from there following the Deurne Canal and finally the Noorder Canal to Nederweert.

The information which O'Connor had received about the German troop movements was to some extent correct, but its implication was quite different. What had happened was that General Erdmann with his staff, and Colonel Goltzsch with his staff, had changed places: the former moved to the front near Venray, so that this sector of the salient came under the 7th Fallschirmjäger Division, whereas the canal front in the southern sector was now the 344th Division's responsibility. Fallschirmjäger Regiment Hübner remained in this sector and was joined by Fallschirmjäger-Lehr Regiment Hermann. The battered remnants of Battalion Paul, badly mauled in the Overloon battle, and thereafter attached to Fallschirmjäger Regiment 21, commanded by Lt. Colonel Loytved-Hardegg, also occupied positions in this southern sector.

One might say that this implied a certain strengthening of the German southern sector, but under the circumstances the forces deployed there would never have been able to beat off an Allied offensive. Why, then, was Operation "Constellation" called off so abruptly after only one phase, "Castor," had been completed? We know Montgomery's aspirations: he wanted to clear the Scheldt estuary, at the same time chasing the Germans from the western part of the province of Noord-Brabant and rolling up the Peel-Maas salient. On October 16 there came an end to his ambition. The order had all the characteristics of an independent decision by the Field Marshal, but in fact Eisenhower had forced him to give up his plans. Eisenhower himself not only ordered that absolute priority was to be given to the opening up of the port of Antwerp, but also referred to even higher authorities to back up his order.

Outranked, there was nothing the Field Marshal or his chirping canary Herbie could do. The day after receipt of Eisenhower's letter, Montgomery replied: "I have given top priority to Antwerp in all the operations of the 21st Army Group. All offensive power will be directed westward against the axis Hertogentosch-Breda. All other offensive operations on a large scale by the Second Army will be terminated." Thus an extremely frustrated General O'Connor received orders to abort "Constellation." The 15th Scottish Division and the 6th Guards Tank Brigade were withdrawn from the Peel sector to support the offensive in the western part of the province of Noord-Brabant. Neither "Pollux" nor "Sirius" nor "Vega" had had an opportunity to sparkle in the heavens.

This change in plans doomed Venray to remain a front-line town. It is true that in the meantime the engineers had built two crossings over the Loobeek, but they no longer served to bring in fresh troops, merely to relieve troops and for mass evacuation of civilians. Venray was full of refugees anxious to go back home. Often all they found on their return were piles of rubble.

One of the refugees was Len Welbers, who had ridden on his bicycle from Overloon to Grave in September, and had obtained permission on October 16 to return to Overloon. There he found his parents' home totally destroyed, only the bicycle repair shop still standing. It took another ten days before the whole Welbers family had been reunited; his parents and his brothers and sisters had survived the bombing of the Jerusalem boarding school. His father had lost all his savings, a few thousand guilders, in the fire and as he stood in front of the destroyed house he saw that everything he had worked for during the past 25 years was gone. He burst out in tears. This was the first time in his life that Len Welbers saw his father weep.

After the liberation the German guns kept hammering away at Venray. Food supplies stagnated. The situation became desperate. In St. Anna the number of dysentery cases grew daily. The 1,700 patients depended entirely on British Army rations and even water had to be brought in from outside. The medical services of the Army, and subsequently Civil Affairs officers, came to take stock of the situation. Sister Marie-Godelieve always saw the same reaction: never before had they been faced with such misery during the war.

The visitors had to go down into the cellars in the pitch dark. There was no power and furthermore the usual stock of candles had been exhausted. One could hear patients scream, but one could not see them. In many cases the inspection of one such cellar, packed with apathetic or cursing women, became too much for many an official. After visiting his hospital on October 19 for the first time after four days, Dr. Schim van der Loeff "had aged incredibly and become a broken man." As he eyed the ruined buildings he said to Sister Marie-Godelieve: "I'll never be able to rebuild St. Anna; I might as well resign." Which he did.

There were twenty-two bodies in the morgue which nobody had been able to bury. When, on October 20, a few nurses and men made preparations for the burial—there was only one coffin—a shell exploded in the morgue, mutilating the bodies terribly. The day before, the sad exodus of the patients had begun: 850 patients were loaded onto trucks in an indescribable chaos. They were taken to institutions in Boekel and Woensel. The next day another transport left for Eindhoven. On October 21 the 80 worst cases were loaded onto trucks on stretchers, some heavily sedated, others fighting wildly and screaming in panic. Finally, emaciated tuberculosis patients were loaded into ambulances. "Hurry up!" the British kept shouting, because their convoy of 30 ambulances and 15 trucks was being exposed for hours to the risk of being shelled by the Germans. No permission was given to take luggage because there was not enough space in the trucks.

St. Servatius also had to be evacuated. This was an even more risky undertaking since this hospital was still in the front line. The evacuation started on October 22. The East Yorks had been occupying positions around the buildings for the past four days. General Whistler, who had visited St. Anna, had decided to evacuate St. Servatius under military control. Major Renison left the implementation of the evacuation order to his second-in-command, "Banger" King. King was full of criticism about the manner in which St. Anna had been evacuated by Civil Affairs, which had kept long, vulnerable columns of trucks waiting for hours inside the grounds of the hospital. At St. Servatius this would be tantamount to suicide.

To the west of the hospital, the least dangerous side, the East Yorks had made a new access road where the trucks would be fairly safe while waiting for the patients. Walking cases were accompanied by medical orderlies and helped onto the trucks. The actual convoy was lined up near the hospital on the western edge of Venray. Only the worst cases were removed from the place by ambulance. Renison was full of praise for the support from the medical staff of St. Servatius and its Mother Superior. Within two days, and without any casualties, all the buildings had been emptied. Renison observed: "The highlight of the procession was the sight of 'Banger' King, whose ideas on the female sex were well known to us, taking his place in a jeep-load of elderly nuns, their black robes billowing round their necks as the jeep drove off."

All this was merely a prelude. On October 25, Civil Affairs was forced to make a far-reaching decision: the whole of Venray was to be evacuated. This was a bitter experience for people who, as refugees without any rights, were forced to live among strangers, dependent on their favors, in the dark as to the fate of their homes and belongings, waiting for who knew how long. "Time is of no importance to refugees," remarked Dr. Schim van der Loeff during the evacuation. He had been right; he would never rebuild St. Anna. At the end of December he died of a heart attack on a street in Eindhoven, fifty-three years old.

The refugees from Venray had at least one consolation, however: they were free. Less fortunate were those who were still in the occupied area of the province of Limburg and for whom the hour of freedom had not yet struck. One of these was Harry van Daal, an Overloon municipal employee. In hiding, hunted by the Germans, he ultimately found shelter at a farm in Oirlo, where on October 14 the Germans set up a field hospital. They forced van Daal to keep the place clean. He had to sort out torn pieces of uniform belonging to the wounded, including their blood-soaked underwear, and make separate piles of them in the stable. The kitchen served as an operating room and at regular intervals he had to scrub the floor. Before the wounded were taken to the kitchen, a portly Feldwebel in the stable took down their name, rank and number.

"A soldier was brought in," wrote van Daal, "a frightened little boy of eighteen, covered with mud from head to toe, his right arm smashed. Lying on the stretcher, he was staring at one point on the ceiling with his dark, keen eyes. Blood was dripping steadily from his sleeve, forming a small puddle on the floor." After the Feldwebel had finished his notes, van Daal took a cup of soup to the wounded young German, made of meat from a freshly slaughtered pig. "Here, try this." The German looked up in surprise. A friendly Dutchman? But as van Daal wrote: "After having stayed for two days among these men, with their smelly wounds and their blood-soaked uniforms, I mellowed and accepted them." The soldier ate his soup, thanked van Daal and, turning around on the stretcher, he said: "I wanted to be an engineer."

In the "operating room" a twenty-eight-year-old doctor worked around the clock. "The minimum of sleep was compensated for by a maximum of wine," van Daal wrote. "Wine was an excellent means of getting rid of the pervading smell of ether and iodine which clung to our clothes." The fat Feldwebel told van Daal that Herr Doktor had not graduated yet, but that picking out shell splinters probably was a better qualification for a doctor than a university degree. Herr Doktor boozed so much that he spent most of the time—night or day made no difference—in a kind of stupor. His dull eyes and the uncertain way in which he moved about left his subordinates in no doubt as to his condition. "In such a state he is at his best at the operating table," remarked the Feldwebel.

Van Daal also saw how a tall soldier with a bayonet wound in his head went berserk on the operating table, kicking the doctor in his belly, rolling off the table onto the floor, screaming and ripping off his bandage, taking a piece of skin from his head with it. He tried to raise his right arm as he shouted: "Heil Hitler, the greatest swindler on earth!" Thereafter he was carried away unconscious. A robust Fall-schirmjäger was brought in. His abdomen had been ripped apart by a shell fragment and he made a wailing sound, like an air-raid siren; van Daal watched with surprise how he was silenced by a gruff "Shut up!" from the doctor. The splinter was removed from the Fallschirmjäger's shivering body, which made the table tremble. The Feldwebel said, "Always the artillery. Courage is of no use here."

As van Daal was sorting out the belongings of a soldier who had died during treatment, he found pornographic photographs and magazines, *Nuits de Paris,* brought from France to the front in the Peel. He also watched another soldier die, a rosary clenched between his teeth, his eyes shining with a strange kind of inner peace, staring at the two bloody stumps that once were his legs. "Like a tornado which threatened to drag me into its vortex, this mass of human misery faced me," wrote van Daal. When, after the fall of Venray, the field hospital had to be abandoned in a hurry, the Germans forced van Daal to go in the direction of the Maas, away from the approaching Allies.

There the refugees waited in great anxiety, uncertain of what the future might bring. Death, destruction, mass evacuation? Or deportation of the men, who were being hunted down by the *Grunepolizei,* to be used for digging defense systems. Failure to report for duty was punishable by death, the Germans threatened, and one could not stay in hiding forever, could one?

Thus, liberation, which had seemed so near, was still to remain beyond reach.

CHAPTER NINE

COUNTERSTROKE
IN THE SWAMP

WHEN OPERATION "CONSTELLATION" was aborted by the Allies, the American 7th Armored Division was in the Peel, south of the British divisions that had participated. The front line ran with erratic meanderings along the Deurne Canal — skirting around Meyel — from Nederweert to Wessem. Nowhere was the Peel swampier than in this area. Small branch canals, past excavations, lakes, pools and tussocks made large areas of it impassable. Where the ground was solid and suitable for agriculture, the soil was soft. The Americans found that when digging foxholes these were easily flooded by groundwater. Another disadvantage was that tanks and other heavy vehicles could not move off the few roads in the Peel, which severely hampered their deployment. The Allies' only consolation was that the enemy faced the same problem.

As it was, the Americans did not believe the Germans capable of launching a major attack. They felt very secure behind the irregular belt of the maze of canals in the marshy Peel. Combat Command A had dug in behind the south bank of the Canal from Wessem to Nederweert, with the Free Belgian Brigade on its right flank. Combat Command B was in position inside the bridgehead near the village of Griendtsveen.

The sector held by the Division was, in fact, about 14 miles long, guarded by the 87th Reconnaissance Squadron. On paper this unit was at battalion strength: 900 recce troops, carried in 43 half-tracks, with 17 tanks at their disposal. But this was a fairly small combat force for a front line of such length. In fact, it was merely a string of outposts, each six to nine men strong, with one machine gun at each. The outposts ranged from 500 to 800 yards, sometimes more, behind the canals. A lot of patrolling was done between the outposts, but infiltrations by Germans from across the canals during the night could hardly be prevented. Other units of the Division—reserve units, supply troops, technical units and such—were stationed in the rear, the bulk in and around the village of Asten. General Silvester's HQ had been established in a little wood near the hamlet of Heusden, south of Asten.

The Americans enjoyed, in what one of them called the "Peel Swamp," a necessary and deserved rest. Between actions the foot soldier could indulge himself in the rare luxury of spending the night in a real house, sometimes a factory or a school, often with Dutch families who treated him as one of their own. The Army Service Corps managed to bring warm meals to the soldiers daily, without being fired at.

Aside from patrolling, now and then the artillery fired a few rounds. It was not very exciting and became part of the day's routine. The Germans had a habit of lobbing over a few shells at four o'clock in the afternoon. One American soldier who had made a date with a Dutch girl, and had been foolish enough to arrange a rendezvous at that time, saw the young lady riding toward him on her bike. Suddenly German shells whizzed past. The girl dived for cover in a nearby ditch and "was not hurt," the soldier said afterward. "Then she jumped on her bike and rode off like mad. I've never seen her again."

Not much else happened. The men of the 7th Armored who were familiar only with Germans in stubborn defense or in chaotic flight had few reasons to think that anything eventful *would* happen.

The assumption on which the Americans had based their false sense of security in their quiet front sector may be considered unjustified, and is comparable with the situation on the eve of the huge German offensive in the Ardennes in December 1944. It was wrong to underestimate the enemy's strength, and equally wrong to believe that terrain could provide a totally protective barrier. In fact, it is not even necessary to point to the Battle of the Bulge. The Germans had already done something similar in 1940, when their forces smashed through the Ardennes and won the battle against France. Exploiting the element of surprise to the full, hitting at a place and at a time least expected by the enemy, was characteristic of German planning.

It has already been point out that, ever since the retreat from Normandy, the idea had ripened in German minds, vaguely at first, but becoming firmer as time progressed, of launching a large-scale counteroffensive of a blitzkrieg nature, as in 1939–42. By October this plan had matured, but what mattered most to the Germans at the moment was to deny the Allies use of the port of Antwerp for as long as possible. After the disaster at Arnhem, Montgomery devoted all his grim energy to clearing the Scheldt estuary there.

It was therefore imperative for the Germans to hold on to the western part of the province of Noord–Brabant and the province of Zeeland. But how long would the German 15th Army be able to resist the tremendous pressure brought to bear on them by the Allied forces? General Model believed he had found a solution. On October 24 he proposed to von Rundstedt to launch a sudden, powerful attack from the Maas salient against the Allies, who would then be forced to withdraw part of their forces from the Zeeland–Brabant front. It was to be a fast, unexpected stroke, similar to those of the daring blitzkrieg days and aimed at the weakest sector of the Allied front: the canal line held by the American 7th Armored Division. The objective, though, was limited: Asten was to be the final topographical destination, with Meyel, the village at the junction of the Deurne Canal and the Noorder Canal as the first target.

On that same October 24, the German High Command discussed a more ambitious plan, which was to go down in history as the Ardennes Offensive, or the Battle of the Bulge. Was the smaller offensive, to be launched from the Maas salient, intended as a preliminary exercise? Perhaps. It turned out later that it had merits as such.

★ ★ ★

On the German side of the canal front most of the Fallschirmjäger regiments of Division Erdmann (now called the 344th Division) were still in their positions. For the German offensive, Model had at his disposal a special force, the 47th Army Corps, commanded by General von Lüttwitz. This corps actually consisted of two divisions, the 9th Panzer and the 15th Panzergrenadier. 47th Corps was to advance through the 86th. In other words, the German paratroops were to stay behind the canals, and the two attacking divisions were to advance through them and assault the opposite canal bank.

First, the panzer division was to attack, with the Panzergrenadiers in their wake. A very large number of guns had been lined up on the German side to support the offensive, which — very rare in this period of shortages — had been supplied with huge stocks of ammunition. The 9th Panzer Division would have to bear the major responsibility for the attack. In examining this unit, the picture that emerges is not unlike that of the 107th Panzer Brigade, which had previously thrown itself against the airborne corridor. The 9th Panzer, too, had been badly mauled in other battle areas, France in particular, and had been pushed back against the German frontier in August, where it had helped stem the American penetrations south of Aachen in September. At the end of that month the Division was allowed to rest. Its commander was replaced by Major General Harald Freiherr von Eberfeldt (he was to die in March 1945 during street fighting in Cologne) and the Division received sorely needed supplies of men and equipment, chiefly through merging with an unattached panzer brigade. Thus the division again obtained the necessary tanks and SPs.

In early October the 9th Panzer Division was again thrown into battle, this time in the Betuwe, an area between Arnhem and Nijmegen. Fierce battles were fought there, reducing its strength to 50 percent, without its having achieved any significant success. On the contrary, the Germans abandoned nearly the whole eastern part of the Betuwe and the 9th, again badly mauled, was pulled out of the line and transferred to the vicinity of Xanten in Germany to be re-equipped. This did not take too long and very soon the Division had been brought up to strength in both light and heavy weapons. It was also supplied with bridge-laying equipment — not without importance for what was to follow.

More difficult to compensate for were the heavy losses in company and platoon commanders. These losses had always been high because German panzer officers were expected, regardless of circumstances, to be shining examples of daring and have contempt for death. It was therefore common for such men to stand erect in the open turrets of their tanks during battle. But in the lower ranks, too, losses had been severe. Despite all this, the Division was brought back to a 75-percent capacity during the re-equipment period near Xanten, and this was, considering the very difficult situation in which the German Army found itself, a remarkable achievement. The 9th Panzer was not completely at full strength, however, nor would it ever be, simply because the staff of one of its tank regiments and its 1st Battalion were stationed in Austria, and for some obscure reason could not be extricated from there.

It is not known how many men and tanks the two divisions of 47th Army Corps had in mid-October, but it is certain that it must have had at least 26,000 men and 50 tanks. Adding the SPs (to the American tanks should also be added their tank destroyers and "assault guns," which were often used as ordinary tanks) the total number of tanks on the German side may be estimated at a minimum of 80. Some of them were the feared Panthers and there were probably also a few Tiger tanks with their notorious high-velocity 88 mm guns. As for the rest of the equipment, 47th Army Corps in this last year of the war was certainly not inferior to its American opponents.

The American soldier Margreiter looked upon his M-1 rifle and the M-7 SP howitzer as better weapons than the German equivalents, but "the rest of their equipment was superior to ours," more efficient and more practical, he felt. The fighting spirit of the German soldier was rated highly by the Americans once they had come to grips with them: "Professional," was the general opinion, "better than later at St. Vith in the Ardennes offensive," according to an American lieutenant. Numerically, this time the 7th Armored Division was facing a superior force.

Were the Americans aware that something was afoot at the end of October? Did the German attack on the 27th, as alleged afterward by the Americans, really come as a "complete surprise"? Due to the bad weather in the week October 20 to 27, Allied air reconnaissance had been virtually impossible. During this period American outposts did spot German staff officers on the opposite bank of the canal from Wessem to Nederweert who were observing the American side at their leisure. Their heads and shoulders were silhouetted above the canal bank and now and then the Americans saw how the Germans were poring over their maps, pointing out certain landmarks. After a while, American gunfire put an end to this bold German display. As it happened, the Germans did not attack in this sector because, according to the Americans, they had made it quite clear they were on the alert.

There were other indications as well. Germans regularly patrolled across the canals. In itself this was not very disturbing, but no one knew whether any of them stayed behind on the American side of the canal. This was a real possibility, since the American line was thinly held, a series of outposts, actually forming more dots on the map than a line. On October 25 a skirmish took place near the canal junction north of the Noorder Canal, and there was another the next day near Budschop, roughly in the same area where an American tank had been destroyed. More ominous was the exodus of the people of Meyel, who acted on their Mayor's orders. Why? Was it merely out of fear of German artillery fire, as the Dutch official maintained, or had he heard something of a pending German attack?

The Americans had also been told by Dutchmen that 2,000 Germans had been transferred from Venlo to the area near Stokers- horst, halfway to the Noorder Canal. Some Americans of the 87th Reconnaissance Squadron took this news and other bits of information very seriously. Unfortunately, the intelligence officer of the 7th Armored, who had been mistaken previously near Overloon, again refused to believe the warnings of a possible German attack. Each indication pointing in this direction was dismissed by him as unim- portant or misleading. A few Americans did nevertheless reckon with a German attack, but with no clue about its nature or its strength.

Generally speaking, there was no question of a thorough preparation on the part of the whole Division for such a contingency. On the night preceding the German attack, the enemy observed that American troops were proceeding from Meyel to Liessel and that they made no effort at all to keep their movements hidden. "The noisy behavior of the Americans," an alert Fallschirmjäger on the opposite side of the Deurne Canal noted, "pointed to troops which either had no combat experience or were feeling very sure of themselves." The Americans were simply being careless, and this would cost lives. There was also a psychological aspect that "plagued" the Division. It had seen its first tough fighting near Metz, and even though the assault near Overloon was an almost complete failure, they had never been overwhelmed by a sudden assault from a well-armed, superior force. This was something very hard for them to imagine. When it did happen, however, it came as a terrible shock. Although no relationship between the German offensive in the Peel and the enemy's counter-offensive in December can be claimed, in hindsight the former looked in many ways like a smaller dress rehearsal for the Ardennes.

The night of October 26/27 was a quiet one — ominously quiet. The morning dawned without the sun being able to lift the fog that limited visibility to less than 50 yards. At 0615 the dormant sector suddenly erupted in a 40-minute German artillery preparation.

Then they came, the Germans. Under cover of fog and artillery they had crossed the Deurne Canal and the Noorder Canal at several spots, looming up in front of the American outposts. A few minutes after the German shelling had ceased, a German officer came in sight, emerging out of the fog less than 40 yards from the American positions. He shouted a few orders and at once 200 Germans rose around him, materializing, as it were, out of nowhere. In three successive waves they stormed toward the American lines, not caring about their losses. Their behavior was so strange that some of the Americans thought they had used drugs.

The first wave was gunned down. Right behind them came the second, which was also annihilated by American fire. But the third wave had more luck: throwing hand grenades they broke through the American line and reached the houses of Meyel. The Americans were forced to withdraw and tried to reorganize west of the town. At 0830 the place was in German hands.

Meyel had been defended by a company made up of only two platoons: Troop C of the widely dispersed 87th Reconnaissance

Squadron. Just west of Meyel, what was left of this weak detachment linked up with Troop B, held in reserve till then. The commanding officer, Lt. Colonel Vincent Boylan, had only one thought: an immediate counterattack to retake Meyel. He placed two companies supported by nine light tanks on either side of the road from Asten to Meyel. He himself stood in the middle of the road and shouted to his men: "Come on, Goddamit! They can't hit you. Move! I want to see a few Krauts bite the dust!"

At 1010 the counterattack was launched. Contrary to what Boylan had shouted at his troops, the German fire from Meyel was deadly accurate. Four American tanks were destroyed; two disappeared into the woods near Meyel and were never heard from again. Boylan tried again, this time with tanks and small groups of infantry armed with bazookas. This, too, turned into a disaster. Again two tanks were destroyed, whereupon the infantry withdrew in disorder.

The Germans had already launched three other attacks that day. The least important one was a thrust over the southernmost canal toward the village of Thorn—an attack promptly repulsed by the Belgian Brigade, at that time attached to the American division. This was merely a diversionary raid by the Germans, however, if its objective had been to keep Combat Command A immobilized behind the canal from Wessem to Nederweert, it was a successful maneuver. From that time onward, the Germans did not make any more efforts to cross this canal, but CCA was neutralized for the greater part of the battle. The second attack in the morning was made by the Germans in the area east of Nederweert and the canal junction near Budschop and Ospel, an attack which they had already prepared for, a few days before, by intensive patrolling. Here, too, the Americans were forced to withdraw, but some stabilization was achieved during the evening of that day.

The German attack at this point was only potentially dangerous if the main German force should succeed in taking Asten. So long as this did not happen, the German forces on the Ospel front were, like their opponents, separated from their comrades by the vast swamps on the northeastern side, called the "Grote Peel" and "Peel de Veluwe." This made their presence in this sector for the time being quite irrelevant to the success or failure of the main German offensive. North of Meyel, near Nederkant, a third German attack was launched, almost concurrent with the assault on Meyel, and almost as dangerous.

Here it was the American Troop D that had to fall back before the numerical superiority and the ferocious nature of the assault. It was the German infantry which, as near Meyel, provided the first shock wave that drove the Americans back. This enabled them to lay bridges over the Deurne Canal by 1100 hours, whereafter heavy German tanks and SP's made their appearance on the battlefield.

Not only near Meyel and Neerkant, but also east of Liessel, heavy German armor had crossed the canal. This at least was what the commander of Combat Command R was told. His unit was largely held in reserve behind the front. He dispatched a small force to find out what was going on, a task force made up of two squadrons of Sherman tanks, one infantry company, and a few smaller units, placed under the command of Lt. Colonel John P. Wemple. Task Force Wemple received orders to throw the Germans back over the canal east of Liessel. As Wemple approached the battle area, he was told by men of the 87th Reconnaissance Squadron how the enemy had attacked on a broad front from Meyel to Liessel. Rolling up German bridgeheads was totally out of the question! Committing forces to do so was even regarded as undesirable.

It was obvious that the German attack was on a much larger scale and on a broader front than appreciated by the gentlemen at HQ in the rear. Wemple had the guts to ignore the orders given him. He realized that in this sector it was imperative to hold the road from Meyel to Liessel, so he decided to distribute his forces at three positions on that road, more or less equally spaced over the entire distance from one town to the other. One of the positions he chose was near the point where the Kanaalstreet, the road from Hogebrug on the Deurne Canal to Liessel, joined the road from Meyel. Wemple establish his command post in Neerkant.

This was a wise decision. But it did not alter the fact that a serious situation was developing for the Americans. Just how serious they did not yet know by midday. It was still possible for the attack to be a local maneuver by the Germans on a fairly large scale. The Americans were unaware that two German divisions were involved. The Germans attacked in three phases: first, with the infantry of the 9th Panzer Division, who made it possible for bridges to be laid over the canal without being hampered; then, by tanks, using three bridges; and finally, but not until the afternoon, by the infantry of the 15th Panzer-grenadier Division, which had a small number of tanks.

The Fallschirmjäger units, on the whole, did not stay east of the canals, but were also used piecemeal in the offensive of 47th Corps. Units from Battalion Paul, temporarily attached to Fallschirmjäger Regiment Hübner after the bloody battles of Overloon, were committed on the less important front near Ospel and Waatskamp. Other units of the regiment, roughly the strength of a company, joined in the fight for Meyel, and later an entire battalion was to cover the German withdrawal near Liessel. These German paratroops played a subordinate role, however; everything depended on the motorized and armored units.

The 9th Panzer Division acted with the familiar German *Schneid,* quickly and vigorously, although not everything went smoothly. The Americans defended themselves ferociously, and the number of German casualties was large. Because of their numerical superiority this did not seem to matter too much at this time, but eventually — the Germans were fully aware of this — they would not be able to replace their losses as the Allies could. Apart from this, a few serious mistakes were made by the Germans. The attack had been preceded by a heavy artillery bombardment, primarily directed at those woods where the Germans had wrongly assumed the Americans to be hiding.

The large number of German casualties was due mainly to the reckless manner in which they launched their attacks, inadequately supported by heavy weapons. The Panzer Aufklärungs Abteilung 9 (Armored Reconnaissance Unit) of the Division under Lt. Colonel Bockhoff was operating near Meyel, while near Neerkant Panzer Regiment 10 under Lt. Colonel Reich was fighting, but these were the only important assault forces the 9th Panzer could muster. Panzer Regiment 11 had not shown up at all! In the evening its commander was replaced by the dynamic Bockhoff, and the units of this regiment were wedged in between the two other assault groups. But by then the damage had already been done. If the Germans had committed all their forces simultaneously in the morning, their success would have been even greater. This was not only a matter of the missing Panzer Regiment 11 but also of the 15th Panzergrenadier Division, which was supposed to have crossed the canal half a day earlier, and could have done so. The Germans realized this only much later.

Toward noon they began to notice a stiffening of the American resistance. The fog had lifted and the Allied air force joined in the battle. The Germans no longer had to cope solely with the weak, dispersed troops of the 87th Reconnaissance Squadron. West of Meyel, where Lt. Colonel Boylan had made his unsuccessful counterattacks, Combat Command R under Colonel Chappuis was now defending the road to Asten. On the road to Liessel the Germans ran into Task Force Wemple. Admittedly it was not a strong force, and Wemple still had plenty of reasons to be worried.

Earlier, three German tanks (always referred to as Tigers by the Allies, but probably Panthers) had approached the junction where the Kanaalstreet merges with the road from Meyel to Liessel. An American armored car, well hidden behind a haystack, let the first German tank pass, and then fired six shells in rapid succession from its 37 mm gun at a distance of 15 yards at the rear of the tank. Crippled by this fire from such a short distance, the tank landed in a ditch and the crew hastily abandoned it and scurried for cover. The two remaining tanks swung back menacingly toward the American armored car, which wisely turned tail. Later, the Americans dispatched three tank destroyers and a Sherman to deal with the Germans; all four were lost. Wemple realized that it would be very hard for him to cope with another German attack.

Northwest of Meyel, CCR went into the attack with the 48th Armored Infantry Battalion and a company of tank destroyers. It was intended that they would also relieve the badly mauled units of the 87th Reconnaissance Squadron. At 1400 hours the Americans started their advance along the road from Asten to Meyel, the infantry on either side of the road up to their knees in water, not an enemy in sight. Slowly they continued their advance, until after a few hours they reached the bend in the road near Berg, only about 1,000 yards from the edge of Meyel. There they were pinned down by heavy rifle and machine-gun fire. There was not a chance of getting through. The American attack had collided head-on with a German one. It would be incorrect to use the word "counterattack," for neither had a clue as to their opponent's intentions. The Germans proved to be stronger, it was as simple as that.

It was a wonder that the Americans were able to hold on to their positions until nightfall. The company north of the road dug in; another company south of the road was in danger of being surrounded and decided to pull out in the dark. This succeeded, but in doing so the men had to wade through peat bogs most of the night, now in the opposite direction. In the head-on collision, the Germans, typical of the war in this part of the Peel, had no more tanks than the Americans, but they did have heavier ones. The bazooka projectiles fired at the panzers by the men of the 48th Armored Infantry Battalion from a distance of less than 100 yards did not even damage the front plates of the German armor. Like disgruntled mastodons they rolled along the metalled road, slowly, sometimes unexpectedly gathering speed, appearing to be almost invulnerable. They were followed on their flanks in the swampy fields by the German infantry.

Sam Sharp, a lieutenant with the 48th, came across a Panther tank that night near a farm about a mile west of Meyel. To Sharp, the Panther seemed a living being, a monster, getting angry and on the point of spitting fire: "It was standing still, ominous and waiting. I could see its angular hull, its wide tracks, tapering turret and long gun with its muzzle. No doubt about it, this was a Panther alright!" The scene was illuminated by the glow from an American tank burning in the background. From a distance of 20 yards Sharp and another soldier fired a bazooka at the Panther. The projectile bounced off the armor without exploding. Had they forgotten the safety catch? "The tank had not been damaged, but it became worried," said Sharp. It turned its gun menacingly as if it knew we were somewhere out there, but did not know exactly where." Sharp's anthropomorphic description sounds so peculiar because he was so close that he could hear the crew's voices inside. One way or another, he managed to summon an M-10 tank destroyer. It lined up in front of the Panther "at a distance of about 40 yards, both tanks firmly planted in the middle of the road, the muzzles of their guns virtually in line. All was quiet, the Panther had not noticed the M-10." The gun of the destroyer was aimed on Sharp's directions, the story goes on.

"Click." Silence.

"Click." Dead silence.

"Click." Unbearable silence.

"Lieutenant, the gun does not work," someone said. Now the Panther realized that something was afoot. It began to move and chased the M-10 into a ditch. The crew managed to get away in the fields alongside the road. Sharp and his buddy retired for the night into the cellar of a farm. As soon as there was enough daylight they decided to take off in Sharp's half-track, "parked" at the back of the farm. The Panther, still nearby, was surprised when the vehicle started to move, but was determined to get it, and fired three shells that failed to hit. Sharp watched one shell whiz over his head like a red-hot football. The half-track roared past German infantry, who were too stunned to react, toward the American lines. By then the sun had risen.

★   ★   ★

Twelve hours earlier, on the afternoon of October 27, it began to dawn upon the American Division staff that the German offensive had great impetus and was not just another small, local attack. Major General Silvester feared that his division would be unable to hold on much longer, and asked the commander of the British 8th Army Corps, O'Connor, for support. What could the British do to extricate the Americans from their unhappy situation?

O'Connor promised to do two things: first, he would send some British artillery as soon as he could (the Americans did not have many guns), and also he was prepared to have the bridgehead near Griendtsveen taken over by the British. This would release Combat Command B to return to the west side of the Deurne Canal and attack the Germans from the north. The promised British artillery did not arrive until the next day, but Combat Command B had already been transferred post-haste to Liessel on the evening of October 27.

Silvester wanted to launch a two-pronged attack in the early morning of the next day. CCB, including Task Force Wemple, were to advance from Liessel to Heitrak and from Neerkant to Meyel, part of the force to turn to the left a few miles south of Liessel to continue along the Kanaalstreet to Hogebrug on the canal. CCR was to attack Meyel from the northwest along the Asten-Meyel road.

On this first day of the German offensive the pattern of fighting in the days to come had already been established: it was a battle for two roads, one from Meyel north to Liessel and then on to Deurne, the other the one running northwest to Asten. The Americans and the Germans, near Budschop and Ospel, were fighting a secondary combat in these decisive days, which, as already explained, would in no way affect the final outcome of the battle because of the geographical situation, so long as Asten remained unoccupied by the Germans.

The road from Meyel to Liessel did not lead, as did the other road, through the peat bogs, but the often soggy ground made deployment of heavy vehicles off the road extremely difficult. It all depended on local conditions, which could vary yard by yard. Many secondary roads were impassable for the American tanks as well. Another disadvantage for the Allies was that the main road was constantly being shelled by the large concentration of German artillery on the other side of the Deurne Canal. Moreover, there were German forces between the road and the canal. Their exact whereabouts was unknown to the Americans. They did know that the Germans had a bridgehead near Hogebrug from which they threatened Liessel and the road to Meyel along the Kanaalstreet.

The road from Meyel to Asten had its own problems. On the American right wing, southwest of the road, there was — and still is — the beautiful natural resort of the fens of the "Grote Peel" and "Peel de Veluwe." Today, signs along the road warn that no one is allowed to enter the area in the period between October 15 and November 15. One might say that this also applied to the same period in 1944, though German infantry did succeed in penetrating even there. On the other side of the road the swamps were smaller and the Germans advancing from Neerkant and Heitrak could bypass them and attempt to continue their advance on more solid ground, to a woods lying between the last stretch of the road to Asten and Liessel, the "Dennendijk Wood."

These were the roads and the area where a battle was fought, first for three days between Germans and Americans, then between Germans and British. The Allied objective was to converge along the two roads on Meyel; the German objective was to fan out from Meyel to reach Asten and Liessel.

A fully detailed description cannot be given of all the attacks and counterattacks which took place on and around these two roads, in the swamps and in the sparse woods. For three successive days the German 47th Army Corps kept pushing against the American 7th Armored Division, which fought an unequal battle, was forced on the defensive and then pushed back — an entirely new experience for them — but was not defeated. Ironically, tanks and all sorts of other armored vehicles were fighting each other for days on ground that was totally unsuited for such warfare. The two forces could not do without armor, but they could not fully exploit it either. Out of necessity, tanks drove in single file in columns; the infantry, leaving the armored personnel carriers behind, tried to advance on either side of the road. This made it possible for two or three tanks, sometimes only one, or a small group of determined men with bazookas, to beat off an attack which in general gained little or no ground.

This was the most typical aspect of the war in the Peel near Meyel during the five days in which 47th Corps battered against the weakest link in the Allied front line in the province of Noord-Brabant. At 7:00 in the morning on October 28, Brigadier General Hasbrouck led the men of his Combat Command B from Liessel along the road to Meyel, driving in single file on the first leg of the route. According to plan, part of the force, mainly made up of tanks and tank destroyers, branched off to the left after some time in order to advance toward Hogebrug along the Kanaalstreet. The main force continued southward.

"It is a strange thing when men are on a start line waiting to attack," wrote John Margreiter, who was in the main force. "Some look at pictures of wives, children or sweethearts. Some just stare at the ground as if lost in thought. Some chain-smoke cigarettes or chew gum very rapidly. There is a minimum of conversation and everyone appears to be nonchalant. Inside, each man is saying to himself, 'I'm frightened to death of what lies ahead and I would like to run away

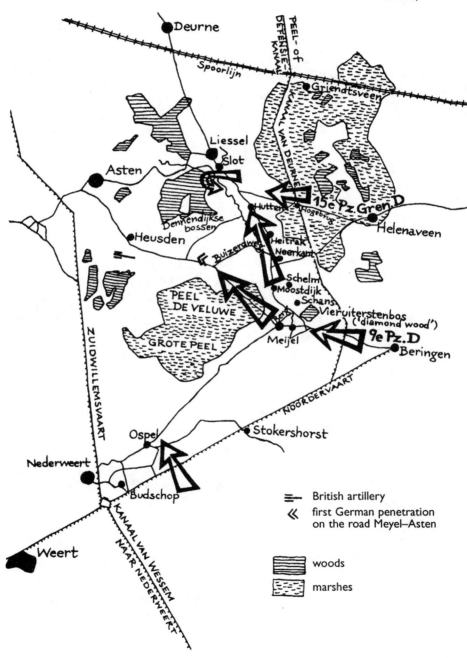

Oct. 27–Nov. 6, 1944

Deurne

Spoorlijn

PEEL- of
DEFENSIE-
KANAAL

KANAAL VAN DEURNE

Griendtsveen

Liessel

Slot

Asten

Hutten

Hogebrug

15e Pz. Gren. D

Dennendijkse
bossen

Heusden

Buizerdweg

Heitrak

Neerkant

Helenaveen

Schelm

Moostdijk

Schans

PEEL-
DE VELUWE

Vieruiterstenbos
('diamond wood')

Meijel

9e Pz. D

GROTE PEEL

Beringen

ZUIDWILLEMSVAART

NOORDERVAART

Ospel

Stokershorst

Nederweert

Budschop

KANAAL VAN WESSEM NAAR NEDERWEERT

Weert

≡− British artillery

≪ first German penetration
on the road Meyel–Asten

woods

marshes

and hide somewhere. But I am ashamed to do something cowardly when all these guys are so brave. They are not afraid, so I must act as if I am not and maybe they will not know how scared I really am.' One learns that bravery is not the absence of fear: bravery is the ability to keep moving forward in spite of fear."

The number of men unable to play this game, incapable of coming to terms with their own fear, was in fact remarkably small. There were a few, though, and they were the outcasts of the troop. Margreiter recalled how one soldier told Sam Goodman, the sergeant of his section, that he could no longer go on. The sergeant took him behind a haystack and a few moments later the others heard a shot. "Well," someone exclaimed, "he finally shot that cowardly little bastard." Goodman walked back to the troop and someone asked him: "Did you actually shoot that s.o.b.?" "No," answered the sergeant. "He said he couldn't go on because his carbine wouldn't shoot. I took it and fired that shot into the air to prove that he was lying. Then he said he couldn't go on because he had hurt his back. I decided that we'd be better off without the yellow-bellied bastard, so I told him go to hell and left him there, crying. Here, guys, split up his ammo."

Later, the situation became more and more confused. Margreiter's platoon commander, a lieutenant who saw his first fighting here, vanished without a trace. The section lost contact with each other. Goodman ordered Margreiter's section to dig in—just in time, because clusters of mortar shells started dropping around them. A Sherman tank drove up and the tank commander shouted from his turret at Goodman: "Sergeant, I have been observing from behind you through a saddle in this ridge. About 1,000 yards from my position I could see a wood and a lot of Krauts were moving about with mortars and machine guns. I notice that you have a mortar and I want you to take it and put some fire on those people."

Goodman looked incredulously at the tankman. Then he shouted: "Go screw yourself! You got a goddamned cannon and we got this lousy peashooter nobody knows how to operate! If you want those goddamned Krauts shot at, then go do it yourself! We don't even know where the rest of our company is!" The tank sergeant spotted another Sherman tank perhaps 200 yards to his left. "There's my lieutenant! I'm going to discuss this with him!" The tank moved off down the road. The two tanks sat side by side for a short time, then the Sherman headed back toward Goodman. Just as it reached Goodman and his men, another mortar concentration forced them back into their foxholes. Margreiter then heard an explosion that sounded different from those made by the mortar shells. When he raised his head he saw the Sherman brewing up. Nobody came out alive. Goodman said: "In the bushes farther down the road I saw two Krauts aiming at the tank with a Panzerfaust." "But why didn't you shoot them, or alert the rest of us?" asked Margreiter. Goodman had no answer for him.

The American attack toward Heitrak had failed. Hasbrouck suffered many casualties. Of the 17 tanks with which the force had started the attack, 13 were lost. The men of Combat Command B who tried to push on to Hogebrug achieved nothing and they too suffered many casualties, including five tanks. Now it was the Germans who advanced on either side of the Kanaalstreet and they threatened to drive a wedge between the Americans there and the main force on the road to Meyel. At 1400 hours Hasbrouck decided to withdraw slightly. Toward evening, the Americans dug in.

The attack by Combat Command R did not get off the ground at all. The German pressure was too great. Two battalions of Panzer Regiment 10 forced their way from the small wood west of Moosdijk and the surrounding area into the "Grote Heide van Asten" (a large heath) and pushed hard against the American left flank.

On the road to Asten, Panzer Aufklärungs-Abteilung 9 also tried to move forward. For this unit in particular it became an extremely hard day. Its attacks were no more successful than those of the Americans, though the Germans did gain some ground by the end of the day, after heavy fighting and with many casualties, mainly from shellfire. They did not know that the shells were not fired from American guns. Early in the morning the British 25th Field Regiment, an artillery unit, had deployed its guns near Heusden and had begun shelling the Germans. It was the first unit to come to the support of the Americans. British fighters strafed the German lines — and sometimes accidentally American lines as well.

But in spite of this it was a tremendous boost for the morale of the

Americans, to whom it had been brought home what it was like to be outnumbered and to be on the defensive. Now the British had come to their rescue!

The sight of British planes swooping down on them was nothing unusual for the Germans, but they were unaware of the field regiment's having joined the battle. It might perhaps be said that the Germans fought so keenly because they underestimated their opponents' strength, and the same probably goes for the Americans. Time and again they launched counterattacks believing that they were opposed by one division only. By the end of the afternoon of the second day of the battle Major General Silvester's HQ was forced to re-evaluate the situation. From information gleaned from prisoners, it became obvious to the Americans that they were also facing the 15th Panzer-grenadier Division near Liessel. Silvester now decided to go over entirely to the defensive.

By nightfall, Combat Command B had dug in a few miles from Liessel. It was expected that it would be able to hold this position for the time being. There was no such optimism for the sector of CCR. Lt. Colonel Chappuis, worried about the heavy German pressure on his front, decided to pull out his most forward companies which, because of the Germans making headway on the flanks, had become exposed and ran the risk of being trapped. Communication with these two units, which had suffered many casualties, was already very difficult. Chappuis sent Lieutenant Avery Tucker with a few men out into the night to act as guides for the two companies, or what was left of them, and to bring them back to the Battalion CP.

It was the intention that at the time the units would start to pull out they would be protected by a box barrage; covered by a screen of shellfire they would be able to return to their own lines. Tucker set out in the dark, but was halted by German machine-gun fire. The men with him had suddenly disappeared so he decided to go back. Thereafter he made another attempt, this time accompanied by a corporal carrying a radio set. When the two men had reached the forward companies, they were to send a message in code on the radio set to Chappuis, and this would be the signal to commence the box barrage on the German positions. Tucker and the corporal succeeded in reaching the two companies, but the radio set turned out to be defective. Another set was fetched, but its batteries were flat. Tucker just managed to transmit the message "Happy Birthday," whereupon the guns let loose. The lieutenant ordered the men he had found to follow him in single file — an episode reminiscent of the withdrawal of the British paratroops from the perimeter of Oosterbeek near Arnhem. A break occurred in the column but, guiding themselves by the flashes of the artillery and two burning houses, the lost group safely reached the American lines.

The confused situation during that night almost became fatal to Margreiter. His company, too, had been ordered to fall back a few hundred yards and dig in for the night. A sergeant asked for volunteers to find the rest of his own men so that they might be warned. Margreiter did not want to go, it was not his own unit, but reluctantly he stood up and went. Abruptly, a German flare was fired in the field in front of him, bathing him in a dazzling light. A sledgehammer blow smashed into his left thigh, the force of it knocking him to the ground. "I'm hit!" he yelled, and lying on his stomach he tried to return the fire. He saw a figure approaching in front of him and raised his rifle to shoot. Fortunately he recognized the familiar shape of an American helmet before he squeezed the trigger. The man asked anxiously: "Goddam, did I kill you?"

Margreiter's leg was numb, and with his arms around the necks of two men he hobbled several hundred yards, finally coming to an asphalt road where the men made him lie down in a ditch on the roadside. "Did somebody get hurt up here?" He recognized Burdman's voice, the lieutenant who had "vanished" without a trace. Margreiter impulsively blurted out: "You're goddamned right! Where the hell have you been all day?" Without saying a word, Burdman turned away and Margreiter never met him again. A shot of morphine soon took care of the pain and shortly afterward, strapped on a litter, he was on his way to the battalion aid station.

For a long time now, both armies had become used to Allied planes prowling in the sky, weather permitting, always on the lookout for prey on the ground. On October 28 the Luftwaffe (whose existence since the bombardment of Eindhoven on September 19 had almost been forgotten) quite unexpectedly re-entered the fray by bombing and strafing Asten. This place, after the unfavorable turn of events that day for the Americans, seemed on the point of falling into German hands.

The American Division now was in urgent need of British support. Would it come in time? Staff Officers of Major General Silvester's HQ saw an unidentified artillery unit approaching them. On asking the unknown soldiers who they were, it turned out that it was indeed the 131st Field Regiment, the second British artillery unit to come to the assistance of the Americans. By midnight, the regiment had taken up positions on the left flank of CCR. British infantry had not yet arrived.

Toward the morning of October 29, an American soldier on guard duty near Liessel heard heavy traffic movement to the east. He wondered who or what was making all the noise, and asked another sentry, who simply replied: "Oh, hell, it's the British!" On the sun breaking through, however, the source of the noise became clear. East and south of Liessel a German force had assembled to attack at 0700 hours. Though the Americans fought desperately, the Germans succeeded in entering Liessel by 0830. The staff and vehicles of CCB had to abandon the village in a hurry.

The German success was made possible because their tanks, though often heavier than the American ones, could frequently utilize sandy tracks on which the Americans would bog down: the German tank tracks were wider than those of the Americans and the ground pressure per square inch thereby materially reduced. On the other hand, a few light American tanks, absolutely no match for the heavily armored German tanks with their large-caliber guns, succeeded in crippling one of these monsters near a road junction by firing at it quite unexpectedly from a very short distance. The immobilized tank then blocked the road for the rest of the column, a typical event in the Peel swamps.

The Americans were forced to abandon Liessel, but the Germans could not continue their advance. The Americans held on to a few positions on the road to Meyel which they defended stubbornly. Early in the afternoon Combat Command B launched an attack against Liessel that was moderately successful: one American company penetrated into the place. At that moment Hasbrouck was informed that British support was on its way but that they planned to take up positions west of Liessel. He ordered the attack to be halted and pulled out all his forces. Liessel remained in German hands.

On the road to Asten things did not go well for the Americans either. There, too, the Germans attacked at sunrise. Regardless of their losses, they smashed through the positions of the Americans astride the road. One German tank put its gun through the window of the house where the company command post had been set up and forced the surrender of the Americans inside. The other American units on the flanks feared that they would be surrounded and decided to withdraw. Here and there panic broke out. Major Frazier watched how the forward line collapsed. He decided to improvise another line quickly in the rear and gathered a small number of tanks, a few tank destroyers and 80 infantrymen. With this small force he set up a perimeter defense around the junction of the main positions which had been overrun.

Soon afterward the Germans approached. Sam Sharp, in position with his men near the road junction, had dug a slit trench for himself at the entrance to a cow shed. He could clearly see the German tanks and infantry coming closer. In front was a Panther, large and menacing — perhaps the same tank, Sharp thought, that he had come across two days ago and whose fire he had narrowly escaped. Between him and the Panther stood an M-10 tank destroyer. If the Germans put the M-10 out of action, Sharp and his men would be overrun. The M-10 fired a number of shells at the front of the Panther. Sharp knew from experience that they would simply bounce off. As if annoyed, the Panther suddenly veered around. Wasting no time, the M-10 hit it on its exposed side, apparently in its weakest spot. There was an explosion and that was the end of the Panther. That same afternoon, the M-10 destroyed another five lighter tanks, Mark IVs, before it was itself struck. Four men baled out of the burning tank destroyer and fled into the bog.

The Germans continued to put more pressure on, and the artillery on both sides stepped up their rates of fire. When shells started to drop

27. On November 5, 1944, a swamp east of Meyel turned into a graveyard for brewed-up
Churchill tanks.

28. Royal Scots preparing to dig in near Moostdijk, November 6, 1944.

29. The 15th Scottish Division supported on its left flank by Vickers machine guns of the Middlessex Regiment; in the background one of the two mills at Liessel.

30. The 6th Guards Tank Brigade during one of its last actions in the Peel. The vehicle on the right had just been hit by a shell.

*31. Argylls and Sutherlands (51st Highland Division) on their way to the
Uitwateringskanaal along a road the sides of which have not yet been cleared of mines.
At right is a burned out German ambulance, November 16, 1944.*

32. Between mud and water: VIII Corps moving along the Deurne Canal to the village of Amerika, November 25, 1944.

33. German troops employed many of the canals in southern Holland for defense.

34. *The village of Leveroy liberated. Villagers, the priest in their midst, cheering a half-track of the 51st Highland Division.*

35. *By 1945, the Fallschirmjäger were still considered one of Germany's elite formations.*

36. *The British 3rd Division advancing against a stream of refugees along the Venray road into Wanssum.*

37. "Cuckoo," a German Panther tank captured in a shed at Overloon, being driven to Geysteren by the Coldstream Guards, November 27, 1944.

38. The Castle of Geysteren during its heyday: a panoramic reconstruction by Anco Wigboldus with bank of the Maas River in the background.

*39. Suffolks watching the ruins of the Castle of Geysteren with sten guns at the ready,
December 1, 1944.*

40. *The offensive against Fortress Blerick begins in the early morning hours of December 3, 1944.*

41. *Sherman flail tanks advancing toward the anti-tank ditch of Fortress Blerick.*

42. One of the flail tanks exploding a mine.

43. Kangaroos, a bridgelaying tank and Churchills assembling for the attack on Fortress Blerick, December 3, 1944.

44. A British patrol near Grubbenvorst in the icy cold winter, January 1945.

45. More than one thousand people from Arcen had to be evacuated within a few hours through twenty inches of snow to Geldern in Germany, January 9, 1945.

46. "Desert Rats" during their assault on the village of St. Joost on January 21, 1945, supported by a flamethrower mounted on a Churchill tank.

Strategisch wichtiger Posten.

llung an der Maas, die durch einzelne Schützen-
her zusammenhängt und von bewährten Fall-
schirmjägern gehalten wird

FALLSCHIRMJÄGER
HALTEN DEN
MAASBRÜCKENKOPF

Rechts: Brücke und Notsteg.

Die zerstörte Maasbrücke liegt unter ständigem
Feindbeschuß; unsere Stellungen sind durch einen
Notsteg verbunden.

*47. German newspaper declaring "Fallschirmjäger Holding the Mass Salient"
shows troops in position opposite Roermond, and the bridge over the Maas
destroyed by bombs.*

48. Infantrymen of the American 35th Division escorting German prisoners with one of their wounded in Venlo, March 1, 1945.

49. *In the City Hall in Roermond, which was surrounded by mines and "asparagus," the Public Prosecutor welcomed the first American liberators on March 1, 1945.*

50. That which remains: the National War and Resistance Museum at Overloon. One of the halls with military equipment.

51. That which remains: the British cemetery at Venray.

all around him, Sharp decided to go back to his trench, which he had left when the Panther blew up. Since then, however, in the heat of the battle, the cows, in their customary routine, had gone back into the stable and Sharp found a calf stuck in his trench. Under shellfire, Sharp tried to pull the animal out by its tail, but all his efforts failed.

The Germans had almost reached the spot where Sharp was wrestling with his calf. They were on their way to Asten, but they did not get beyond this point—and never would. What eventually halted them was not only the small group of bravely fighting Americans near the Buizer road, but also the artillery: American, and especially the British.

★ ★ ★

Did the guns of the 25th and 131st Field Regiments, with hardly any forces in front of them, prevent Asten from being taken by the Germans, as the British afterward alleged? This suggestion would be unjustified and an injustice to Major Frazier, who managed to set up a defensive position in the nick of time, and to the crew of the tank destroyer which, according to Sharp's observations, destroyed six German tanks before it was itself hit. Even if the M-10 had only finished off half that number, it still would have had an important effect.

The decisive factor? In any battle it remains an abiding question what or who tipped the scales, and one probably comes nearer the truth if one regards the battle as a chain of events in which no single link can be ignored: not the stubborn defense by the Americans near Buizer road, not the support from the British artillery, which faced an alarming shortage of shells in the morning (the 131st Field Regiment could spare only 10 shells for each gun), so the Germans advanced. In the afternoon, when fresh ammunition supplies arrived, the German advance bogged down right in front of the hastily improvised position of Major Frazier. The fact remains that all the Americans of the 7th Armored Division, from general to private soldier, were convinced that only British support could save them.

"Hold on!" the British told the Americans, "we're coming!" And the Americans did hold on, until deep into the night. What had the

British been doing during that time? On October 28 the town of Tilburg had celebrated its liberation, which had begun the day before, thanks to the 15th Scottish Division. Tens of thousands of residents of Tilburg, men, women and children, had gone out into the streets and were exuberantly celebrating their freedom with the Scots, when suddenly news spread of a big German offensive: Meyel had fallen! The Scots were literally dragged away from the festivities. Infantry, pontoneers, tank crews searched for their officers and comrades, climbed on their vehicles, griping because they would miss all the fun. Not only the Scottish Division, but also the 6th Guards Tank Brigade received orders to leave.

The first units arrived in Deurne during the night of October 28/29, and other units were dispatched to Asten, such as the Scots Guards tanks, which had already moved the day before. Deurne was the assembly point for all sorts of British staff and units, and on the morning of October 29 they were in a state of near panic. The village of Liessel had fallen, so that the road to Deurne lay open to the Germans, who now might even get beyond Deurne! In Helmond (not without cynical comments among the lower echelons) preparations were made for the evacuation of the HQ of the British Second Army and in Deurne German tanks were expected at any moment.

Halfway through the morning, more alarming news was received: one and a half miles south of Deurne, Tiger tanks had been spotted. Nothing had been heard from the American division. Had it been defeated already? The British decided to establish a defensive line south of Deurne with units from various divisions from in and around the town. Before this, early in the morning, Major General Barber, Commander of the 15th Scottish Division, had held a meeting with Lt. General O'Connor and Major General Silvester. The British and American commanders were all agreed that the Scottish Division was to proceed to the front as quickly as possible to relieve the exhausted American 7th Armored. This was to be withdrawn from the main battle scene and to confine itself to the much smaller sector east of Nederweert where at that time a small part of the Division was fighting a secondary battle against the Germans near Horick and Ospel. A British brigade would be positioned between Combat Command A and the Belgian Brigade on the canal from Wessem to Nederweert. The front sector where the decisive battle was being fought, the triangle Asten-Liessel-Meyel (almost squeezed together to the line Asten-Liessel), was to be taken over by the 15th Scottish Division with its three brigades. The Americans were to hold on until the Scots arrived. Barber also paid a visit to Hasbrouck and Chappuis. Both men promised to hold on until the evening, but it became obvious to Barber that the Americans were on the point of collapse. Time was running out.

Barber did not believe that Deurne was in immediate danger. He felt it more likely that the Germans would not try to advance to the north from Liessel but would push to the west to Asten. The American and British units southeast of Asten would in that case be attacked from the rear. Afterward, it appeared that working on this assumption proved to be correct. Barber planned how to deploy his forces. They were to dig in one mile behind the American line. After dark the Americans were to pull out through the British lines. Most of the Scottish units were on their way, and because of the fluid situation Barber had to continually revise his plans. But he stuck to the main plan and by the evening all that he had intended was accomplished.

The Scots took up position between Asten and Liessel, in the villages of Voordeldonk, Rinkveld and Leensel, and, more important, in the Dennendijk woods between Asten and Liessel. The Glasgow Highlanders, temporarily attached to 46th Brigade, had to venture into the woods and occupy the northeast corner, facing Liessel, without benefit of any reconnaissance and without any support from tanks or other heavy weapons. All in all, it was a risky job! Behind them, on the left, the Royal Scots were in Leensel. The Glasgow Highlanders had partial flank protection there. But the south side of the wood was undefended, so that they had no cover at all on their right flank. The 227th Brigade occupied positions southeast of Asten.

"The British are coming!" Sharp was told by an American soldier of a recce platoon which had accompanied the Scots to the front. "Scottish troops in checkered trousers, who only wear their helmets when the going gets tough." They were marching in columns of four. The American guide, a man named Bob, tried to convince the company commander (from a safe position in a ditch alongside the road) that he should spread out his men, but the officer would not hear of it, as it "wasn't done." So the men continued the advance in marching order. On the night of October 29, with full moon, the Americans, both near Liessel and Asten, performed one of the most difficult maneuvers in warfare: disengaging themselves from an enemy in close proximity of their front. That casualties were so few during that night was thanks to the British and American guns that were putting up a continuous screen of shellfire between the retreating forces and the Germans.

For three days the Americans fought hard to beat off the German offensive. On this last day alone the Division reported 233 casualties, including those missing or taken prisoner. Between 50 to 58 tanks were lost, not including tank destroyers and SPs. The Germans had lost 30 tanks. Despite smaller losses on the German side, the enemy staff was fully aware that these were causing a heavier drain on their dwindling resources.

The Germans were unaware that the American 7th Armored Division was being relieved by the Scots, though von Rundstedt's intelligence officer had a vague idea. But firm indication that the object of the German offensive was being achieved—the withdrawal of British forces from the front where they were containing the German 15th Army—was fully expected.

Field Marshal Model was therefore not dissatisfied with the way the battle was going. Possibly there might be more in the offensive than was initially anticipated! The preceding day, October 28, he had asked von Rundstedt to reinforce the successful 47th Corps with another panzer division and an entire artillery corps. Model knew exactly which panzer division and which artillery corps he wanted. The name "corps" was somewhat exaggerated, but the unit Model had in mind owned quite an impressive number of guns, varying from 75 mm to the very heavy 210 mm howitzers. What did Model intend to do with two panzer divisions, one panzergrenadier division and all those heavy guns? Unfortunately no records to substantiate this exist, but most likely he was already thinking far beyond Asten and Liessel, and probably beyond Deurne as well, unlike von Rundstedt.

Von Rundstedt, the highest commander on the western front, was a cautious man — cautious with his armies and even more so with himself. Though there had been times when he had dared to differ in opinion with his Supreme Commander, the Führer, these disputes had never been allowed to blight his career. Although he was privy to the plans for an officers' revolt to overthrow Hitler, he refused to commit himself. When the assassination attempt failed, the conspirators were cast out of the Army by "kangaroo courts" and handed over to the notorious *Volksgerichtshof* (People's Court) which sentenced them to death. Von Rundstedt was used as chairman of this so-called "court of honor," thereby sealing the fate of his fellow officers, who were all hanged or shot.

As a strategist, the Field Marshal was generally inclined to follow a conservative course. Rommel's plans in the spring of 1944 to destroy the Allied invasion forces on the beaches of Normandy were found to be too risky for von Rundstedt. He believed that one should always have reserves. Never venture too far forward was his motto.

He held similar views on the offensive of 47th Corps, and as it turned out he was probably right. At 1115 hours on October 29, von Rundstedt sent a signal to Model which had the effect of a cold shower on the more swashbuckling field marshal. The offensive was to be halted at once, for persistence "promises no result in relation to the effort. It is even more than likely that the 9th Panzer Division and the 15th Panzergrenadier Division will suffer losses in men and equipment which cannot be replaced within the foreseeable future." Presumably von Rundstedt was unaware of the fact that only a few hours before, the signal was sent that Liessel had been taken, but it must be doubted whether this would in any way have influenced his decision. The only thing Model was able to achieve was a continuation of the attack to obtain a better front line. Exactly the same thing had happened to O'Connor on October 16 with his operation "Constellation." That the Germans had achieved nearly all they could on that day, Model was still unaware.

Unobserved by the Germans, the Glasgow Highlanders had established themselves in the Dennendijk woods that night, facing Liessel. At 0815 on the morning of October 30 they saw that near Slot, a hamlet on the southern edge of Liessel, a German force (from the 15th Panzergrenadier Division) was assembling in an open field, obviously unaware of the prying eyes in the woods. The German officer in command quietly smoked a cigar, and for this reason may have been particularly annoyed when, suddenly, he and his men found themselves being fired at.

The Germans, of course, could not let this go unpunished. Besides, as predicted by Barber, they wanted to advance to the west, to Asten. This made it necessary for them to occupy the woods. Especially after the unexpected Scottish fire, this had become even more imperative.

What now followed was the battle for the Dennendijk woods, which was the farthest point reached by the Germans in the offensive that had already been countermanded by von Rundstedt. What happened afterward was not really of importance, nor were the local attacks and counterattacks elsewhere. The drama of the German counterstroke in the Peel found its real end in the thick pinewoods of Dennendijk and on the sand tracks which criss-crossed the woods. When the Germans, who no longer were allowed to carry out offensive actions, realized that they were at the end of their tether, they still held out for two days, but without conviction, since by then it was becoming obvious that they would have to yield the ground they had gained.

Yet the Germans succeeded in entering the woods; attacking from the north, they overran the forward Scottish platoons and also occupied the southern part of the woods. Bitter fighting went on for hours, mainly between infantry hidden behind trees and shrubs, and between a few German tanks rumbling down the sand tracks and British anti-tank guns which had been dragged in among the trees but were hampered by the limited fields of fire. The situation initially developed in favor of the Germans until finally, in the afternoon, a tank squadron from the Grenadier Guards came to the support of the Glasgow Highlanders; two companies of Royal Scots followed behind the tanks. This became the turning point. Slowly but inevitably the Germans were driven out of the woods. A few managed to hold on, especially in its southeastern part, which was not cleared until the next day.

The Germans had lost the initiative for good. Moreover, von Rundstedt had now forbidden them to go on the offensive again. The two German divisions did not have a real mission any longer and to continue the battle made no sense. Yet the Germans were reluctant to give up the ground they had taken with so much effort and so many casualties. More out of habit than because of strategic consideration, they continued to defend themselves stubbornly for a few more days.

The Scots now attacked Liessel from the north and west; the Borderers, the Royal Scots Fusiliers and the Glasgow Highlanders launched their attack from Deurne, supported by a tank squadron from the Grenadier Guards. The Cameronians advanced from Asten with two tank squadrons from the Coldstream Guards. After heavy fighting, Liessel fell on October 31. The Scots did not advance much farther, primarily because of the continual shelling of the line in advance of Meyel by German guns behind the Deurne Canal.

The Scots Guards supported the 227th Scottish Division east of the village of Heusden. On the night of October 30, two troops of tanks were bivouacing in a wood called De Witte Bergen, approximately one mile ahead of their B Squadron. In the light of dawn the tankmen saw a few gray figures sneaking away toward the German front line. No doubt our Argylls and Sutherlands, they thought. Half an hour later it was found that they had shared their bivouac with a company of German infantry! In order to prevent this sort of infiltration from happening again, 227 Brigade asked for "a good stonk" to be brought down on the wood, which virtually uprooted every tree. Afterward, De Witte Bergen was avoided by the Germans.

One thing the Germans were convinced of was that they had been successful in drawing an entire British division and a tank brigade onto their front! This had been brought home to them in a manner not to be misunderstood in the Dennendijk woods. What was happening to the Germans at the front, near Asten? Panzer Regiment 10 sent out a patrol there on the night of October 31 and in the early morning the patrol did indeed spot soldiers wearing the typical British tin hat, so different from the American helmet. So the British were there too! That their presence near Asten did not materially lessen the pressure on their 15th Army was something the Germans did not know, nor did they care to realize. The operations section of Model's HQ noted that the objective of the German offensive had been achieved, and that as a consequence 47th Corps was to pull out, holding on to a bridgehead around Meyel. This was rather Model's effort to save face; when von Rundstedt ordered the offensive halted, the Germans had not yet noticed the British presence, and in fact there was hardly any at that time.

★   ★   ★

Two events on the night of October 31—"afterburners" of the German counterstroke in the Peel marshes—merit some comments. The first event was the construction of a small bridge by the Germans over the canal from Wessem to Nederweert, right in the sector of the American front where virtually nothing had happened all this time. An American patrol was sent to find out what was going on that very same night, and two soldiers succeeded in planting an explosive charge underneath the bridge while under German fire.

Well-directed American gunfire set off the charge. The bridge was destroyed completely and six German soldiers were killed. Probably the Germans, in order to withdraw their badly mauled divisions without interference, merely wanted to use the bridge as a means of diverting the American's attention and to create anxiety among the Allies. If that was their intention, they were highly successful. O'Connor became worried about a German offensive across the canal and considered Weert and even Belgian towns like Kinrooi and Bree as being in danger. The vigilance which had been lacking so sadly on the eve of the German counterstroke was now being exercised, quite unnecessarily. But the Germans did not think at all of an attack there, because by now they were preparing their withdrawal.

At midnight of that same October 31, the highest-ranking victim fell as a result of the German offensive: Major General Lindsay MacDonald Silvester was sacked as commander of the 7th Armored Division by General Bradley. Hasbrouck became his successor. Why? O'Connor gave as his opinion that "Silvester was already a somewhat older man who did not have the necessary feeling for modern, mobile warfare." It can be argued whether this gives Silvester enough credit.

Shortly afterward, Bradley wrote that he had "lost confidence in Silvester as a division commander," an observation which merely raises other questions.

Was it due to differences of opinion about the manner in which the division had been handled in France, as Silvester himself suspected? Silvester *had* disappointed him near Melun, wrote Bradley afterward. Or was it because of the surprising blow dealt by the Germans in the Peel? Another officer of the division, who later became a general himself, stated that Silvester had generously taken the blame in the inevitable recriminations to protect his intelligence officer, who had repeatedly failed. Hence his dismissal. When Silvester went to see Bradley to protest, he also lost his two stars and was demoted to colonel. A military court of inquiry which investigated the case after the war upheld Bradley's verdict. After some time, Silvester was reinstated to the rank of Major General.

On the next night, the German 47th Army Corps withdrew behind the web of canals as quickly and silently as it had crossed them during the attack, leaving a garrison behind, in and around Meyel. By the following night, the corps had already recrossed the Maas and was moving at high speed back to Germany to be re-equipped. On the banks of the canals in the Peel stood, as before, those who had spearheaded the attack into Holland in May 1940, and who in 1944 had formed the backbone of the thin screen of troops who had delayed the Allied advance: the German Fallschirmjäger.

CHAPTER TEN

FROM THE PEEL TO THE MAAS

T HE AUTUMN OF 1944 was one of the most depressing weather periods on record in the past 80 years, characterized in particular by a very unusual amount of rainfall. In Roermond, the average precipitation measured was 53 mms in October, 56 mms in November and 53 mms in December. In 1944 these figures (measured at Venlo and Sevenum) were: 81 mms in October, an unheard-of record of 132 mms in November and 73 mms in December.

Not only in the province of Limburg, but all along the western front, the weather was dismally wet and gloomy, with disastrous consequences for the Allied advance. Everywhere the motorized and armored units ground to a halt in seas of mud, making proper deployment impossible. The low, dense clouds also made it difficult to benefit from the Allies' favorite trump card: air superiority. And, finally, the infantry remained exposed to continuous discomfort, damp quarters and soggy foxholes.

The front could be characterized by one word: stagnation. It is true that the island of Walcheren had at long last been liberated (actually, inundated) in this first week of November, but the clearing of the Scheldt estuary had been delayed for so long that it precluded any further offensive actions in the west. Though Aachen fell on October 21, there was no question of a forceful thrust toward the Rhine from that sector. After bitter fighting, the Americans had reached the Ruhr River in early December. It was swollen and the ground flooded, so they found it impossible to ford. By that time

Patton's Third Army had just entered the Saar (it had taken him ten whole weeks to seize the city of Metz). Farther south the Free French and the American forces had had more luck in this bleak November month and succeeded in liberating a large area of Alsace.

There was no denying that great successes had not been achieved that autumn. Shortages in manpower and ammunition became painfully manifest. On average, the Allies' supplies in November increased only from 25,000 to 28,000 tons a day, which was insignificant for an army that was steadily increasing in numbers and was trying to prepare for a campaign in which winter clothing would be high on the list of priorities. Each attack in this miserable autumn had a detrimental effect on the logistics of any simultaneous or successive attack elsewhere. It seemed as if Eisenhower's "broad front" strategy simply lacked enough material backup to achieve its main objective — the destruction of the Wehrmacht west of the Rhine.

In the Peel and Maas regions the German defense, as on the Roer and elsewhere in Holland, such as in the Betuwe and the other land between the big rivers, utilized the abnormally wet season to raise the water level, to block water ducts and to breach dikes. Limburg was spared the latter. In spite of these German countermeasures the Allies succeeded here in eventually reaching the Maas, but the story was the same as with the Rhine and the Ruhr: there would be no prospect of a crossing so long as the land was flooded.

On November 1 — with the Scheldt operation almost completed — Eisenhower gave his approval to regroup the Allied forces. The American units in Holland, including the 7th Armored Division, were attached to Bradley's Army Group. In the Peel, the British XII Corps joined VIII Corps. When the two corps attacked, German resistance inside the Maas salient was bound to collapse. Naturally, time was needed to make the necessary preparations: two weeks of relative quiet on the front — except, as we will see, near Meyel.

Within the scope of our story, much suffering must remain unmentioned. In the wake of what happened on the front between the Peel marshes and the Maas, after four and a half years of German occupation, oppression and terror were still the order of the day. After the ruthless manhunts on October 8, the roundups went on until the very last few days before the salient collapsed. Always the cry "Raid!" was heard, which forced men over sixteen to go into hiding. There was not a single family that did not live in constant fear. People were always worrying that one day the Germans would order the mass evacuation of the entire area.

At the end of October the whole population of Griendtsveen, Helenaveen and Amerika were forced to leave their homes at one hour's notice in an uncertain exodus to the east. On November 8 the British authorities, too, resorted to the evacuation of villages in the western Peel. What will we find left of our homes and belongings on our return? This question was on the minds of every family that was evacuated. On the German side of the front, though not on the scale of the planned pillage that characterized the evacuation of Arnhem, looting of cattle and furniture by retreating soldiers was commonplace.

It is sad to report that in the liberated parts of the battle area the situation was the same. The war had not left the moral standards of the Allies unaffected and, to them, "to liberate" had often become a euphemism for "looting." Major Renison clearly realized how far they could go when he noted: "We succumbed to the temptation of a looted bottle of wine which 'Banger' produced from a nearby cellar. The Boche had done a good deal of looting, but we had to be very strict, especially in the case of a well-stocked chemist's shop opposite D Co.'s HQ." But despite all measures, despite all signs proclaiming "Looting Is a Serious Crime," pillage cast a shadow on the liberation.

It may well be true that it was not the front-line soldier who misbehaved, as may be gathered from experience not only in the liberated areas behind the Allied front line but on the German side as well. Much of the pillage was attributed to troops passing through or to those who stayed in the rear. Sometimes Dutch citizens were to blame and, in the case of Arnhem, systematic pillage was conducted by German civilians controlled by Nazi Party officials.

Brother Ivanus Krol made an entry in his diary as early as October 27, the day when Major Renison's East Yorks left St. Servatius Psychiatric Hospital: "We have nothing but praise for these soldiers;

so far they have been the only Englishmen we can't complain of. On the contrary, they have done everything within their power to help us. On leaving, the Sergeant-Major warned us to hide all our valuables. When we asked why, he answered rather embarrassed: 'English soldiers steal!' It was very hard for us to believe such a thing, but later events proved to our dismay that it was the truth. In cellars and in attics the brothers and three civilians who had stayed behind tried to stash away furniture to protect it from being thrown outside by soldiers who felt that it was in the way. Their efforts were wasted. After a day of hard work they found the next morning that all the locks and doors had been forced open. Innumerable protests addressed to official agencies such as Civil Affairs and Military Police had little or no effect. Often the soldier caught red-handed in the act of looting or wanton destruction would say 'Sorry' and that you were right in reprimanding him, but as soon as the coast was clear he resumed his activities."

Pillage on a large scale actually began when the front started to move up a little and the soldiers found themselves in deserted and destroyed areas with empty houses that were often heavily damaged. The soldiers had been in Venray long enough to know where they could easily get what they wanted or what would meet their immediate needs. Trucks were chartered to load the things they desired. Very soon this was mainly done during the night, for the soldiers quickly learned which were the most convenient hours. Truckloads of tables, chairs, spring mattresses and other pieces of furniture vanished. In particular, spring mattresses — at that time better known as "Aupings" — were in great demand. They were easy to find, easy to take away and they were very comfortable to sleep on: they were much to be preferred to sleeping on the hard ground. Thus, pieces of furniture were scattered in every direction!

To protest against it or to try to prevent it was impossible. The soldiers were like flies, swarming all over the place at the same time. If a Dutch citizen protested against pillage and looting in one place, the "gentlemen" quietly waited inside their trucks until he or she moved on to protest in a different place, then took advantage of the situation and quickly loaded anything they had set their minds on and disappeared at full speed with their loot. It was hopeless. Even officers and M.P.s who were asked to call a halt to the ransacking were powerless, which they frankly admitted.

Another nuisance were the soldiers who went on leave. Every other ten days or so the tired soldiers were allowed to go on leave in the civilized world. Apparently many of them needed money or presents for their entertainment or for girls. Hundreds of curtains, sheets, pillow cases, towels and other items that were easy to take away disappeared in this manner. Even a complete brass band with a value of many thousands of guilders was stolen, including the uniform caps. A typical phenomenon was the widespread habit of converting chairs into comfortable toilets.

As soon as a new group of soldiers arrived, a big trench was dug. Then a number of chairs were collected — the state they were in did not matter — the seats were knocked out and thereupon they were placed over the trench and the toilet was ready for use. Each group that arrived wanted different chairs. Those which had done their service were used as firewood.

Father Beda Verbeek, of the monastery of the Franciscan Friars, wrote that the safe in the sacristy had been forced open within three weeks after the liberation: "Much was stolen and deliberately destroyed at that time." This case was typical of so many others. Doctor Havermans, of St. Servatius Psychiatric Hospital, gave an account of the situation in Venray after he had been allowed to return there for a few days: "Words cannot describe how appalled I was when I saw how the town had been pillaged and destroyed. I spoke to an elderly English officer whose words speak for themselves: 'I'm very sorry and deeply ashamed; the Army has lost its reputation here.' Every house I went into I found smashed furniture, drawers pried open, their contents scattered on the floors, kicked-in panels, marble mantelpieces broken to pieces, chandeliers torn from the ceilings, a piano standing in the pouring rain. Valuables had vanished. And I spoke to Englishmen who without any embarrassment told me that down in the cellars things were even worse!"

In March 1945, the Group Commander of the Dutch Constabulary of Venray drew up a protocol which phlegmatically listed all it had recorded of pillage by German troops. They had mainly targeted cattle, horses and harnesses; also stoves, blankets and office appliances; occasionally they had also opened a safe. But all this was peanuts compared with the conduct of the Allied troops. Ten policemen had been left behind in Venray and about thirty men of the Orde Dienst (voluntary police force). By sending out patrols into the town they had tried to prevent looting, but from six o'clock in the evening until six in the morning there was a curfew, and during that time they were not allowed to go into the streets: that was the time when the looters struck—in the darkness. At dusk and during the night, sometimes even in broad daylight, military trucks stopped at random places, whereupon the occupants searched the houses, according to said protocol. Everything was forced open, even the floors were broken up, underneath which clothing, linen, radios, china, jewelry and other valuable items had been hidden to keep them out of the hands of the Germans. The liberators did not respect these personal belongings.

In the village of Leunen near Venray, members of the Orde Dienst found that in this village alone thirteen safes had been cracked open. Soldiers of the Royal Engineers who were clearing the streets of rubble had loaded wood, furniture, stoves, sewing machines onto their trucks, and even thirteen truckloads of brown coal. The Mayor of Venray sent this damaging protocol to the Claims Office at Eindhoven—the beginning of a lengthy administrative procedure. Forty thousand such claims were registered for the entire area—to a large extent, "English damage," as the pillage was called in those days.

Seldom has this aspect of the liberation been discussed openly in The Netherlands since the war. Did the Dutch prefer to suppress the bitter taste, to whitewash the conduct of soldiers supposed to be friends, or did they feel a sort of substitute shame, similar to that shared by the elderly British officer? Whatever the case may be, this dissonance did not fit the typical image, also upheld long after the war, of friend and foe, the former being incapable of any evil and the latter incapable of any good.

★ ★ ★

In a battle area, fear of death or mutilation, by soldiers and civilians alike, outweighs the concern for purely material things. Thus the citizens of Venlo and Roermond lived in perpetual fear because of the continuous threat of air attacks. Between October 13 and November 19, eleven air raids were made on the bridges of Venlo. Large areas of the inner city had been destroyed by near-misses, but the bridges remained in use. Roermond heaved a huge sigh of relief when eventually its bridge was hit by the Allied airmen so that finally the raids could cease.

On November 2, the 15th Scottish Division began its operations to retake Meyel. It was supported by tanks of the Guards Tank Brigade. Advancing along the straight road, the Scots were able to seize the hamlets of Heitrak, Neerkant and Moostdijk, but their frontal attack foundered in a screen of German artillery and mortar fire.

Meyel would have to be outflanked and this required tank support. But tanks, too, were unable to get around the town. The Germans had dug in in the Vieruitersten Wood (called "Diamond Wood" because of its shape), between Meyel and the Deurne Canal, from which they fired at anything that moved. One SP of the tank destroyer section left behind by the 15th Panzergrenadier Division destroyed three flail tanks and three Churchills.

A renewed effort was made two days later, the plan being for the 2nd Squadron of the Grenadier Guards to outflank Diamond Wood, to advance parallel to the canal, under the very noses of the Germans on the opposite bank. This would only be possible if the artillery could put down an effective smokescreen to provide cover for the tanks. The Scottish infantry would attack astride the straight road. Continuous downpours caused the attack to be postponed for one more day, until Sunday, November 5.

After a soaking night with plenty of shellfire, dawn broke, the sky for once bright and unclouded. The Scottish infantry could see the Germans moving about in their positions two miles in front. It was 0730 when the 19 Churchills set out on their perilous advance along the canal. All eyes were focused on them. A bad omen: one of the tanks hit a mine right at the start. Once on the move, the column, protected by the smokescreen on the left, seemed unstoppable and the tanks rapidly approached the farthest point, where they were to make a sharp turn around Diamond Wood.

Then fate struck. The advance of the squadron ended abruptly in the treacherous soft soil in which tank after tank bogged down. Their engines roared, their tracks churned vainly in the mud, digging themselves deeper and deeper into the ground. To make matters worse, five were destroyed by German mines. Though the artillery kept up an uninterrupted smokescreen, the din of the engines had given the position of the tanks away to the enemy. Volleys of shells hurtled through the smokescreen and well-directed anti-tank gunfire destroyed another three machines. The squadron commander had no alternative but to give the signal to retreat. Only four tanks managed to return to the start line — 800 yards to the rear — of which two were no longer fit for action. The rest of the Squadron — 14 tanks — lay helplessly in the crossfire from the other side of the canal and from Diamond Wood. In the course of this Sunday three tanks eventually managed to "survive" and to continue their fire from their precarious positions near the German lines. The remaining eleven crews were forced to leave the relative safety of their vehicles and search for cover in the open fields.

The frontal attack by the Scottish infantry bogged down as well. The supporting tanks ran into a minefield, which made a mockery of any further help they might have given to the infantry. Five Churchills were lost. The infantry came across Schü mines. Borderer Officer Robert Woolcoombe watched the men of his platoon and the stretcher bearers who came to their rescue being blown into the air one after the other. "Strange: time went by as usual, and for one brief moment you looked at the sky and felt a touch of wind. Then there was a man who tried to get up and stand on the stumps of his legs. More men came forward to clear the mines and a sergeant threw himself to the ground, stabbing away with his bayonet to reach his wounded men. A mine blew up in his face. This was a brief, absurd play, enacted in a crazy world, where bodies, sinisterly quiet underneath blankets, were carried away one by one on stretchers. As I watched one of them, I heard the man stop gnashing his teeth. A grin appeared on his face which made me sick. His eyes rolled upward in their sockets. The sergeant-major who stood next to me turned away brusquely and shook his head: 'No, Sir. No, Sir.' There was nothing else to say."

Not only mines but also artillery played havoc with the Scots of the Lowland Brigade. The firing from the other side of the canal became so heavy that in spite of it a troop of Churchill tanks decided to come to the Lowland Brigade's support. The four tanks were destroyed by German anti-tank guns. It became clear in the early afternoon that pursuing the attack against Meyel was unthinkable. All that mattered now was trying to save whatever could be saved.

At 0330 hours the Recce Platoon of the Grenadier Guards was sent forward in an effort to bring the surviving tank crews safely back to their own lines. Six Honey tanks under the command of Lt. Greville Selby-Lowndes were dispatched to do the job. His Honeys were lighter than the Churchills and carried lighter weapons, too. Only Selby-Lowndes left with a complete crew (he himself, a gunner, a driver and a machine-gunner) in case the weapons would be needed. The other Honeys only had a driver and a commander on board in order to be able to carry as many stranded crew members as possible.

Selby-Lowndes had a rough idea of what the ground looked like. The troop of Honeys advanced with great caution through the fields, following the tracks made by the Churchills. The smokescreen was very thick. Selby-Lowndes was on the point of getting lost when suddenly he saw the commander of a still fully manned tank waving to him indicating that he should try to get his tank as close to the Churchill as he could. Three of the six Honeys bogged down. Though halved in number, the troop carried out its orders: they made a number of sorties to save the Churchill crews. The men were hoisted from inside their prisons, clinging to the hulls with frightened faces. Artillery shells and mortar bombs exploded all around them and occasionally an 88 mm shell whizzed past. The Honeys lumbered on among corn stacks from which Selby-Lowndes saw a few anxious Germans peering at them. They turned out to be harmless.

At dusk the operation had to be suspended. Nearly all the survivors had been rescued, including fourteen wounded, as well as wireless codebooks and secret instructions. Nine men were still missing, but a further search was useless. Whoever was still alive in that dark no-man's land would have to make his own way back to the British lines. The nine, of whom four were wounded, actually succeeded in doing so the same night. Eleven dead were left in the fields.

While all this was happening, the decision had been made to discontinue any more attacks against Meyel. Sunday, November 5, had been a disaster for the British, but for Venlo this day was even worse. Gradually the population had become used to the bombardments, from mid–October onward. The sixth air raid was made on November 3.

"It's not the bomb explosions themselves," wrote Gijs Bertels, a journalist, in his diary, later published under the title *Die Swaere Noodt*, "but the moments before that are unbearable. The quiet, steady drone of the airplanes like the humming of bees in a flowering shrub, peaceful, soothing and venomous at the same time. Out of that weak, monotonous sound which has a mesmerizing effect that makes you forget the booming of the ack-ack guns there swells a vague, rumbling noise which grows into a screaming crescendo of falling bombs, a terrifying noise that seems to blot out the whole outside world. People in the cellars were reduced to miserable little bundles of fear, the horrifying noise freezing the marrow in their bones. When the bombs strike, the ground trembles underneath the foundations, the walls sway, pieces of brickwork begin falling around you and gray and yellow dust enters your lungs. High up in the air the horrible, shrieking noise of another bomb-carpet starts up again."

Twice the bombers appeared over the Venlo bridges on November 4. Again it was the town itself that received direct hits. At four o'clock on Sunday afternoon, the ninth air raid set the town center on fire. "Huge flames tower above the city," lamented Bertels, "our beloved hometown is burning, and in the restless breath of the night wind the fiery glow reflected by the low-hanging clouds can be seen all over the land of Northern Limburg and people know: the town of Valuas, of St. Maarten is burning. The big St. Martinus Church is a pillar of fire. It seems as if the town is totally deserted and is left to itself to burn away, crackling, collapsing, emitting sparks and groaning, a thunderous orgy of fire." During the night it started to rain, which probably prevented the total destruction of Venlo.

"It seemed, when things were at their worst, that the tiny hand of our Lady of Genooi [a statue of Mary] called a halt to the firestorm," Bertels wrote gratefully in his diary. He still could not find words to express the horrors of that day. Another citizen of Venlo, an ex-teacher, simply noted: "We received general absolution from the chaplain. Frightened to death, we squatted on the ground in the shaking cellar, closely packed together, in indescribable terror."

After November 5, Meyel still remained in German hands. To the British it seemed advisable to wait until the village could be outflanked by the coming offensive. This Sunday had been the bleakest day for the Grenadier Guards in their entire campaign in Europe. The battered battalion was pulled back to Helmond to recover; 29 tanks and other vehicles were left on the battlefield. The Scots Guards Battalion, too, was temporarily relieved. The Peel had turned out to be a graveyard for tanks. From now on, we will only find tanks being used in a supporting role for the infantry.

To the west, the American 7th Armored Division had succeeded in advancing along the Noorder Canal to about halfway between Nederweert and Meyel; on that same Sunday the Americans got stuck as well. Three days later, the "Lucky Seventh" disappeared from the Noord-Brabant theater of war for good. Its nickname had acquired a bitter taste here. After the disillusion of Overloon, the German counterattack had completely surprised them. The Division had suffered 106 killed, 344 wounded and over 300 missing, most of whom must have been taken prisoner, but in defense it had shown great fighting spirit. General Dempsey, commander of the British Second Army, showed his unreserved appreciation in an order of the day giving the Americans a farewell salute. Nobody knew then that the 7th Armored, after Overloon and Meyel, was to face even worse trials in the near future. The bitter experiences in Noord-Brabant would turn out to be valuable when the division was called upon to stem the German offensive in the Ardennes.*

*During the Battle of the Bulge in December 1944, the 7th Armored Division demonstrated what an effective fighting machine it really was. The Germans found themselves forestalled at St. Vith by the Division and Brigadier General R.W. Hasbrouck became one of the great men of the Ardennes. It is believed that but for the stand made by the 7th from 18 to 21 December, the Germans would have moved directly through the gap between St. Vith and Bastogne. By holding until December 21, First Army had time to move forces via the gap and block the Germans in the rear of the positions held by the 7th Armored.

Troop movements were taking place all along the front, one unit taking over guard duty from the other. Not everywhere was this such a cushy job as near Griendtsveen, where patrols wading through the swamps in the direction of the village of Amerika were merely disturbing pheasants and ducks. The area around Veulen and Leunen was under constant German artillery fire. A unit stationed in Leunen compared its existence with scenes from *Journey's End,* the famous play about trench warfare. It was a subterranean existence, or in a house with thick walls. Just like their fathers or uncles, the soldiers were on "stand to" at sunrise and sunset: then all the positions were fully manned and men were staring across no-man's land with their weapons at the ready. And as in the old days, the daily ration of syrupy rum was the only thing to look forward to. The civilian population, not used to being in a front line, was considered a nuisance.

Hence, the decision that all of Leunen must be evacuated. The next day a sad procession of men, women and children slowly walked away from their homes, some trying to take a few head of cattle with them. Horses and cows posed no problems, but pigs with their erratic behavior simply could not be taken along. Poultry, too, was impossible to control. The soldiers watched with mixed feelings: pity, but also the very tempting prospect of the best food of the campaign — every day fresh pork and chicken breast galore. Good food brought some variety to their daily routine. Now that the unbearable strain of the fighting had suddenly ceased and the advance had been halted, other tensions came to the surface.

Jan Ledeboer watched how a soldier, a veteran of the Italian campaign, abruptly refused to go out on patrol. He objected violently, had to be held and was then dragged away. What Ledeboer witnessed here was one of the symptoms of that much dreaded syndrome: battle exhaustion. During and after the fighting for Overloon and Venray it was in particular the 3rd Division that was faced with such cases. Medical reports for the month of October, in addition to 839 wounded, listed 212 cases of battle exhaustion, a ratio of 1:4. This, however, was a better figure than for the months in Normandy.

The divisional staff had the syndrome analyzed and took pre-cautions which were effective. This analysis distinguished three types of exhaustion: first, the "Windy Willy," who usually arrived in the R.A.P. (Regimental Aid Post) two or three hours after a battle had started, showing signs of great fear, but who was not a true case of battle exhaustion. Then there was the nervous type, walking into the R.A.P. shaking all over, who keeps his helmet on under all circumstances, diving for cover at the slightest noise. Third, there was the man who was physically exhausted after three or four days of fighting and who no longer had any control over his nerves, mainly because of lack of sleep. The doctors found that there were relatively fewer cases during an attack, when the soldier seemed to have more control over his fears, but that symptoms did occur as soon as additional factors played a part, such as when an advance bogged down. At these times, men had to dig in and were exposed to continuous shellfire, while forced to remain idle and helpless, wet, cold, dirty, with irregular meals and a chronic shortage of sleep. As Margreiter remarked: "At the front you find ourself more or less in a kind of trance, only faintly aware of what's going on, yet very alert."⋆

This state did not last long. A front-line soldier, after having overcome his initial fears, gradually started to function better; but the peak of his performance, which he usually reached after about three weeks, could not be maintained for long, a few weeks at most. Then he slowly started showing signs of battle exhaustion.

In the case of the "exhaustion" of the 3rd Division it should be remembered that between June 6 and October 31, 1944, it lost 8,758 men (the most depressing peaks being 3,508 in June, 2,504 in July and 1,308 in October); the majority of the casualties were in the rifle companies: 4,500 men. In theory, this meant that each front-line soldier during these five months had already been replaced twice by a newcomer. Admittedly this is only partly true, because as a man's battle experience increased, his chances of survival improved. Concern for newcomers, keeping active, comradeship and motivation (being

---

⋆Army Doctor W. C. Menninger's book *Psychiatry in a Troubled World*, dealing with military psychiatry in the years 1941-45, mentions as the most prominent symptoms of a soldier under fire: palpitations (over 50 percent), queazy stomach (40 percent), vomiting (25 percent), chills and perspiration (20 to 25 percent). Remarkably, though, "Dirtying one's trousers because of fear rated at only 5 to 10 percent."

proud of being a soldier and of his own unit) should, according to the doctors, have been ingredients to build up the Division's morale. Outside attention for the Division as a whole was a factor. Unfortunately, the 3rd had never received much publicity, explaining why the men had ironically nicknamed themselves "the unspectaculars" or "the contemptibles." (The latter designation echoed the nickname used by the British Expeditionary Force in 1914, after remarks by the German Kaiser about that "contemptible little army.")

The 51st Highlander Division, however, was anything but "obscure." They had been the heroes of El Alamein and many millions had watched them on the screen marching in the desert behind nightly barrages, to the sound of exciting bagpipe music. The pipers were there again on November 14 when the 51st got ready for the first of its three attacks on the German bridgehead which had been aptly dubbed the "Nutcracker." Between the closing jaws of two army corps the enemy front line would shrink and his resistance would eventually collapse.

Two brigades were to supply troops to establish the first bridgehead across the canal from Wessem to Nederweert. They were supported by a barrage of 450 artillery and anti-tank guns: 2,000 rounds a minute. In assault craft and in Buffaloes (armored amphibious vehicles that could carry 30 men and even a Bren gun carrier), a trial crossing was made first, for the equipment had to be carried to the canal bank on sledges and then lowered into the water by hand. The Gordon Highlanders had a guest in the person of Chester Wilmot,* who made a live report of the crossing. Near Wessem the banks were found to be too steep to launch the Buffaloes, but the Cameronians, accompanied by their piper, succeeded in floating theirs. "The advance toward the canal," wrote an eyewitness, "was an unusual sight, reminiscent of mobile units in the desert. Infantry on tanks, on Buffaloes, on foot, all spread out along a front of 800 yards with a terrifying barrage screaming over their heads."

---

*Famous BBC newsman and author of *The Struggle for Europe*, one of the outstanding books written on World War II.

What followed next was an anticlimax. German opposition turned out to be of a nominal nature from November 14 onward. Only one German division, made up of the Fallschirmjäger Regiment Hübner and Fallschirmjäger Regiment Hermann, each two battalions strong, were facing the Allied divisions on the canal front: four battalions of Fallschirmjäger vastly outnumbered by the Allied forces. The Germans could do little more than pull back and fight rearguard actions. *"Hinhaltende Verteidigung"* was the fancy name given by the Germans to such delaying actions, but these skirmishes could not halt the Allied advance for long. Again it was the terrain and the countless minefields that slowed down the Scots. After a few days they had reached the Uitwateringskanaal. For the first time, albeit briefly, the German defense made itself felt. Their artillery fire was so heavy that the commander of the 154th Brigade, returning from a visit to the Black Watch Battalion at the front, on being asked what it was like over there, merely answered: "John [the battalion commander] put his tin hat on."

According to the historian of the division, the Germans even went so far as to launch a counterattack, "displaying the utmost courage," against the bridgehead across the Uitwateringskanaal, under cover of concentrated artillery fire, the worst the 51st Division had experienced since Normandy. The attack was beaten off and the advance in the direction of Baarlo was resumed.

On November 19, soldiers of the 154th Brigade came across a number of Dutchmen near the village of Helden. They were exhausted, unshaven and dressed in threadbare overalls. The Scots had heard rumors of a group of resistance men hiding in the woods with German prisoners. The hour these had so eagerly waited for during ten long, anxious weeks had arrived at last. Their task was finished. They handed over to the Scots twenty-three dirty, half-starved Germans, covered with lice and fleas.

Most of the Germans had been captured by surprise during the confusing days of September by a group of "Wood Partisans of Baarlo," composed of members of local Resistance organizations, reinforced by two groups from Schijndel and from the area between the rivers Maas and Waal. Immediately after "Mad Tuesday" the

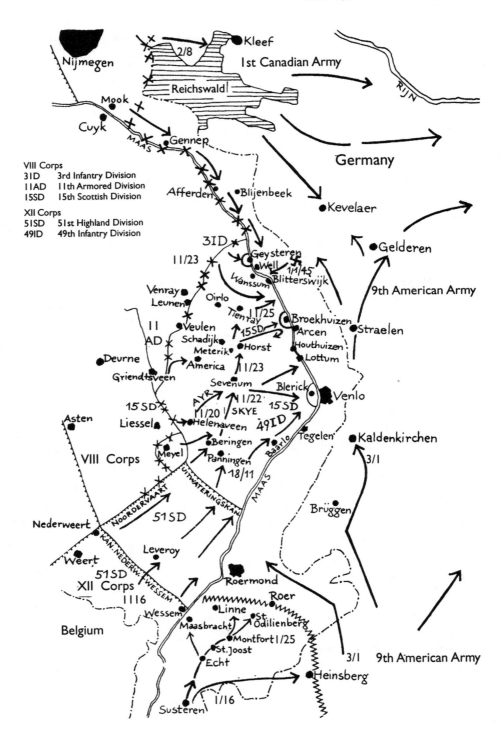

Nov. 12, 1944–March 1, 1945

Kleef

Nijmegen

1st Canadian Army

2/8

Reichswald

RIJN

Mook

Cuyk

Germany

Gennep

MAAS

VIII Corps
3ID   3rd Infantry Division
11AD   11th Armored Division
15SD   15th Scottish Division

XII Corps
51SD   51st Highland Division
49ID   49th Infantry Division

Afferden

Blijenbeek

Kevelaer

3ID

Geysteren

Gelderen

11/23

Well

1/1/45

Wanssum

Blitterswijk

Venray

9th American Army

Leunen

Oirlo

Tientray

11/25

Broekhuizen

11
AD

Veulen

15SD

Arcen

Straelen

Schadijk

Houthuizen

Meterik

Horst

Lottum

Devrne

America

11/23

Griendtsveen

Sevenum

Blerick

Venlo

15 SD

AYR

11/22

1/20 | SKYE

15 SD

Asten

Helenaveen

49ID

Kaldenkirchen

Liessel

Beringen

Baarlo

Tegelen

3/1

VIII Corps

Meyel

Panningen

18/11

Brüggen

UITWATERINGSKAN.

MAAS

Nederweert

NOORDERVAART

51SD

KAN. NEDERW.

Leveroy

Weert

9th American Army

51SD

WESSEM

Roermond

XII Corps

1116

Roer

Belgium

Wessem

Linne

St.

Maasbracht

Odilienberg

Montfort 1/25

St. Joost

3/1

Echt

9th American Army

Heinsberg

Susteren

1/16

Dutchmen had gone to Venlo in order to seize the bridges over the Maas. Their plan had failed utterly and the group went into hiding at the farm "Boekenderhof" near Baarlo. Using the farm as their base they first captured ten Fallschirmjäger, followed by another batch of eleven. On September 27, after a brief skirmish near the farm, three Germans were killed. The group left the farm in a hurry, just in time. That same afternoon the "Boekenderhof" was surrounded by a strong force of Germans and burned to the ground.

There were no other reprisals, possibly because the front was too near and the Germans had other things to worry about than gruesome reprisals like those taken by them at about the same time against the village of Putten in the Veluwe. The "Wood Partisans" moved from place to place, taking their prisoners with them. One day two deserters joined the group. They seemed to be very keen on surrendering themselves. Then one morning, when they were washing themselves, one of the Resistance men saw that the two men had been tattooed with the SS rune, and with the aid of a cooperative Czech prisoner they were exposed as infiltrators. Both were found to have a dubious past, the death sentence was pronounced, and they were shot on October 2.

Hunted down by a growing number of Germans, the group tried to get in touch with the Americans in the Peel. Those were the days of the German counteroffensive and "along the road from Kessel to Meyel long columns of tanks advanced, passing us closely. It's a miracle the Germans did not spot us," one of the partisans related. There was not a chance of getting through, and gloomily, after many deprivations in the hostile peat bogs, they went back to the woods of Baarlo. Diseases and exhaustion had affected their morale badly, but each time the alternative of getting rid of their prisoners came up, this idea was rejected. They even captured two more Fallschirmjäger, who rode a motorbike with sidecar. The adventures of the group, arrests of helpers and breathtaking narrow escapes have all been described in the captivating memoirs of J.W. Hofdijk, who himself was one of the Wood Partisans at that time. (Similar P.O.W. camps were run by the Resistance during that autumn in the Biesbosch and in Salland.)

On the night of September 17, a few, among them Jacques Crasborn, commander of the underground group in Limburg, and

Paul Weemering from Rotterdam, who was the commander of the group, succeeded in getting in touch with the approaching liberators and warned them. On handing over the Germans to the Scots, the Dutchmen saw to their surprise that the prisoners were forced to give up everything they had formerly been allowed to keep, such as watches, photographs, wallets and other personal belongings.

Baarlo was liberated on November 21. Thereafter, the 51st Division disappeared from the scene. It was relieved by the 15th Scottish Division, which, a week earlier had taken Meyel. The town was virtually deserted by the civilians and there was no enemy resistance. But the toll paid by the division in the preceding battle had been high: 127 killed and 583 wounded. On November 19 the 15th crossed the Deurne Canal. From an intercepted German radio message it became evident that the enemy was withdrawing to the east. One brigade marched via route "Ayr" to Helenaveen, another via "Skye" to Sevenum. Within a few days both "Ayr" and "Skye" turned into a big mud pool.

The historian of the division referred to the roads as "a trial similar to that which our troops had to face in the winters of World War I, a sheer nightmare of dampness and cold, muck and deprivation, there came no end to it. In front of us the Germans burnt down farms and villages. In the dark, fires lit up the entire horizon. All day long, sad columns of refugees came our way, heading west, tired, their few belongings loaded in prams and wheelbarrows, or simply being carried on their backs, plodding through mud and rain, to us an unforgettable picture of abject human misery."

The floodgates of heaven continued to unleash torrents of rain on friend and foe alike. Divisional histories record how the roads turned into tracks of oozing mud and how each detour chosen soon turned into an impassable barrier. Columns of exhausted soldiers stood knee-deep in the mud wrestling to get their bogged-down vehicles back onto solid ground. Sometimes a Churchill tank was the only answer to the problem, but it was not unusual for a tank to rip off the front of a bogged-down vehicle. At one point, four men were needed to pull one of their comrades out of a mud hole in which he was slowly drowning.

The Scots reached the deserted village of Helenaveen via "Ayr" on November 20. Sevenum and Horst were liberated on November 22. The day before, Fallschirmjäger—a few who had taken an overdose of "Dutch Courage" (gin)—had established positions near Sevenum, but in the early morning orders were given to move again. "Wake up, men, don't sleep, or we'll all be killed!" shouted their captain. To the villagers he said: "Your friends will be coming soon, your Tommies. But we'll be back in the spring! See you then!" Among the last Germans to leave, unfortunately, was the demolition squad, which blew up the proud Gothic church tower.

Horst, too, received its share of shellfire. Forty-five refugees had found shelter in the cellar of a large farm. Among them were Father and Mother Ernst with their eight children. They had been chased from their home in the village of Amerika at the end of October. There they had already been bombed and shelled. Their cellar had swayed like a ship at sea—at least that was what it had felt like to their nine-year-old son Jan. When it had grown quiet, he had crawled out of the cellar and it seemed to him as if it had grown dark already; the sun was hidden behind a cloud of dust and sand. When they had to leave Amerika, he had watched how the Germans started tearing doors from their posts to use them as covers for their foxholes and how they carried furniture outside to make their positions more comfortable.

Once in Horst, the Ernsts had fairly quickly found shelter with the prospect of receiving regular meals, sometimes even meat when a shell killed a sheep or a few chickens. But now in Horst, too, the shelling had increased to a crescendo of fear. The men had gone into hiding in the fields in case the Germans would start hunting again for "diggers." Jan was tossing in his sleep among the mothers and children, when suddenly the whole ceiling came crashing down. Jan saw a large fireball, emitting sparks. There were people lying next to him on the floor. Two were killed, six badly wounded. One of his brothers died six months later as a result of this direct hit. Jan was to suffer from feelings of anxiety for the rest of his life, in particular during a thunderstorm.

The Scots made contact with the 11th Armoured Division near Horst on November 23. This division—wisely enough, virtually without tanks — started its advance on the road from Griendtsveen to Amerika on November 22, not without casualties, however. The captain of a company of Shropshires went through a horrifying experience. Cautiously he was advancing to Amerika when there was a series of sudden explosions. Eight soldiers were lying in the mud with blown-off feet. Schü mines! The captain asked for further orders, but the battalion commander told him to push on. He regrouped his company in single file, himself in front. With death literally stalking him, he carefully prodded the ground in front of him for mines. Each man trod in the footsteps of the man in front of him. Despite this precaution an ear-shattering explosion occurred, this time right behind the captain. Again a casualty — and thereafter a man was so unfortunate as to stumble. He fell with his hand on a mine and lost his arm. Pushing on would be tantamount to suicide. There was nothing else they could do but to return by the same track — and this time luck was with them. One of the casualties died; the others were crippled for the rest of their lives.

After the 11th Armoured had advanced from Amerika to Horst, they realized that there would be very little room left for them to establish a front line on the Maas. They were literally squeezed out of their positions by the Scottish 15th which had taken over the front sector of the 51st Highland Division near Baarlo. This division approached Blerick and the Maas on November 25. Pressure had also been brought to bear on the 11th Armoured by the 3rd Infantry Division on the left since November 23. When refugees had reported that there were no more Germans in the area, the troops of the 3rd Division had left their positions between Veulen and Vierlingsbeek. Moving out in pouring rain, all they came across were deserted villages and foul-smelling carcasses of cattle.

Now that the salient was being rolled up from the south, General von Obstfelder had decided to restrict himself to delaying tactics in the north with two Fallschirmjäger units (Grasmehl and Menzel) which had been sent to him as reinforcements. Resistance of any significance was met by the 3rd Division at Geysteren only — more about this village to follow — and between Wanssum and Blitterswijk, where the Ulsters lost seventy men on November 30 and December 1. The

Division reached the Maas on a fairly broad front. The young Lieutenant Norman Scarfe wrote a poem called "The Stygian Maas," realm of the dead:

> War has suspended
> Even the cultivation of the soil:
> Cows are not milked nor sluices attended
> The Stygian Maas
> And the cold "beeks" have left their
> appointed course.
> Here you can see despair,
> The glimmering waste of years,
> Sense the frustration.

On November 15, the 11th Armoured Division pulled two of its infantry battalions out of the front. The Monmouths were left behind, totally unaware of what was in store for them. In the meantime, the 15th Scottish Division had fanned out from Horst to the Maas. They reached the river from Blitterswijk to Houthuizen within two days. The advance from Meyel to Sevenum had been a very tough one and the divisional historian had every reason to refer to the Peel as "the abomination of desolation."

On November 26, Operation "Nutcracker" came to an end for the Scots as well. Yet this same day they were to pay dearly. Though British forces were now to be found practically all along the Maas, there were still German pockets west of the river. Three positions were being held by the enemy and each was destined to write its own grim story.

CHAPTER ELEVEN

TWO CASTLES
AND A FORTRESS

THE THREE POCKETS where the Germans still held out on November 28 with their backs against the Maas were, from north to south, the castle of Geysteren, the castle and village of Broekhuizen and, last but not least, Blerick, a suburb of Venlo which, by a network of trenches, strongpoints and anti-tank ditches, had been turned into a fortress. Within six days these "last ditch" positions would all be taken by the British. In the actions against these strongpoints we find two examples of how they should not have been fought and one example showing what good and sensible planning could achieve: a victory without unnecessary bloodshed.

Most tragic was the battle for Broekhuizen. The Scottish Division was to be relieved on November 28, but the commander of the battalion of Cameronians for no apparent reason felt that he should undertake a successful action just before he left. Broekhuizen castle lay southwest of the village, which the Germans had ordered to be evacuated on November 21. The castle was deserted; its owner, Mayor Berger of Venlo, because of shortage of building materials, had only had the roof patched up, and the remainder of the building was in a poor state of repair. A handful of Fallschirmjäger—no more than fifteen—had installed themselves within its walls. They were an outpost of the village, which had itself been fortified during the past month by minefields, trenches and barbed wire; the sides of its streets were connected with each other by a system of trenches, and nearly every house had been turned into a strongpoint.

Orders had been issued to the garrison—a company of about 150 men of Regiment Grasmehl—to fight to the last man. Why were the Germans so determined to make a last stand in this little hamlet in northern Limburg? The most plausible explanation is that the German command feared the Allies would cross the Maas straightaway and that it might then be useful to retain small bridgeheads west of the Maas around the Broekhuizen and Blerick from which to hamper any such attack. But then again, it might well have been one of those weird orders thought up by General von Obstfelder at Hillenraad Castle.

The first Scottish recce cars came very close to the castle of Broekhuizen on the afternoon of November 26 when they reached the hamlet of Stokt, which consisted of fourteen farms. The farmers warned the Scots that ahead were a strong German garrison and minefields. This sealed the fate of Stokt. The recce cars turned back and the people were promised that the infantry would come to liberate them in a few hours. Unfortunately, the infantry did not show up.

On the contrary, in the evening a number of Germans entered Stokt, chased the people from their homes and, in retaliation for their contact with the Scots, set fire to the houses. Half the number of farms and all the barns were burned down. The next day the Cameronians arrived—too late. Was their attack an act of revenge, a belated attempt to do something against the Fallschirmjäger in retaliation for burning down the houses? Be that as it may, the Scots' attack went ahead. Not by a company, no; only a platoon advanced toward the castle, preceded by a section of engineers who were to clear mines. Together they were hardly more than forty men.

Once within firing range of the castle, the Scots were mowed down by withering machine-gun fire. On pulling out, they were shelled from the other side of the Maas; from the village of Well the enemy had an excellent view of what was going on in Broekhuizen on the opposite river bank. Eight or nine Scots returned to their outfit unhurt, eleven or twelve wounded. Sixteen wounded were probably captured and ferried across the Maas by the Germans; four were listed as killed. Only one of the Germans was killed.

Immediately after the Scots were relieved that day, the Monmouths Battalion of the 11th Armoured Division, Lt. Colonel Stockley its commander, planned an action that was to lead to the capture of both the castle and the village. In order to break through the defenses of the village which was protected in the rear by the swollen waters of the Maas, it was necessary to assault the castle first. A squadron of tanks, stationed in Deurne, and ten flail tanks were to support the attack. Artillery fire was to be put down on the castle for a period of one hour in order to soften up the defenders and lay down a smokescreen between it and the village. Thereafter, from 1000 hours till 1045 two platoons from A Company were to take the building, and the tank squadron, firing all its guns, was to advance with the infantry. Fifteen minutes later C Company was to start the attack against the village, supported by tanks and artillery. The plan looked very good on paper, but the reality of November 30 was quite different.

At first, everything seemed to be going as planned, although one flail tank became hopelessly stuck (currently on view in the Museum grounds in Overloon), but the remaining flail tanks of the Hussars did reach the start line on the road from Stokt at 1000 hours. The shelling had been going on then for about one hour. Nobody knew that the Germans had retreated into the cellars of the castle, only to quietly slip back into their positions once the shelling had ceased. Among them was Helmut Dettinger, eighteen years old. The Fallschirmjäger had sworn to save the last bullet for themselves to avoid being captured alive. To their dismay they watched how the flail tanks quickly beat a path through the minefield. Seventy-five yards away from the castle, the flail tanks halted and turned back. The other tanks, spraying the castle with machine-gun fire, did not go any nearer. As was the case two days before, the infantry was left to itself to cover the last 75 yards, spread out in a thin line. The Germans watched in awe how the British advanced as if on a walking tour.

What now happened was a small-scale repetition of July 1, 1916, when the British on the Somme, in long lines and almost casually, approached the German trenches, with the same disastrous results. The Germans allowed them to come within firing range and then blasted away with everything they had, mowing the British down. Schü mines exploded and dead and wounded soldiers were lying all over the field. Within a few minutes A Company had been decimated; only one officer survived. The flat, open fields offered no cover at all. Wireless communications with the battalion's command post broke down. Another attack from the west by one platoon from D Company failed as well, when two flail tanks bogged down. Nobody had any idea of the magnitude of the tragedy. Lt. Colonel Stockley ordered his intelligence officer to go forward and try to find out what had happened. He was killed, too. Then the second-in-command of the battalion was sent forward. As soon as he climbed out of his carrier he fell to the ground, mortally wounded.

In the meantime, German artillery on the other side of the Maas had zeroed in on the edge of the wood where the soldiers of the other companies were waiting for the order to attack. In spite of all these setbacks, the action against the southern edge of the village of Broekhuizen was commenced at 1100 hours by C Company — as if the castle had already been taken. The attack collapsed in heavy machine-gun fire from the edge of the village. A panzerfaust knocked out one of the supporting tanks. The survivors of A Company lying in the field were exposed to a hail of shrapnel fire. Stretcher bearers could not get through to them. Not until noon, when the commander of one of the flail tanks came to report that there were quite a few dead and wounded lying in the fields in front of the castle, did Stockley realize how serious the situation was.

What to do next? Ask for more tanks or more artillery fire on the village and the castle? No, he decided to go and have a look for himself. Jumping into a ditch where Major R. Payne, the only survivor of A Company, had taken cover, Stockley remained standing there and ignored the shouts from his men to take cover. He calmly surveyed the situation and shouted back, "They haven't got me yet, have they?" Leaping out of the ditch, he drew his revolver and cried, "Come on, off we go!" Major Payne and fifteen survivors left their cover and followed Stockley. They ran straight into German machine-gun fire and Stockley and Payne were killed on the bridge of the castle. Those who survived this useless display of heroics eventually returned to the start line uninjured, under the command of a sergeant.

With Stockley gone, the brigade commander himself arrived on the scene two hours later to take things in hand. He ordered what was left of A Company to assemble for another attack against the castle. Two platoons of D Company were to attack the village, this time from the west. Both attacks were to be supported by a newly arrived squadron of tanks and two Cromwell tanks as mobile artillery. First the tanks advanced, then D Company followed them and turned to the right in front of the castle in order to take up positions in the orchard and the kitchen garden, the tanks blasting away point-blank at the castle.

The shells forced Helmut Dettinger and the other Germans down again into the cellar of the castle, where they were almost blinded by the grit and dust showered on them by the explosions. Holes were blasted in the solid walls. It seemed as if their last hour had arrived. Finally, an eighteen-year-old soldier lost his nerve, ripped his tunic off and shouted: "I want to live!" His comrades watched him with stupefaction. The boy tied his shirt to his rifle and, standing up in the cellar's exit, started waving it. The other Fallschirmjäger shook off their lethargy and one after another left the cellar under the protection of the waving flag. If the survivors of A Company had had their way, they would have shot all the Germans on the spot. Tankmen of the Hussars intervened, however, and saved their lives. On the double the prisoners were driven in front of a menacing tank toward the road to Stokt.

In the meantime, C Company had managed to hold on to the southern edge of the village. They had rushed a few fortified houses and had lost three officers. Many British and German killed and wounded were lying in the trenches. Medical aid could not be given because the access road to the village was covered by German artillery fire from the opposite bank of the Maas.

By 1500 hours, the tanks, no longer hampered by the castle in their rear, approached the western edge of the village, continuously firing their guns and machine guns. Sixty men from D Company left their cover and dashed after the tanks, slithering along on the muddy field. Nearing the trench system, the attackers started throwing hand grenades at the defenders, and these were often thrown back at them. The tanks plowed through the gardens, and house after house was attacked and taken by small groups of infantry. Within an hour all organized resistance had ceased and fifty Germans had surrendered.

Not until then were the sad remnants of D Company relieved from their precarious position, but the roads were in such a bad state that it was well after midnight before the wounded could be taken to the rear.

In the early morning, the number of prisoners had risen to over 100, although an unknown number of Germans managed to get back across the Maas. Three captured Monmouths were forced to join the Germans in their rubber boat. It was too small to hold them all and the British were put overboard in shallow water and left there. Dripping wet, they returned to their unit.

The sacrifice made by the Monmouth Battalion in this action was the bloodiest of the whole Peel campaign. Of the three companies — about 300 men — which carried out the attack, 140 were killed, wounded or missing. D Company, which took the village of Broek-huizen, suffered only two killed and 15 wounded. The battalion commander, the commanding officers of A and C Companies and five other officers were killed. Seventy percent of these units were put out of action.

Broekhuizen is an example of overestimation of one's own strength and underestimation of what a determined, well-entrenched enemy is capable of.

★   ★   ★

The 3rd Division also found a castle in its way. But here its capture would cost hardly any human lives. It is its wanton destruction that makes one wonder whether this was really necessary from a military point of view. On November 24, a group of Bren gun carriers came across a few horse-drawn carts east of Venray. They held a group of refugees from the German lines: 12 children and 10 adults, among them Baron and Baroness De Weichs de Wenne. The day before, they had left their Geysteren Castle under the protection of a white flag. This proud building stood between Maashees and Wanssum on the left bank of the river. It had gone through wars before; it had been occupied by Dutch troops in 1580 in the Dutch-Spanish War, retaken five years later by the Spaniards, deserted a fortnight later and burned down. Not until safer times arrived, with the Peace of Münster, was it rebuilt with an inner court that was unique in Holland — a square with three arcades, each side supported by Tuscan pillars.

De Weichs de Wenne, whose Westphalian ancestors had owned Geysteren Castle for nearly 150 years, was not only the owner of large areas of land, he was also the Mayor of the Municipality of Meerlo and Wanssum and an honorary chamberlain to Queen Wilhelmina. Because of his German ancestry and his having studied in Germany, he had received permission in World War I to volunteer for the Kaiser's army. He was wounded in Alsace. His past, however, did not prevent the Germans during the occupation of Holland from arresting him in 1943 and holding him as a hostage for a time in a camp at Haaren.

At the end of September, Kampfgruppe Walther had established its HQ at the castle. Walther, a rude fellow according to De Weichs de Wenne, showed great respect for Herr Baron, which was understandable: the Dutchman was a tall man of fifty-six, with aristocratic features, who, as an ex-officer with combat experience, could bellow at the Germans in their own language. Thus Herr Baron succeeded in talking the Germans out of their plans to evacuate the populations of Meerlo and Wanssum across the Mass to Germany. His own family, including a number of people who had been hiding at the castle from the Germans, and a few other refugees, were allowed to stay. All the household activities, however, were to take place in the cellars of the castle. Once a day the children were taken into the courtyard, where De Weichs de Wenne made them go through a program of physical exercises to the tune of patriotic songs.

A varying number of Germans occupied the beautiful rooms upstairs. Staffs came and went. On the whole the Germans behaved correctly — sometimes even more than that. One day the *Grune Polizei,* who systematically combed out the area in their manhunts, were stopped in the front courtyard and not allowed to enter the building: "Halt! Military Area!" On the neighboring farm, called the Spiekert, Fallschirmjäger had placed a crate on top of the trap door under which a number of people were hiding from the Germans. Whenever the *Grune Polizei* raided the place, the soldiers would be sitting around the crate playing an innocent card game. The household of De Weichs de Wenne used to receive food from the field kitchen: every day a shell provided meat from a killed animal.

But then again, the Germans could be less friendly. During nightly drinking bouts the family often heard the Germans smashing valuable furniture and glasswork or breaking the large Louis XV mirror to pieces. This was merely a prelude to the total destruction that was to follow. One evening, a German unit passing through had occupied the cellar next to the one in which De Weichs de Wenne's family was staying, in order to recover from the hardships at the front. Suddenly a British shell crashed through the wall and exploded among the soldiers, setting off their ammunition stacked against the cellar walls. The explosion blocked the cellar exit. The screams and moans of the wounded soldiers could clearly be heard in the adjacent cellar.

De Weichs de Wenne, realizing that nobody was coming to help the men, decided to go upstairs. The other cellar could be reached via a trapdoor on the terrace. On opening the door, De Weichs de Wenne saw a horrible sight. A few survivors rushed past him into the open air, covered with blood from themselves and from their comrades. Some were in such a state of panic that they jumped into the Maas. The Baron had to use all his persuasive powers to get a medical orderly to give first aid: "That's not a unit of ours, you see." With the Germans themselves unwilling to help, a few civilians started clearing up the cellar. The children were kept away from the scene. Wheelbarrows with torn-off limbs and bloody remains were rolled out of the cellar. Ten bodies were recovered.

Worried to death, the family tried to make the best of it in the cellar, which was lit by a small oil lamp. The older people kept their thoughts to themselves but they realized that their chances of survival were very slim.

In the early hours of November 21, sixty Fallschirmjäger entered the castle. A subaltern was in command, with five other subalterns under him. One of them was an Austrian, Walter Pens, who was in charge of the staff section. He informed the Baron of their disastrous plans: Geysteren Castle was to be defended to the last bullet. Pens seemed to be very concerned about the art treasures of the castle. "Could we not try to save at least your collection of paintings?" De Weichs de Wenne showed him a hiding place in the ducts of the heating system in the cellar. It was also agreed that the family silver should be stored in a safe.

On trying to lock the steel door, the key broke and the safe remained unlocked. The Baron fetched the German commander. The latter had his men lined up in front of the safe. "Anyone who dares to take anything out of this safe will be shot." Not an idle threat. At about the same time, a Fallschirmjäger near Broekhuizen, who was caught in the act of taking a wristwatch from a prisoner, was executed on the spot — in sharp contrast with the habits of the British soldiers described earlier, who on this point completely disregarded the Geneva Convention.

On November 24, all the inhabitants of the castle safely reached the British lines, where the Baron gave out very useful information. He argued desperately that there was only a relatively small group of some sixty men inside the castle; they had hardly any food supplies and were unlikely to receive any from the other side of the Maas. He insisted that the castle be surrounded and the defenders starved into surrender. But his plea fell on deaf ears. The day after his risky crossing of the line, the first shells were fired at Geysteren. On November 25, D Company of the Suffolks advanced toward the castle. Their attack was preceded by an air raid by Typhoons. But a sudden hailstorm prevented the planes from locating their target, which had been marked by the artillery with red smoke. By the end of the afternoon the infantry attacked. Walter Pens saw them come nearer. The Fallschirmjäger held their fire to the very last moment. The Suffolks suffered twelve casualties, two of them fatal.

One of the killed was Dr. Erwin Rothbart, a thirty-two-year-old lecturer from Cambridge, a pioneer in the field of econometrics. Being a German Jew, he had emigrated to England, where he made a quick scientific career and, after a brief internment as a "German," volunteered in 1943 under the assumed name of "Rivers." Rothbart died near his PIAT and, though mortally wounded, he still tried to help a wounded comrade.

A few days earlier he had written in a letter to England: "Compared with the majority of the men who are here 'because there's a war on,' I have the privilege of knowing why I'm fighting. I say this without any feelings of complacency. It is a fact and it is a great help. To me this chaotic killing and suffering is not meaningless. My feelings do not depend on the outcome of the war. Fighting this war has been worthwhile, simply because it gives mankind an opportunity to solve its problems, which is a very valuable thing, even if nobody has any great expectations of what people will make of it."

And in another letter: "Since my previous letter we've had a rough time. I was greatly relieved to realize that if you know what you're fighting for it really helps to overcome the primitive anger that fills any normal being when he is suddenly faced with the real death that lurks behind the soothing mechanism of orders, positions and movements according to plan."

In spite of the casualties, the second-in-command of the Suffolks Battalion wanted to pursue the attack. But Hugh Merriam, commander of D Company, refused to obey the order: he felt that it would end in a bloodbath.

The Germans had also suffered casualties. The same morning, a patrol sent out to the edge of the village had been ambushed. The Germans managed to bring back their four dead comrades. They were wrapped in canvas and laid in one of the pillared arcades of the main courtyard because the artillery fire was too heavy to bury them properly outside the castle walls.

In the meantime, the water level of the Maas kept rising. The castle became isolated from the land and the Fallschirmjäger were forced to abandon their positions in the castle park. There were fifty-two men left on November 26.

That day, the first air raid was made. Ten Typhoons fired away at Geysteren Castle with rockets and machine guns. There was a great deal of deliberation on the English side that Sunday: the brigade commander not only wanted to use infantry, but artillery, air force and tanks as well in a final effort to take the castle. On November 27 Churchill tanks from the Coldstream Guards took up positions in sight of the castle. But their 6-pounder and 75 mm guns failed to blast holes in the thick walls; only tanks fitted with a 95 mm gun were able to do so, and hence a Panther tank captured by the battalion near Venray and appropriately nicknamed "Cuckoo" joined in the shelling.

The small German garrison suffered more casualties. During that night a few severely wounded men were ferried across the Maas — "only to die there," Walter Pens mused. An air attack was postponed because of the weather.

The next day, watched by a great many curious spectators and reporters, the integral program could at last be performed. At nine o'clock in the morning two squadrons of tanks began to fire, joined until lunchtime by the artillery. In the afternoon, shell after shell continued to hit the unfortunate castle. Then two waves of seven Typhoons attacked, each dropping 1,000-pound bombs. Spellbound, the spectators watched how the leading airplane swooped low over their heads firing its guns at the castle. The first bomb hit the building. Red-colored clouds of dust rose into the air. One bomb fell closer to the public "grandstand" than to the target, and with German shells from across the Maas falling all over the place the audience hastily scurried for any muddy hole they could find. Six bombs were direct hits on the castle.

That evening the *Daily Mail* printed the heading: "Tanks and Typhoons in the strangest battle of the war: castle surrounded by moat mocks British Army. Germans fight from castle's parapets with bazookas and mortars." A more down-to-earth entry in the 3rd Division's diary said: "The castle is receiving radio and press publicity out of all proportion to its military significance."

Geysteren Castle was in the process of being turned into a rubble heap. The west wall of the pillared arcade had collapsed, finally burying the four dead Germans. A cross was placed on top. The tower had partly collapsed and could no longer be used as an OP for the artillery on the east bank of the Maas. The heaviest weapons inside the castle were a few mortars and two heavy machine guns. In the garden there were still three or four men in outposts, up to their knees in water. In the house only the cellars remained fit for use. The meager food supplies stored in the kitchen could no longer be used because of a collapsed wall. A few Fallschirmjäger had almost been trapped in one of the cellars but had managed to get away to safety by climbing through a window and crossing a steel girder, whereupon they jumped into their foxholes again. The German regimental HQ asked in vain for permission to withdraw. The order still stood as before: fight to the last man.

In the evening, D Company of the Suffolks advanced once more toward the castle. On their approach a flare went up and machine guns commenced firing. An entry in the war diary of 8 Brigade read: "Those Jerries cannot be finished off!" The British did not know that during the night the German regimental commander had crossed the river in a speedboat to pay a visit to Geysteren Castle. He spent two hours with the men underneath the steadily crumbling ceiling of the cellar. When he left, he promised to plead with his superiors to abandon the castle.

The spectacle was continued on November 29. Again, tanks and artillery hurled shells through the sad ruins and once more Typhoons—two this time—roared over low to drop their bombs. Later, four more Typhoons fired their rockets and guns at the castle and its surroundings. By dusk the Germans were summoned by loudspeakers to surrender. There was no reply. That same evening the decision was made to storm Geysteren Castle during the night by assault boat. A company of the Suffolks assembled at the edge of the flooded castle park and six boats were carried toward the water. But a German shell fired from the east bank of the Maas damaged five boats. Not until midnight did another five or six arrive from the rear. The tanks started harassing fire in order to mislead the German artillery. The boats crossed the water and the infantry stormed the northeast wall of the castle.

Then came the anti-climax. The castle was found to be deserted. A few hours before, the survivors, in the nick of time, had been ferried across the Maas under cover of artillery fire. One of the shells fell short, blowing off both feet of the last two Germans to leave the castle. Their comrades bandaged their wounds as best they could in the dark and carried them to the boats. One of the two lost so much blood that he died on reaching the other side.

At sunrise on November 30, the Austrian subaltern Walter Pens turned around and looked back at the sad ruins of Geysteren Castle among the bare treetops on the other side of the river. A feeling of deep sadness and anger about the war overwhelmed him as he walked away from the Mass toward an unknown future.

Neither the castle of Geysteren nor that of Broekhuizen have been rebuilt since the war. Among the ruins, De Weichs de Wenne found all his paintings: Pens had carefully removed the frames and safely stored the canvasses in the place pointed out to him. He also dug up the safe, with all the silver—bent by the heat—still inside. British soldiers out on a patrol watched his recovery of the hidden items with such a wistful look in their eyes that he wisely decided to keep a close watch on the goods.

In a niche he found the roll-call lists of the Fallschirmjäger for November 25 and 26. It had been their senseless defense of Geysteren Castle that had induced the British to destroy it. Had its *destruction* been as senseless? From a military point of view, the tower of the castle was an artillery OP for the Germans and its destruction was necessary. But this might also have been achieved by demolishing the tower with guns firing at close range. Instead, the total destruction of this irreplaceable monument had become a matter of prestige to the British.

★   ★   ★

The only bridgehead on the west bank of the Maas now left to the Germans was "Festung Blerick." They had worked for months to turn Blerick into a fortress and they had every reason to be proud of it. The "Festung" ran around Blerick in a crescent shape with the Maas in its rear; it was three miles long and its greatest depth was one and a half miles. The garrison numbered some 300 men, strongly entrenched. A deep anti-tank ditch formed the outer barrier of the fortress, protected by double or triple barbed-wire entanglements, a number of minefields and a trench system with strongpoints. Nearly every house had been incorporated into the defense system.

There was no way back for the defenders, for what thirteen Allied air attacks had been unable to accomplish the Germans themselves did on November 25: they blew up the Maas bridges between Venlo and Blerick. On the higher east bank of the river some 100 guns had been massed and pointed their muzzles at the low-lying, bare fields on the other side of the river. The attackers, on the other hand, had to descend from the Blerick hillocks toward the river, without any cover, and within firing range of the Germans.

At the end of November, the 15th Scottish Division had taken over this front sector from the 49th Infantry Division. It was the Scottish Division's 44th Brigade that was ordered to wipe out this last German stronghold west of the Maas. At first glance, it was a far from enviable task.

The brigade commander, General Cummings-Bruce, came up with an ingenious plan, mentally putting himself in the place of the German defenders. The obvious place to expect the British attack was in the northwest. There the anti-tank ditch was cut by the railway tracks Boxmeer-Venlo and Helmond-Benlo. Not only did the railway embankment offer some form of protection to any attackers, but there were also some woods there, the only ones in the area. Cummings-Bruce decided to make the Germans believe that the attack would be launched from there—but the real attack would come in from the west. He also wanted to fool the German artillery. The exact position of their guns was to be located, and they were to be destroyed first, before the British infantry would make its appearance.

On the night of December 1, loud noises from moving tanks were heard coming from the woods. German artillery reacted promptly and started pouring shells into the area. As the number of shells increased, the tank noises grew fainter and after some time complete silence had returned. A great success for the enemy: all armored British units had been destroyed even before the attack had begun!

The Germans did not know that the only things they had destroyed had been gramophone records. There had never been any tanks, only soundtracks of tanks. A few armored cars had carved deep tracks through the wood to make the enemy believe that a massive buildup was going on.

The next night, the Scottish patrol activity in that same area was intensified. Bangalore torpedoes blew holes in barbed-wire entanglements and the sounds of bridge-laying equipment being brought forward and of bridges being laid could clearly be heard. Again German artillery responded. And again they had been fooled by recordings. The result was twofold. The enemy batteries firing at imaginary targets had given away their positions to the British observers, which made it easy for the guns to be destroyed within a few hours when the time would come. Moreover, the Fallschirmjäger garrison was now watching in the wrong direction.

Late in the afternoon, Cummings-Bruce transferred his HQ to the vicinity of the real start line. The troops were assembled behind the Blerick hillocks. Every man knew exactly what to do. In mock-ups the whole operation had been rehearsed. The attack was to be preceded by an artillery barrage, not only from the 72 25-pounders of the division but from the artillery of the whole corps as well, some 400 guns in all. The attack was to be supported by a squadron of Churchills and two reinforced squadrons of flail tanks, each with bridge-laying and fascine-carrying tanks and two sorts of armored vehicles rarely used in this theatre of war: Crocodiles and Kangaroos. The former were flame-throwing Churchill tanks, the latter served as infantry carriers.

First the Churchills, firing all their guns, were to drive straight up to the anti-tank ditch. Then the battalions of Royal Scots and Royal Scots Fuseliers were to advance in their Kangaroos through lanes cleared of mines by six flail tanks. They were not to leave the carriers until they had reached the streets of Blerick, whereupon the Kangaroos were to drive back quickly to pick up the other two battalions that were to form the second wave of attack. The Crocodiles would have to intervene in the street fighting. The attack was to start in the early morning of Sunday, December 3.

On Saturday afternoon it began to rain again, soaking the already wet ground. Would tanks be able to get through? There was some uncertainty as to whether the attack could go ahead or not, but at 2100 hours that evening the rain ceased and the commander of XII Corps, General Neil Ritchie, gave the go-ahead at midnight. Plan "Guildford" could proceed.

The crews of the two squadrons of flail tanks tried to get some sleep inside the cold, damp hulls. Here and there guns were firing, seemingly at random. By the light of the moon, preparations for the attack commenced at 0300. Red pilot lights glowed on the electric circuits. Headphones began to crackle as the wireless sets were tuned. With stiff fingers, the crews of the flails and tanks checked their instruments, the faint smell of gasoline and engine oil mingling in the cold night air.

Two hours later the engines were started, white vapor plumes trailing behind the exhausts. Searchlights were switched on—Monty's moonlight—which paled the light of the moon. The flails slowly began to move ahead. Now and then, gunfire sounded in the distance and sometimes a flare soared nervously into the sky. Yet again the Limburg mud took its toll. On their way to the starting line the tanks of one squadron bogged down. A whole troop had to be replaced. The other squadron, with the loss of one flail tank, safely reached the start line.

By 0530 the British artillery unleashed all its fury. And the targets were known, thanks to the excellent cooperation from the German batteries, whose end was now near. At 0745 the guns switched to the opening line of the barrage, moving forward 100 yards every two minutes. Smoke shells were dropped on Venlo to hamper German observations. Shells poured down into "Festung Blerick," not just from ordinary artillery but also from Bofors ack-ack guns which fired shrapnel shells that exploded in the air with a sharp bang, spreading lethal fragments over the area. The Canadians had lent the British a new weapon: six of their rocket launchers, nicknamed "mattresses," each of which fired 350 shells at a time, covering an area of 200 square yards.

The German defenses could not be breached everywhere. In the center of the attacked sector all efforts failed. Too many flail tanks had bogged down there. In most places heavy German fire was encountered. Shells, mortar bombs, machine guns and bazookas fired from the trenches. In the northern lanes, tank crews were sometimes forced to abandon their tanks to assist in towing them out of the mud. But by 1015 most of the tanks had entered the anti-tank ditch and kept firing away, waiting for the infantry. It took 45 minutes before the Kangaroos came rolling through the breaches.

Not all went according to plan. The Royal Scots safely reached the outskirts of Blerick in their Kangaroos. But those carrying the Scots Fuseliers threatened to bog down in the mud. The battalion commander made a risky decision. As he had not encountered any German fire yet in his corner, he decided to let his men dismount and allow them to advance on foot inside the anti-tank ditch. Otherwise the delay might cause the other two battalions to arrive too late in Blerick.

By doing so, all four battalions managed to enter Blerick on schedule.

To the troops mopping up, Blerick was a maze of small, winding streets, but after the first few barriers had been taken, German resistance was found to dwindle rapidly. The German artillery and mortars on the east bank were fully aware by now of what was going on in Blerick and they began to saturate the place with shells and mortar bombs, which caused casualties among the Scots. By 1600 hours, however, all organized resistance had collapsed. With the Borderers bringing in their last prisoners that evening, the total bag was 250. A small number of Germans had managed to get away across the Maas.

The Scots were now standing on the bank of the Maas and were able to look into Venlo. The last operation west of the Maas had been completed and was already proclaimed to have been the "perfect battle." In the future it would be a favorite subject at military academies. And for good reason: "Guildford," because of the cunning plans of Cummings-Bruce and by brilliantly coordinated teamwork by artillery, engineers, tanks and infantry, had cost no more than 22 killed, 85 wounded and 12 men missing. On that day in Blerick, more than 3,000 civilians crawled out of their cellars, where they had survived the artillery bombardments.

From entries in diaries kept by citizens of Venlo, which also suffered heavily from the artillery fire, we know how nerve-racking the bombardment must have been for the population of Blerick. Gijs Bertels noted in his diary: "Volleys of shells slammed into the town: from afar, from nearby. Ominously nearby, in rapidly increasing succession, until a hurricane of steel and fire raged over our heads. There seemed to be no end to it. Every Sunday for the past few weeks has been full of misery. This Sunday is pure hell, with one continuous roar of exploding shells. Sometimes a direct hit briefly drowned the hissing and moaning sound made by shells, followed by the noise of breaking roof tiles and windows and chunks of masonry falling down. Thousands have spent this Sunday without food in unlit cellars, closely packed together, standing on cases and boards because of the groundwater. Over our heads our homes were blown to pieces, but in spite of this and the danger we were in, we lived in the expectation that our liberation was at hand."

Many shared the same feeling. One of them was the ex-teacher mentioned earlier, who had found shelter at a farm south of Venlo. Mass was read in the large kitchen that Sunday. Never before had the words of Luke 21 been more appropriate as on this day with the guns roaring in the background: "Upon the earth men will faint with terror at the thought of all that is coming upon the world, for the powers of Heaven shall be shaken. And when these things begin to come to pass, then stand upright, and lift up your heads, for your liberation draws nigh."

In Tegelen, another suburb of Venlo, young Anna Werps attended early Mass in the cellar of the St. Anthony Monastery. After making an act of contrition, 250 refugees received general absolution while having a cup of coffee and a sandwich. During lunch the news came: the English had crossed the Maas, there was street fighting going on in Venlo. "Our shouts of hurrah and clapping of hands were quickly silenced lest the Germans might be provoked."

The truth was different as recorded by Bertels: "When toward noon the intensity of the firing grew weaker and one could hear occasional small-arms fire only, we were convinced that the British had crossed the Maas and would soon make their appearance in the streets of Venlo. After five hours, a kind of hush fell over the town. We were able to relax again and look outside. Not a house was undamaged, roof tiles gone, walls pitted with bullet holes, windows broken. Direct hits and near misses—but no Tommies."

As another citizen of Venlo jotted down on that 3rd of December: "A day of joyful expectation which ended in despair." For Venlo's deliverance was still far from near.

CHAPTER TWELVE

WINTER ORDEAL AND LIBERATION

B Y DECEMBER, the Dutch in the German-occupied area of the province of Limburg on the east bank of the Maas had given up every hope of an early liberation. Venlo and Roermond would have to wait another three months before the last German would be gone.

During those three months the population suffered terribly, and most other Dutchmen have, to date, remained ignorant of the hardships the Limburgers on the east bank had to endure. A detailed account of the fate of this unliberated area behind a static front line is beyond the scope of this book; however a few figures speak for themselves. Of the 26,000 citizens of Venlo it is estimated that 11,500 were forced to leave the town in the bitterly cold third week of January 1945, stumbling through the snow on the slippery road to Kaldenkirchen and Straelen in Germany. Often they had to wait there for days in primitive makeshift accommodations before being carried elsewhere in unheated freight cars so crowded that people had to stand all the way; only the sick, the elderly and children could lie down. The train journey lasted from 24 to 48 hours, a journey into the unknown, the refugees being unaware of their final destination.

In Venlo at least 14,000 people defied the evacuation orders given by SS Colonel Leffler. In Roermond the situation was different. There Fallschirmjäger Major Ulrich Mattheas had 13 people who were found to be hiding executed on December 26 after a so-called "drumhead" court martial. At the same time, he announced that every man between 16 and 60 years of age who had not reported to the German authorities by December 30 for work in Germany would be treated likewise. The result was that 2,800 men, intimidated by the German threat, reported and left on foot that same day for Germany on a bitterly cold night.

The remaining 17,000 citizens of Roermond received the order for a mass evacuation on January 19. Nearly 13,000 of them walked for 13 miles through severe cold to Brüggen in Germany to wait for a train. Nobody knew where they were going. When the trains had left, they were repeatedly attacked from the air on their slow journey through a Germany that was already in chaos. At least twenty-five evacuees were killed, not including the babies and sick who did not survive the journey. All this made a mockery of the instructions given by Himmler in his telex message which authorized his SS to carry on with the evacuation of civilians of Limburg, stating: "The people must be treated well as you should bear in mind that they are of the Germanic race and will be part of the German Reich in the future!"

Most Limburgers found a place to stay in the three northern provinces of Holland. Their exact number is unknown, the most reliable estimate being 70,000. Their deserted homes were looted and pillaged by soldiers and sometimes by citizens as well, though not as systematically as the German pillage of Arnhem. In Venlo in particular there was a shortage of all the necessities of daily life. Gijs Bertels, quoted before, had a job with the food-supply organization and cites a few moving examples in his book *Die Swaere Noodt*: "Not only food shortages, but also lack of fuel, power and water. Coal stocks were depleted; the power supply from the Krefeld power station in Germany was very erratic and broke down completely for 21 days. The water supply broke down as well and people had to make do with eleven wells in Venlo." The town was in a state of indescribable squalor, and it is a miracle that prevailing diseases like dysentery, in combination with malnutrition and physical exhaustion, claimed relatively few victims.

In Roermond, now practically deserted, the situation was somewhat better. The town had not suffered so much from acts of war as Venlo, where friend and foe could see and hear each other on either side of the Maas. Throughout the Dutch river area where the front had been stabilized, both sides restricted their activities to patrolling.

On December 16, in the Ardennes forest to the south, three American divisions, supposedly in a quiet sector, were taken completely by surprise by an unusually large and ferocious German counteroffensive. In various tactical details, though on a much larger scale, it resembled a repeat of the unexpected German counterstroke near Meyel. This time the entire Allied front reacted to the threat, though it was not until ten days later that the great "Bulge" created in the American front was stabilized.

On New Year's Day, the Germans added a series of "afterburners" to their offensive (which by then had already failed its strategic purpose). A surprise attack in the nature of a swan song by the Luftwaffe against Dutch and Belgian airfields took place, and several counterattacks recovered ground in the northeast of Alsace and, to a lesser degree, on the Maas front. This was operation *Schneemann* (Snowman). There the Germans established their *Brückenkopf Wanssum* (Wanssum Bridgehead), much publicized in the Nazi press, in the sector guarded by the British 3rd Division. The South Lancashire Battalion lost dozens of killed and wounded in an attack on the wooded area between Wanssum and Blitterswijk, where German grenadiers had dug in. In cruel weather conditions these Germans were supplied from across the Maas by inflatable rubber boats and small motor craft.

Two companies from the Suffolks were given the task of wiping out the bridgehead, within sight of the enemy's artillery observers on the opposite bank of the Maas. The men were carried into the battle area in Kangaroos. Their attack commenced on January 8 in a severe blizzard. The supporting tanks kept sliding off the road, but luckily the bad weather prevented the German artillery from intervening. When the tanks were getting ready to shell the wood, they found the Germans keen to surrender. The Suffolks took 20 prisoners and counted 136 dead Germans inside the wood, nearly three times as many as their own casualties in killed and wounded.

During the winter, regular Dutch forces — Stoottroepen — made their appearance on the Maas. The British admired their fighting spirit, which was not affected by their being underarmed or by their shabby uniforms. Lacking proper winter clothing, a soldier on sentry duty frequently had to be taken back to his billets numb with cold.

In the meantime, the front south of Roermond began to move on January 15. Within two weeks the British XII Corps drove the enemy from what was called the "Sittard Pocket," or the "Roermond Triangle." Snow and ice hampered the advance. The first objectives were Susteren and Echt. The main attack was launched on January 16 when the British 7th Armored Division, known in North Africa as the "Desert Rats," swung to the northeast toward the German town of Heinsberg. By this maneuver Montgomery hoped to cut off the bulk of the enemy divisions in that area from the river Roer. But here again it was the Fallschirmjäger (including Regiment-Hübner) which delayed the British armor. Heinsberg did not fall until January 24. Thereafter, the British advance through the Dutch border villages encountered fierce opposition, and it took two days of tough fighting before the village of St. Joost could be liberated. Simply disastrous was what happened to the village of Montfort. So many refugees had tried to find shelter there that the population had grown from 1,700 to nearly 7,000. Three days of artillery fire and air bombardment had pulverized the village. One hundred and eighty-three people were killed, placing Montfort at the top of the list, along with Vierlingsbeek and Breskens, in fatalities. A very questionable sacrifice, for, although there were Germans around the village there were hardly any inside. Why, then, this senseless destruction? Initially the orders were to block the routes of communication, but eventually the fliers reported, "Village obliterated, nothing left but rubble and smoke," thus implying what their mission had actually become.

The badly damaged village of St. Odiliënberg was liberated on January 28, as was Linne. North of the latter, the Fallschirmjäger held on to their positions on the south bank of the Roer River. Montgomery disregarded this narrow strip of ground and considered the operation finished. The sector was then transferred to the American Ninth Army.

During the last days of January the British 3rd Division, and south of them the 11th Armoured Division, received orders to increase their patrolling activities. These nightly reconnaissance trips across the Maas, based on information from Dutch line-crossers who often paid for crossing the Maas with their lives, had not been planned merely to keep the troops out of mischief. Their main objective was to divert

German attention from the sector between Nijmegen and Mook, where Montgomery had already made preparations for an attack in early October — since then twice postponed, the last time because of the Ardennes offensive. He was planning for the final major offensive against the Germans to be launched from the Nijmegen sector.

Montgomery and Bradley were to work closely together in this battle for the Rhineland. Montgomery was to attack in the north on February 8 and two days later the Americans were to cross the Roer. Thus the Allies hoped to trap a large German force west of the Rhine and to lure the German High Command into a decisive battle that would deplete their last resources in men and equipment.

From a tactical point of view the Allied operation did not develop according to plan. Bradley had to postpone his attack across the Roer until February 23; the Germans had blown up a dam which made it impossible for the river to be bridged due to the high water level. The Canadian, Scottish and English Divisions in the north had to fight hard for every yard of German soil. Among the British divisions were those which had fought their way through the Peel and Maas areas. Strategically, however, the Allied plan was a complete success. The battle for the Rhineland, which was fought between February 8 and March 10, was the last phase of the campaign on the western front where the Germans still maintained a cohesive defense.

The place where the Allies were expected to attack was a matter of dispute within the German Command. Both the Supreme Commander on the western front, Field Marshal von Rundstedt, and General Blaskowitz, Commander of the Army holding the Dutch sector, were of the opinion that the Allies would attack in the south: first, the Americans south of Roermond; then, the British near Venlo. Beyond Venlo the 7th Fallschirmjäger Army had dug in. Its commander had been the only one who believed that the main thrust would be made between Mook and Gennep. When the Canadians did actually attack in this sector on February 8, even if a little farther to the north than he had predicted, it took more than twenty-four hours before he was given permission to transfer his Fallschirmjäger from Venlo to the Reichswald.

Why this desperate last stand by the Germans *west* of the Rhine, a natural barrier behind which they could easily have withdrawn as a coherent force? Not only had Hitler categorically forbidden any withdrawal behind the Rhine, but von Rundstedt, too, was convinced that there was no other choice. He had to stand and fight in the Rhineland because any retreat behind the great river would render it useless as a supply line for the Ruhr industrial area, which was so vital to the German war effort.

As part of the attack on the Reichswald, the 51st Highland Division, and thereafter the 52nd Lowland Division, advanced along the east bank of the Maas. The 51st took Gennep, which had been deserted ever since October. The 52nd encountered fierce opposition near Afferden. Following two days of fighting, the Scots captured the village on February 17. But beyond Afferden there was an anti-tank ditch within firing range from the Castle of Bleyenbeek. At first it appeared that the story of Broekhuizen would repeat itself. A mere 20 Fallschirmjäger armed only with machine guns defended the old castle so skillfully that the Scots, first a platoon, then a whole battalion, were beaten off with heavy casualties.

Sadly, on February 21 and 22, however, it was the episode of Geysteren Castle that was repeated. Four squadrons of Typhoons fired their rockets at the castle and finally razed it to the ground with 22 500-pound bombs. Aerial photographs of the destruction, greatly enlarged, were presented to Churchill in person as "the classic attack of the week." Even so, the advance bogged down again beyond Bleyenbeek. At the same time, the American offensive across the Ruhr had been launched. Unlike Montgomery's forces they met crumbling opposition. From their bridgeheads, three corps of the American 9th Army advanced to the northeast. Field Marshal Model, who time and again had salvaged near-hopeless situations for Hitler, committed suicide in the ruins of the Ruhr.

The people still living in the Maas area longed for the hour of liberation. But in spite of this piece of good news Mien Meelkop entered in her diary on February 26: "We no longer rejoice at whatever good news we hear, afraid as we are to be disappointed again."

The next day, however, when Gys Bertels (who was still running trucks to supply Venlo with food) was making a trip to Roermond, he saw scenes that made him realize the end of the German occupation was near: disorderly bands of front-line soldiers dragging carts loaded with furniture and sheep. During the night on his return trip he saw "guns, a slowly moving column of trucks, a fast car with officers," and finally, near Keldenkirchen: "men on foot, in small, scattered groups, heavily loaded, plodding on in the night. Sitting on our flour sacks in the truck we peered into the darkness, wondering who those passing figures were. Suddenly we realized that they were members of the *Grüne Polizei* from Venlo."

Shells began to fall in the streets of Roermond during the last few days of February, this time American ones. XVI Corps of the Ninth Army was to advance northward across the river to protect the left flank of the tank spearheads which, far to the rear of the German front on the Maas, were pushing ahead and posed a threat to Mönchen-Gladbach. These were to contact the British and Canadian forces approaching Kevelaer. On February 26, Americans forced their way into the small German bridgehead on the Maas southwest of the mouth of the Roer.

In Roermond the Germans knew that they were on the point of being trapped, and made preparations to abandon the town while the escape route to the Fatherland was still open. In the wake of the German evacuation a demolition squad entered the town. Explosions shattered the relative quiet on this last morning of February. The bridge over the Roer was no longer there. The power station and the town's telephone exchange were destroyed. An explosion ripped the tower of the Gothic cathedral in half, the two columns of stone rising above the rooftops like a huge tuning fork.

The Mariamunster Church, one of the unique Romanesque monuments in Holland, was, oddly enough, spared. Why? An eye-witness stated that the demolition squad hesitated to get near the church that afternoon because American shells were dropping close by. Another story has it that the same squad, upon informing the deputy mayor that the church was to be blown up, was invited by him to have a drink first, which resulted in the squad's soon becoming incapable of carrying out its task. So both Roermond and Venlo entered the night unaware that this was to be the last of their ordeal.

In the early morning of March 1 the first vehicles of the 15th Reconnaissance Squadron reached the demolished age-old bridge over the river which led to the southern town center of Roermond. It was strangely quiet in the town. When it grew lighter, a sergeant, Vincent van Hencke, cautiously crawled across the ruins of the bridge to the other side of the river. Not an enemy in sight. More soldiers followed him. There were plenty of roadblocks in the streets, but no shots were fired. Within no time the Americans were surrounded by civilians, awakened from a restless sleep in their cellars by unusual noises. They warned the soldiers about mines in the roads. No vehicles could reach the town center and the Americans had to enter it on foot. The highest Dutch authority still in the town was the public prosecutor. He welcomed the Americans with a speech in the courtyard of the City Hall.

From the southeast vehicles could enter the town without any problem. Another recce unit drove past the *Eiermijn* (Egg Market) where some 500 people were waiting for their liberators. In the cold store, Pierre Willems, a Red Cross worker, was serving as an acolyte at early Mass. A fellow citizen came in and whispered in his ear: "Pierre, the Americans are here, we're free!" The acolyte tugged at the priest's sleeve and told him the happy news. Later Willems said: "I've never known Mass being read so quickly. We went outside. Two armored cars were standing opposite the Egg Market. There they were at last, the Americans. At first we did not know for sure whether we were free. They were recce cars, the men taking a quick look and likely to dash off again. They gave us cigarettes. Deeply inhaling the strong tobacco smoke, I thought I would faint."

In the convent of Kloosterwand the head of the Red Cross told the news to the Mother Superior of the Sisters of Mercy. She hurried down into the crypt where the sisters and a number of refugees had been sheltered during the bombardments. They embraced one another, sang and danced. During evensong the *Te Deum* was sung in the crypt chapel. The Americans were welcomed enthusiastically and were given wine that had been hidden from the looting Germans. Nurses and sick people received full-cream milk, corned beef, biscuits — unheard-of luxuries in those days.

The deputy head of police warned that the hospitals were overcrowded and that mines and booby traps had been planted all over the town. After the liberation these fiendish devices were to kill nine citizens. Household refuse had not been collected for months and lay scattered in the streets. There was no gas, no power, no water. But everywhere the red, white, blue and orange flags were fluttering in the wind, as a correspondent of the Dutch Press Agency reported in London after his visit to Roermond.

In the meantime, the American XVI Corps had dispatched units of its 8th Armored Division and its 35th Infantry Division north, to Venlo. Before noon, the 784th Tank Battalion crossed the border near Kaldenkirchen, so the liberators, followed by infantry from the 35th Division, entered the town from an unexpected direction, the east.

"A mild spring day," reported Bertels in his diary. "The air seemed to be filled with a strange tension. Toward four o'clock there was shouting in the distance with people running excitedly in that direction. It couldn't be, I couldn't believe there were shouts of Americans being in our town. Was this a joke?"

Heavy tanks had parked beneath the trees on the Kaldenkirchen road. Broad Negro faces peered outside, their eyes filled with suspicion. How were they to know that this strip of ground was Dutch soil? Some tanks carried a crucifix in front. Infantrymen appeared from behind the tanks and almost noiselessly entered the town on their rubber soles. The signs "*Achtung Minen*" near the German roadblocks came as a complete surprise. There was an exchange of bullets across the neglected rose garden of the town. Tanks hurtled shells through the railway shed near the Pope lamp factory, across the road into Germany and against the walls of the factory where Herr Ortskommandant (Town Commandant) was said to have his HQ. A few captured German soldiers stood trembling against a wall. Shaking with fear, they asked: "When will we be shot?" Their lieutenant had told them that the Yanks shot all their prisoners, even Red Cross soldiers. But Herr Lieutenant was no longer there to confirm his story.

All the forces available to the German Town Commandant were 200 infantrymen, mostly boys of sixteen to eighteen. Thus did "fortress" Venlo fall. The 320th Infantry Battalion combed out the town. The whole "fortress" yielded 130 prisoners who had nothing but small arms, four machine guns and one Panzerfaust.

Some people simply refused to believe the good news. At St. Joseph's Hospital a few student nurses waving orange flags ran down the steps of the crowded cellar, which was lit by bicycle lights. "We've seen Americans on the Kaldenkirchen road! Negroes, all of them with orange flags on their tanks!" But people shouted at them to shut up and, crying with disappointment, the girls went back upstairs.

From Blerick, too, liberators came to Venlo: British soldiers who had left their trenches on the west bank of the Maas and who tore down the gray fences in the ruined streets beside the river with their grim warnings: "*Achtung! Feindeinsicht!*" (Attention! You Are Under Enemy Observation!)

Liberation did not imply that everything was all right. At least that was what Jacques Guns found out, hiding at a farm northeast of Venlo. At the end of October he had helped as a volunteer in the bombed town; he had seen wounded groaning, with seeping bandages; he had carried a stretcher on which was a woman whose head had been crushed to a bloody pulp; less than two weeks ago he had had to hide from three men of the *Grüne Polizei* who had searched the farm. "I could hear my own heartbeat and the blood rushed to my head," he wrote later in his diary. But now it was all over — at least that was the way it looked.

"Suddenly we heard a few machine guns, now and then heavy explosions. People had left their homes and were standing in the streets shouting: 'They're here!' From the windows we could see the Americans on the Kaldenkirchen road. The people were wild with joy, shouting and shaking hands with one another. Flags appeared from the windows and everyone wore orange badges and our tricolor. On the corner American tanks were draped with orange and red, white and blue flags and bunting. An American climbing out of his tank was hoisted on our shoulders. We were absolutely mad with delight; even the monks danced for joy."

In the distance Jacques Guns could still see Germans. One even came down the street on a bike, quite at ease, but on seeing the American tanks he turned around. Guns, who had fled inside, went

went out into the street again. "A German in a small Red Cross car passed me. He drove on, suddenly stopped and reversed as fast as he could. The tank standing near the Waterleidingssingel fired its machine gun at it. I saw the bullets hit the road and the car. We all dashed back into the cellar. Once inside, we heard shells explode, and occasionally a direct hit on the house. We started to count: one, two, three, and after eight there were more shells and we no longer bothered to count them. Everyone was praying and our last hour seemed to have come; clouds of dust and the smell of cordite filled the cellar. Pieces of brickwork came falling down and we held wet handkerchiefs against our mouths."

After things had quieted down, Guns went upstairs. "A white flag was stuck out of the front window, and on seeing this the Yanks stopped firing. At the back of the house I climbed across a heap of rubble. There I saw the horse which had been blown out of its stable, hanging over the fence, still alive. It could not be saved, however, and with a big knife we cut its throat. It tried to stand on its legs again, stumbled and collapsed."

On March 1 the last Germans had not yet left. On either side of Venlo stragglers were trying to get away. At 9:30 in the evening the ex-teacher mentioned earlier, hiding at a farm near the German border, saw "two Jerries suddenly enter the room. They asked for boys to drive their horse wagons but were told that the boys were already driving for the Wehrmacht. The German retreat lasted all night. With stolen horses and carts, on bicycles, in prams, pushcarts, and any other vehicle one could think of, they tried to carry their loot back to Germany."

The next day tanks thundered past the farm on the road from Venlo to the German village of Straelen. Liberation had come at last to Guns' hiding place, too. On this same March 2 an armored column entered Tegelen, which had miraculously escaped mass evacuation. From the turret of the leading vehicle the column's commander sourly watched the overjoyed crowd. Why were these Germans so hypocritical as to cheer them? Then it dawned on him. "Is this Holland?" he asked. Yes, it was, and within a few moments grinning faces appeared from the tank hatches, hands were shaken, cigarettes, chewing gum and chocolate were handed out. Similar experiences were enjoyed by the people of Venlo. Barkeeper Sjang Cornet heard somebody shout:

" 'They're here! We're free!' But then Negroes with their guns at the ready and with a grim look on their faces cautiously walked past our house, taking us to be Jerries."

In Venlo, ex-Mayor Berger — one of the first mayors to resign in 1941 in protest against the Occupation — could take over civil control of the town. In January he had left his hiding place in St. Joseph's Hospital to be with his wife and children during the evacuation period, but the Resistance had managed to locate him, captured by the Germans, just before he boarded the east-bound train. He and his family had been taken by car back to a safe house outside Venlo.

Mayor Berger was faced with a tremendous task. The town had been reduced to ruins: 5,686 out of 7,420 buildings in Venlo and Blerick had been either severely damaged or destroyed. In addition, 851 horses, 6 churches, 3 schools, 31 industrial buildings and 54 business premises had been damaged beyond repair, and 441 citizens had been killed. But now it was the survivors who posed a problem. "We may not return to the *Sperrgebiet* (area out of bounds to civilians)," wrote Mien Meelkop on March 4 in her diary. "We badly want to go back, for we hear stories that the Americans are not averse to using furniture from the deserted houses as fuel, and they seem to steal a lot as well."

Food was the foremost priority. Within twenty-four hours the first trucks with food supplies arrived in Roermond. In Venlo, where the situation was worse, 30 tons of food arrived on March 2 and 3. Posters stated that there would be a free issue per person of 1,000 grams of biscuits, 250 grams of salt, 50 grams of chocolate, 250 grams of sugar, 125 grams of margarine, 1 tin of meat and vegetables, 50 grams of coffee, 1/4 bar of soap and 3 kilos of potatoes — and 1 tin of condensed milk for the children. Mien Meelkop listed all these delicacies in her diary with exclamation marks.

The last place to be liberated in the province of Limburg was Well, where the Scots were welcomed on March 3. That same day the American 35th Division made contact with forces of the First Canadian Army between the German towns of Geldern and Kevelaer. This event finally brought an end to the Peel/Maas battle. The Allies continued their advance, and in the last week of March the Rhine was forced on a broad front, supported by gigantic air landings, this time close behind the enemy lines. The lesson of Arnhem had been learned. The tank columns, without meeting opposition of any significance, could push on into the North German plain. Within six weeks Nazi Germany was destroyed for good.

On May 8, 1945, church bells were tolling all over Europe and the United States to celebrate Victory in Europe, VE-Day. Many of the Allied soldiers who had set out on their hazardous journey from the Normandy beaches did not live to see this day, however. One of them was Major "Banger" King, with whom this story started on June 6, 1944: "He that outlives this day, and comes safe home . . ." In April 1945 his jeep hit a mine. His death illustrates what many infantry officers wrote after hostilities had ended: "Those of us who fought in Normandy and survived until VE-Day could be counted on the fingers of our hands."

For many years to come the war, that had ravaged this area was to cast its shadow on a cumbersome period of reconstruction. But the dedication of the people to their own towns and villages, their devotion to the piece of land where they had lived and toiled, in due course erased practically all traces of devastation from the face of Limburg. "Out of the rubble flowers will bloom again," sang all Venlo a year later.

Outwardly today there is very little to remind one of the "forgotten battle" fought here—a "backstage' in the theatre of war. Memories, nevertheless, are still vividly alive in the minds of those whom we met when writing this book: not only the local people of those days, but also the Allied soldiers. What were your recollections of the Dutch people? we asked them. A Dutchman is loath to boast of himself or of his national spirit, and it will suffice to say simply that we have been overwhelmed with moving stories of the friendliness met in Holland, the help and hospitality, the food and drink saved for emergencies being shared with the liberators.

One quotation out of many came from the American Lt. Colonel George Dahlia, whose tank battalion reached Venlo on March 1: "The liberation of Venlo will live on in my memory as one of the greatest events it has been my privilege to witness in the war. The deepest impression made on me during the fighting for Venlo was not the military victory, but the people of Venlo. In the faces of these people who had lived for five years under the iron boot of the Germans I saw true courage, strength and determination. This above all proved to me that even though Venlo had been occupied by the enemy, the spirit of freedom which lives in every strong and determined nation can never be broken."

What has been left to us is the Museum at Overloon. The object of the Museum is not merely to remind us of the battle, but also to warn the youth of future generations with an educational display of documents and photographs covering the occupation, persecution and terror. The Chapelle-Ardente at the exit of the building provides a peaceful place to remember those who gave their lives for our freedom.

Then there remain the dead. The number of soldiers and civilians killed in the liberation of the Peel and Maas area can only be guessed at. As a direct result of the war, over 1,000 civilians must have died. Unlike the civilians, the soldiers who were killed — on the Allied side at least 1,100 — have their own war cemeteries, or a corner of their own in a Dutch graveyard. All the Germans killed in Holland were buried in the Peel village of Ysselstein near Venray — more than 39,000 graves with marble crosses. The Americans, too, have one central cemetery. Those who fell found a last resting place in the village of Margraten in South Limburg: long rows of crosses marking those who came from the United States to fight for this soil. The British dead have been distributed among many small cemeteries in the immediate vicinity of where they fell. Their graves, each with its own headstone, are lined with autumn flowers — asters, dahlias, chrysanthemums — which in the very season in which these men met their death come into full bloom every year.

BIBLIOGRAPHY
AND SOURCES

C correspondence
I   interviews
M O National War and Resistance Museum (Overloon)
R I O D National Institute of War Documentation (Amsterdam)
W O War Office
t s   typescript

Regional Topics, General
Alberts, W. Jappe., *Geschiedenis van de beide Limburgen,* 1974.
CBS, *Bevolking en Oppervlakte der Gemeenten van Nederland op 1 januari 1940,*
 1940.
Chorus, A., *De Nederlander uiterlijk en innerlijk,* 1965.
Kemp, M., *Geschiedenis van Limburg,* 1944.
Keuning, H.J., *Het Nederlandse volk en zijn woongebied,* 1965.
Kunstreisboek voor Nederland 1965; *Teegenwoordige Staat der Vereenigde*
 Nederlanden, deel II, 1740.
Wijnen, Jo., *Rondom Peel en Maasvallei,* 1980.

War Years
Jong, L. de., *Het Koninkrijk der Nederlanden in de Tweede Wereldoorlog,* 1980.
Kemp, M., *Limburg in den Wereldbrand,* 1946.
Altes, A. Korthals., *Luchtgevaar/luchtaanvallen op Nederland 1940-1945,* 1984.
Nierstrasz, V.E., *De verdedig van Noord-Limburg en Noord-Brabant, mei 1940,*
 1953.
Onderdrukking en verzet, Nederland in Oorlogstijd, 1947-1954.
Paape, A.H., *Donkere Jaren, episoden uit de geschiedenis van Limburg 1933-1945,*
 1969.

Local

Anonymous, *Dagboek Venlo,* ts, RIOD.

De Slag bij Overloon, Eerste fase 30 sept.–8 oct., 1944, 1974.

Anonymous, *Serum in den Oezel,* 1946.

Billiau, Sister Marie-Godelieve, *St. Anna vlagt, St. Anna rouwt, St. Anna bouwt,* 1946.

Baghus, P.J.H., *De Slag in de Roerdriehoek,* 1981, 1985.

Blondel, M. (Bertels, G.J.), *Die Swaere Noodt,* 1945, 1980.

———, *Oorlog en Herstel in Noord-Limburg 1940-1950,* 1950, 1975.

Burgt, J.J.A. van den., *Van Duisternis tot Licht,* 1945.

Cammaert, A.P.M., *Tussen twee vuren/frontlijn en evacuatie van norrd en midden Limburg,* 1984.

Daal, H. van., *Venray's ondergang en bevrijding,* 1969.

Derix, Jan., *De Bospartisanen van Baarlo,* 1980.

———, *Vriend en Vijand, de memories van Bert Poels,* 1977.

Goossens, C.M. and Goch, J.A.M. van., *Oorlog en bevrijding in de gemeente Oploo c.a.,* 1969.

Govers, F., *Corridor naar het verleden, Veghel 1940-1945,* 1983.

Grinten-Schrijnen, E. van der., *Dagboek 25 augustus 1944-13 mei 1945,* ts, Venlo archive.

Guns, J.L.L., *dagboek,* ms, RIOD.

Havermans, Dr.mr. F.M., in: *Maandblad voor de Geestelijke Volksgezondheid,* July 1946, pp. 180-187.

Hofwijk, J.W., *Verzet/de 66 dagen van Baarlo,* 1982.

Keulards, H., *Bombardementen op de Maasbruggen te Venlo, oct.-nov. 1944,* 1984.

Kikken, R.G.W., *Veurdet bleumkes oet puin ginge bleuje, Venlo in de laatste oorlogswinter,* ts 1981.

Kroel, Broeder Ivanus, diary, ts, Venray archive.

Laugs, Jan., "Sluipvlucht naar het Noorden," *Maas en Margry, K., De bevrijding van Eindhoven,* 1981.

Meelkop, Mien., *diary,* ts.

Peller, P.R.O., *De kliene oorlog, bezetting, evacuatie en bevrijding van Roermond,* 1947.

Pasier, Father P.M. Tarcisius, *Vier maanden in de vuurlinie, dagboek 15 augustus-3 maart 1945.*

Smeets, M.K.J., "Enkele aspecten van de bevrijding van Roermond," in *De maas-gouw,* 1970.

Tomlow-Steegmans, M.A., *Toen ons Harrieke kwam 1944-1945.* ts.

van der Steen, "Slagveld tussen Maas en Roer," in *Heemkalender der Roerstreek,* 1970.

van der Zanden, *Slag om de Peel* (1949).

Veld, N.K.C.A. in't. "Sport en Spel, de voorbereiding voor de brugover-vallen," in: *Bericht van de Tweede Wereldoorlog,* vol. 13 (1970).

Werps, A.E.M. *Twee maanden schuilkelderleven vóór Nederland's Bevrijding.*
Westerhuis, W.A.A. "5 september 1944–1 maart 1945, een zware tijd voor de stad Venlo," in *Slag om de Peel,* 1949.
Willemsen, W. *Peel en Maas,* October 12, 1984.

Correspondence and Interviews
Mevrouw D. Crooymans, Overloon (I); Sjaak Janssen, Holthees (C); Mevrouw C.W.H., Bilthoven (I); G.C. van Dam, Venray (I)(C); G.G.P. Tomlow, Heerlen (I); L. Welbers, Overloon (I)(C); H. van Daal, Overloon (I)(C); C.W.J. Baron de Weichs de Wenne, Geysteren (I)(C); Baron and Baroness De Smeth van Deurne-Snethlage, Massbommel (I); R.M.P.J. Wolterink, Roermond (I); P.W.L. Weijs, Broekhuizervorst (I); J.A.J. Peeters, Vecht (I); J.W. Hofwijk, Haarlem (I); W. Willemsen, Venray (I)(C)

Allied Campaigns, General
Chalfont, Alun. *Montgomery of Alamein,* 1976.
Didden, J. and M. Swarts. *Eindoel Maas,* 1984.
Ellis, L.E. *Victory in the West,* Vol. I, 1962; Vol. II, 1968.
Harrison, L.E. "The Peel Marshes," in *The American Army in World War II,* 1951.
van Hilten, D.A. *Van capitulatie tot capitulatie,* 1949.
Horrocks, Brian. *Corps Commander,* 1977.
Koning, B. *De bevrijding van Nederland 1944–45,* 1949.
Letschert, A.M. and van Osch, G. *De Slag in het Rijnland,* 1962.
Liddell Hart, B.H. *History of the Second World War,* 1970.
Moulton, J.L. *The Battle for Antwerp,* 1978.
Pogue, F.C. "The Supreme Command," in *The American Army in World War II,* 1954.
Powell, G. *The Devil's Birthday: The Bridges to Arnhem,* 1984.
Stacey, C.P. "The Victory Campaign," in *The Canadian Army 1939–1945,* 1960.
Thompson, R.W. *The Montgomery Legend,* 1967.
_____. *The 85 Days,* 1957.
Wilmot, Chester. *The Struggle for Europe,* 1952.

British Campaigns, Units (in order of appearance)
Montgomery, B.L. *Normandy to the Baltic,* 1946.
Headquarters 21st Army Group, G. Branch, WO file 205, no. 120.
Jackson, G.S. *Operations of Eighth Corps,* 1948.
Headquarters VIII Corps, WO file 171, no. 288.
MacNish, R. *Iron Division,* 1978.
O'Connor, Lt. Gen. Sir Richard, KT, GCB, DSO, MC (C).

Scarfe, N. *Assault Division,* 1947.

Smyth, Sir John. *Bolo Whistler: A Study in Leadership,* 1967.

3rd Infantry Division, G-Branch, WO file 171, no. 411.

Tapp, Sir Nigel. KBE, CB, DSO, DL (C).

Adams, T.H. *76th Field Regiment, (C).*

History of the 3rd Reconnaissance Regiment (date unknown).

Kemp, P.K. *The Middlesex Regiment 1919–1952,* 1956.

3rd Division. *Monthly Medical Bulletin,* Oct. 1944.Jan. 1945, WO file.

8th Infantry Brigade. *War Diaries,* WO file 171, no. 611.

Nicholson, W.N. *The Suffolk Regiment 1928 to 1946,* 1947.

1st Suffolk Battalion. *War Diary,* WO file 171, no. 1381.

Regimental History of the 2nd Battalion The East Yorkshire Regiment (date unknown).

Nightingale, P.R. *History of the East Yorkshire Regiment,* 1952.

Renison, J.D.W. *Experiences in B.LA. with the 2nd Battalion The East Yorkshire Rgiment* (unpublished mss.)

Roebuck, L.M. Diary, MO.

Mullaby, B.R., *The South Lancashire Regiment in North Western Europe,* ts.

Current Reports from Overseas no. 84, Jan., 1945.

9th Infantry Brigade, *War Diaries,* WO file 171, no. 617, ts.

Griffin, J.A., *The History of the Tenth Foot (Royal Lincolnshire Regiment),* 1953.

Larkin MC, Lt. Col. S.J. (C).

Grunning, Hugh, *Borders in Battle, The War Story of the K.O.S.B.,* z.j.

Graves, Ch., *The Royal Ulster Rifles Regiment, III,* 1950.

185th Infantry Brigade, *War Diaries,* WO file 171, no. 703, ts.

Cunliffe, M., *History of the Royal Warwickshire Regiment,* 1956.

Kemp, P.K., *History of the Royal Norfolk Regiment 1919-1951, III,* 1953.

Wilson, MC, Lt. Col. H.M. (C).

The History of the First Battalion, The Royal Norfolk Regiment during the World War 1939-45, 1947.

Radcliffe, G.L.Y. and Sale, R., *History of the 2nd Battalion The King's Shropshire Light Infantry,* 1947.

Forbes, P., *6th Guards Tank Brigade, The Story of Guardsman in Churchill Tanks,* 1955.

Nicholson, Nigel and Forbes, P., *The Grenadier Guards in the War of 1939-1945,* 1949.

4th Battalion Genadier Guards, *War Diaries,* ts.

Selby-Lowndes, Lt. G. (I) (C).

Howard, Michael and Sparrow, J., *The Coldstream Guards 1920-1946,* 1951.

Milbank MC, Major Sir Mark. (C).

Jeffrey, Sergeant T. (C).

Craddock MM, Sergeant J., (C).

White, Sergeant P. (C).

4th Battalion Coldstream Guards, *War Diary*, ts.

Erskine, D., *The Scots Guards 1919-1955*, 1956.

Alldred, Sergeant J. (C).

I.W.I.P., *Taurus Pursuant, A History of the 11th Armored Division*, 1946.

11th Armored Division, *War Diaries*, WO 171, no. 456, ts.

Roberts CB, P.B., DSO, MC (C).

Barclay, C.N., *The History of The Royal Northumberland Fuseliers*.

Brownlie, W. Steel., *The Proud Trooper: The History of the Ayrshire Yeomanry*, 1964.

Young, I.A. Graham., *A Short History of the Ayrshire Yeomanry*, 1947.

The Story of the 23rd Hussars 1940-1946, 1946.

Norman Cuff, *The War Diary of H. Company, 8th Battalion, Rifle Brigade*.

Kemp, P.K., *The History of the Battalion K.S.L.I. 1745-1945*, 1955.

Thornburn MC, TD, MA, Major U. (I) (C).

Eardley VC, MM, Sergeant G.M. (C).

Operations of the 4th Bn. K.S.L.I. in Holland, MO.

How, J.J., *History of the South Wales Borderers and Monmouthshire Regiment*, IV, 1954.

Campbell, Captain E.A., MO.

Martin, H., *The History of the Fifteenth Scottish Division 1939-1945*, 1948.

15th (Scots) Division, *War Diaries*, WO 171 nr 466, ts.

Baggeley, J.R.P., *6th (border) Battalion K.O.S.B. 1939-1945*, 1946.

Woolcoombs, Robert., *Lion Rampant*, 1955.

Salmond, J.B., *Fifty-First (Highland) Division*, 1953.

Independent Units

The Story of the 79th Armoured Division, October 1942-June 1945, 1945.

Birt, R., *XXII Dragoons 1760-1945*, 1950.

Pakenham–Walsh, R.P., *History of the Corps of Royal Engineers*, IX, *North West Europe 1944-45*, 1958.

Taggart, A.F., *Needs must . . . The History of the Inns of Court Regiment 1940-1945*, 1949.

Anonymous, *History of the 25th Field Regiment*, 1980.

Grant, Ian., *Cameramen at War*, 1980.

Surveys of Reports of Foreign War Correspondents on the Battles at the Overloon Front

Ledeboer, H.J., Enschede (I) (C).

Neuerburg, F.K., Rijswijk (C).

Janssen, J.A.M.M., Groen, P.M.H. and Schulten, C.M., *Stoottroepen 1944-1984*, 1984.

Air Force
Thomas, H. Neville, *146 Wing, Operational History,* Air 37, no. 993–995, ts.
Thomas, Chris, aviation research, Wokingham (C).

American 7th Armored Division
From The Beaches To The Baltic, The Story Of The 7th Armored Division, 1945.
23rd Armored Infantry Battalion, October 1944–November 1944.
87th Cavalry Reconnaissance Squadron, September 1944–November 1944 (via Michael G. Furlich, Sioux City, Iowa)

Correspondence
Knowlton, General William A., 87 Rec. Squad., West Springfield, New Hampshire.
Wemple, Lt. Col. John P., 17th Tank battalion.
Kominsky, Cpl. Harold, 17th Tank Battalion, Tomah, Wisconsin.
Chapin, Lt. Neil M., Field Artillery, Petersburg, Virginia.
Keil, Fred, Tank driver, 40th Tank battalion, Wappingers Falls, New York.
Danielson, Sgt. Kenneth R., East Point, California.
Boykin, Calvin C., Soldier, 814th Tank Destroyer Battalion, College Station, Texas.
Margreiter, John L., 23rd Armored Infantry Battalion, Chesterfield, Missouri.
Cowan, Steve. Technician/chauffeur, 23rd Armored Infantry Battalion.
Sharp, 2nd Lt. Sam H. 48th Armored Infantry Battalion, Antlers, Oklahoma.
Thiede, Sgt. Harvey L. 48th Armored Infantry Battalion, Dearborn, Michigan.
Tucker, Lt. Avery V. 48th Armored Infantry Battalion.
Watkins, Lt. Col. Benjamin C. Anti-aircraft battalion, Midlothian Virginia.
Fackler, Glen R. 38th Armored Infantry Battalion, Farmington Hills, Michigan.
Matcocks, Lt. Carl K. 38th Armored Infantry Battalion, Farmington, Connecticut
Wood, Lt. Robert Morse. 38th Armored Infantry Battalion, Annapolis, Maryland
Krask, Harry. Medic.
Fahl, James C.
Keating, L.H.
Osias, Irving.
Jones, Norman G.J.

German Sources
Schramm, Percy Ernst. *Die Invasion 1944. Aus dem Kriegstagebuch des Oberkommandos der Wehrmacht,* München 1963.

Kriegstagebuch des Oberbefehlshabers West, Anlagen: Befehle, Meldungen, etc. 14 sept.–17 dec. 1944.

Kriegstagebuch der Heeresgruppe B, Anlagen: Befehle, Meldungen, etc. 15 sept.–15 nov. 1944.

Kriegstagebuch des LXXXVIII AK, najaar 1944.

Kriegstagebuch van Fallschirmjäger-Regiment-Hübner, met Anlagen, 6 sept.–31 dec. 1944.

(many other diverse documents)

Articles, correspondence, interviews

Pens, Walter, Fahnenjunker-Unteroffizier (at Geysteren); von Brockdorff, Lt. Cay Graf, 107th Panzer Brigade; Loytved-Hardegg, Lt. Col. Rolf. Commandant Fallschirmjäger-Regiment 21; Kerutt, Mjr. Helmutt. Commandant I./Fallschirmjäger-Regiment-von Hofmann; Volz, Lt. Heinz. Adjudant I./Fs.Rgt.-von Hofmann (bataljon-Kerutt); Weber, Heinz. Feldwebel I./Fs. Rgt.-Greve (bataljon-Paul); Jansen, Oswald. I./Fs. Rgt. von Hofmann (bataljon-Kerutt); Schiffer, Gert (C); Dettinger, Helmut (C).

Postwar Studies Commissioned by the American Armed Forces

Blumentritt, Günther. B-634, *Kämpfe der LXXXVI. AK an und westlich der unteren Maas zwischen 3. und 12.10.1944.*

Schlieper, Fritz. P-157 II, *Das LXXXVI. Armeekorps in der Zeit von Mitte September bis November 1944.*

Küster, Götz. *Die Panzerbrigade 107 im Kampfraum Brückenkopf Venlo, 18 Sept.–5 Nov. 1944.*

Meindl, Eugen. B-093, *II.FS-Korps. III. Teil: Rheinland (5 Sept. 44–21. März 45).*

Schacht, Gerhard. P-188 I, *Die Kämpfe der Gruppe 'Walther' vom 13.9.1944 bis zum 12.10.1944 in Südholland.*

Sixt, Friedrich. P-188 II, *Die Kämpfe der Div. Kampgruppe Gotzsch im Maasbrückenkopf Venlo vom 12. Oktober bis Ende November 1944.*

Sixt, Friedrich. P-189, *Die Kämpfe der Panzer-Brigade 107 im September und Oktober 1944.*

Jolasse, Erwin. P-161, *Der Eisatz der 9. Panzerdivision im Oktober und November 1944.*

The authors have endeavored here to list the majority of sources for this book, although some may have been inadvertently omitted. For further research, the primary sources collected by the authors have been bestowed to the National War and Resistance Museum, Overloon, and to the National Institute of War Documentation, Amsterdam, The Netherlands.

Photo Credits

The authors are indebted to the following individuals and institutions for use of the photographs in this book.

The Imperial War Museum, London: photos 3, 4, 5, 6, 11, 12, 18, 19, 20, 21, 26, 27, 28, 29, 30, 31, 32, 34, 36, 37, 39, 40, 41, 42, 43, 44, 46.

Gemeente-archief Roermond: photos 1, 2, 47 49.

Gemeente-archief Arcen en Velden: photo 45.

Bundesarchiv Koblenz: photos 15, 25.

U.S. Army: photos 7, 8, 9, 48.

Nationaal Oorlogs- en Verzetsmuseum Overloon: photos 13 and 50.

Print and Photos Division, Library of Congress: photo 35.

Office of War Information: photo 33, cover.

Dagblad (News) voor Noord-Limburg: photos 17, 38 (the collection of C.W.J. Baron de Weichs de Wenne, Geysteren), 51.

Col. J.D.W. Renison, D.S.O., Heswall: photo 23.

F.J.M. Schmidt, Margraten: photo 22.

A. Korthals Altes, Maarssen: photos 10, 16.

INDEX